Palgrave Games in C

Series Editors
Neil Randall
The Games Institute
University of Waterloo
Waterloo, ON, Canada

Steve Wilcox
Game Design and Development
Wilfrid Laurier University
Brantford, ON, Canada

Games are pervasive in contemporary life, intersecting with leisure, work, health, culture, history, technology, politics, industry, and beyond. These contexts span topics, cross disciplines, and bridge professions.

Palgrave Games in Context situates games and play within such interdisciplinary and interprofessional contexts, resulting in accessible, applicable, and practical scholarship for students, researchers, game designers, and industry professionals. What does it mean to study, critique, and create games in context? This series eschews conventional classifications—such as academic discipline or game genre—and instead looks to practical, real-world situations to shape analysis and ground discussion. A single text might bring together professionals working in the field, critics, scholars, researchers, and designers. The result is a broad range of voices from a variety of disciplinary and professional backgrounds contributing to an accessible, practical series on the various and varied roles of games and play.

More information about this series at
http://www.palgrave.com/gp/series/16027

Nicholas Taylor • Gerald Voorhees
Editors

Masculinities in Play

Gerald Voorhees
Managing Editor

Editors
Nicholas Taylor
Department of Communication
North Carolina State University
Raleigh, NC, USA

Gerald Voorhees
Department of Communication Arts
University of Waterloo
Waterloo, ON, Canada

Palgrave Games in Context
ISBN 978-3-319-90580-8   ISBN 978-3-319-90581-5   (eBook)
https://doi.org/10.1007/978-3-319-90581-5

Library of Congress Control Number: 2018953331

Cover credit: "Target Practice" (2008) by Team Macho
Cover design by Fatima Jamadar

This Palgrave Macmillan imprint is published by the registered company Springer Nature Switzerland AG
The registered company address is: Gewerbestrasse 11, 6330 Cham, Switzerland

The image on the volume's cover has been graciously provided by Team Macho, a collective based in Toronto, Ontario, Canada. Nick first encountered their work (and this piece in particular) one day while on break from his dissertation fieldwork, studying a group of aspiring professional gamers. Something about the image stuck then—and obviously, still sticks. We have a female authority figure (mother? teacher?) whose labour is clearly supporting the young boy's mediated target practice, but who is nonetheless peripheral to the all-important relationship between him and the screen. We have the young boy himself, dressed in the uniform we associate with a certain kind of earnest, mid-twentieth century white boyhood. The shells scattered around him speak to long hours of training. The entire apparatus is at once deeply earnest, fundamentally unsettling, and utterly absurd—much like the contemporary formations of masculinity addressed in this book.

Acknowledgments

This volume would not have been possible without the generosity and insight of our team of reviewers. We are incredibly grateful to Jessica Elam-Handloff, Cameron Kunzelman, Charles Ecenbarger, Milena Droumeva, Christopher Kampe, Jen Whitson, Chris Paul, Sarah Evans, and Joel Schneier.

We also thank our fellow editors on the other volumes in this trilogy: Kishonna L. Gray, Emma Vossen, Meghan Blythe-Adams, and Todd Harper. While we believe these volumes stand on their own as separate and valuable contributions to the field of games and gender, it is important to acknowledge that this volume—much like masculinity studies itself—owes much of its dynamism and vibrancy to parallel work in feminism and queer studies.

We would be remiss to overlook the editorial team at Palgrave Macmillan, notably Shaun Vigil, whose support made this ambitious project possible, and Glenn Ramirez for laying out clearly how to make it actual.

Nick thanks Danielle and Ben, for constantly challenging me to be a better (more feminist) partner and parent. I also thank Jennifer Jenson and Suzanne de Castell, for their tremendous guidance over the years.

Gerald also thanks colleagues who provided advice, encouragement, criticism, and even resources to help make this project happen, including Vershawn Young, Jennifer Simpson, Jennifer Roberts-Smith, Kim Nguyen, Neil Randall, Jennifer Jenson, and Suzanne de Castell. I reserve my most special gratitude for Kim and Quinn for their patience during this project, but more importantly for their sustained encouragement to better practice feminism in my everyday life.

Contents

Notes on Contributors

Michael Austin is Assistant Professor of Media, Journalism, and Film, and Coordinator of the Interdisciplinary Studies Program in the Cathy Hughes School of Communications at Howard University, USA. His research is focused on sound and music in emerging and interactive media.

Gregory Blackburn has a PhD from the University of Massachusetts, USA. His primary area of interest is the interplay between media violence, power, and portrayals of masculinity, and how the consumption of such mediated depictions can impact thoughts, attitudes, and affect regarding aggression and gender roles. Additional areas of interest include media effects theory and the application of traditional effects models to new and interactive media.

Derek Burrill is an associate professor in the Department of Media and Cultural Studies. He is author of *Die Tryin': Videogames, Masculinity, Culture* (2008), the first text to explore the relationship between games, gaming, gamers, and masculinity. His second book, *The Other Guy*, was published in 2014. Additionally, he has written numerous articles and book chapters, and works as an artist, musician, and filmmaker.

Shira Chess is Assistant Professor of Entertainment and Media Studies at the University of Georgia, USA. Her most recent book, *Ready Player Two: Women Gamers and Designed Identity* (2017), interrogates how video game design and advertising construct an idealized vision of women players.

Steven Conway is Course Director of Games & Interactivity at Swinburne University of Technology, Melbourne, Australia. Steven received his doctorate from the University of Bedfordshire, UK, in 2010 on an AHRC National Award Scholarship. His research interests focus on the philosophy and aesthetics of play, games, and sport.

Mark Cruea is Assistant Professor of Communication and Media Studies at Ohio Northern University, USA. Past publications have examined the political economy of the video game industry, including planned obsolescence, externalities, and industry business models as well as the third-person effect in relation to male and female representations in video games. Mark has also been involved in Great Ideas for Teaching Students (GIFTS) at the National Communication Association and is past chair of Central States Communication Association GIFTS.

Nicholas A. Hanford is a PhD candidate in the Department of Communication and Media at Rensselaer Polytechnic Institute, USA. He is also editor-in-chief of the *Journal of Games Criticism*, an open access, peer-reviewed game studies journal. His research focuses on the role of player action in meaning-making in games and rhetorical effects of data mining.

Robin Johnson is Director of the School of Journalism and Mass Communication and an associate professor at the University of Idaho, USA, with research interests in gender, technology, and media and the production of video games and digital media. He is also on the editorial boards of the *Journal of Communication Inquiry* and *ADA: A Journal of Gender, New Media & Technology*.

Kyle Moody is Assistant Professor of Communications Media at Fitchburg State University, USA. His research interests include how video game fans and consumers are involved in the production and dissemination of fan and journalistic content. His ongoing research includes online communities of users and players of video games, new media design, social media applications, ethnography, cultural studies, and media production.

Alexandra Orlando is a freelance writer and academic Twitch streamer. She writes on topics of gender in esports, Twitch streaming, and narrative in games.

Marc Ouellette is author (with Jason C. Thompson) of *Post 9/11 Video Games: A Critical Examination* (2017) and is writing a book on masculinity in video games. He is a Learning Games Initiative Research Fellow.

Valerie Palmer-Mehta is Professor of Communication in the Department of Communication & Journalism at Oakland University, USA. Her research can be found in a variety of venues such as *Communication & Critical Cultural Studies, International Journal of Communication, Women's Studies in Communication, Communication, Culture & Critique, Text and Performance Quarterly, and Journal of American Culture*.

Sam Srauy is an assistant professor in the Communication and Journalism Department at Oakland University, USA. His research area includes the political economics of video game industries and narratives of inequality.

Nicholas Taylor is Assistant Professor of Digital Media in the Department of Communication at North Carolina State University, USA. He is also Associate

Director of their Communication, Rhetoric and Digital Media (CRDM) PhD program. His work applies critical, feminist, and socio-technical perspectives to experimental and mixed-methods research with digital gaming communities.

Aaron Trammell is Assistant Professor of Informatics at University of California, Irvine, USA. He was Provost's Postdoctoral Scholar for Faculty Diversity in Informatics and Digital Knowledge at the Annenberg School for Communication and Journalism at the University of Southern California, USA, and he received his doctorate from the School of Communication and Information at Rutgers University, USA, in 2015. Aaron's research reveals historical connections between games, play, identity, and the US military-industrial complex. He is interested in how military ideologies become integrated into game design and how these perspectives are negotiated within the imaginations of players.

Gerald Voorhees is Assistant Professor of Digital Culture and Communication in the Department of Communication Arts at the University of Waterloo, Canada. His research is on games and new media as sites for the construction and contestation of identity and culture. In addition to editing books on role-playing games and first-person shooter games, Gerald is co-editor of Bloomsbury's Approaches to Game Studies book series.

Rebecca Waldie is a PhD student in Communications at Concordia University, USA. Her current research involves representations of mental illness and masculinity in video games. Her master's thesis research focused on the representation of hegemonic masculinity in horror video games using an intersectional content analysis, and her past work explored digital identity and identity construction in digital spaces.

Lily Zhu is a PhD candidate in the English department at the University of Texas, Austin, USA, studying the British novel in the long nineteenth century. Her primary research focuses on the invasive, foreign figure of the chemist across nineteenth-century fiction and modern video games. She is also developing a game criticism website, *Culture Bytes Back*.

List of Figures

List of Figures

List of Tables

1

Introduction: Masculinity and Gaming: Mediated Masculinities in Play

Nicholas Taylor and Gerald Voorhees

The Empire's New Bros: Gaming, Masculinity, Power

What is our responsibility as scholars of masculinity and games in the contemporary moment—which is to say, a time when the most pernicious, reactionary, and destructive expressions of straight white masculinity stalk the highest political office in the United States, and where the path to a mythic greatness is to double down on patriarchy's deep-seated investments in environmental, military, economic, and racial subjugation?

It is tempting to say games—and game studies—seem trivial in such a time of crisis and upheaval. But to do so would ignore the inextricable and numerous ways in which games have historically served (and continue to serve) neo-colonial white-supremacist capitalist patriarchy (hooks 2003). The games industry is international and powerful, capable of enriching and/ or impoverishing whole regions of production through its cutting-edge experiments in highly mobile (e.g., volatile) development studios and precarious pools of globalized labor (Dyer-Witheford and de Peuter 2009). Its connections to the military-industrial complex are multiple and complex, and predate the advent of digital technologies by centuries, according to

N. Taylor (✉)
North Carolina State University, Raleigh, NC, USA

G. Voorhees
University of Waterloo, Waterloo, ON, Canada

© The Author(s) 2018
N. Taylor, G. Voorhees (eds.), *Masculinities in Play*, Palgrave Games in Context,
https://doi.org/10.1007/978-3-319-90581-5_1

histories linking both tabletop and digital games to the development of military training simulations (Deterding 2009), not to mention the ideological support that "militainment" has traditionally provided Empire (see Stahl 2010, as well as Gregory Blackburn's chapter in this volume). And in the last few years, particularly misogynist elements of geek culture—a culture which itself bears legacies of gender- and race-based exclusion (Kendall 1998; Turkle 1997), not to mention shared origins with gaming in the military-industrial complex (Miller 2012)—have found potent political agency first in the form of the gamergate hate campaign and, more broadly, in an adulation (and energetic online advocacy) for President Trump and his overtly sexist, racist agenda.

Around the same time we began putting together this volume, a rash of "think pieces" came out linking (and then unlinking) the rise of Trump to gamergate. Some did so in overt fashion, arguing that the online communities, media platforms, and communicative strategies involved in the hate campaign against feminist game designers, critics, and scholars were redirected toward promoting Trump, and seeing lawmakers', politicians', and industry leaders' responses (or lack thereof) to gamergate as emboldening the alt-right (Lagomarsino 2017).

We do not seek to draw a straight line of causality between any one gamic representation of masculinity and the current crisis in American culture and politics; exaggerating the social impacts of games is arguably as detrimental as an approach that views them simply as leisure technologies, as artifacts of (a now indefinitely prolonged) boyhood. Rather, it is important to recognize that the relationships between games and their broader cultural milieus are characterized by "overdetermination," Louis Althusser's (1969) term describing how most social formations are animated by multiple, contradictory forces that both affect and are affected by one another (p. 101). And so it is with games and game cultures; while it does little good to simply label the alt-right "gamergate on a national scale" (Marcotte 2016), there are numerous technological, ideological, and sociocultural relations between gaming's recent hate offensives and the 2016 US election that bear noting. In this vein, commentators position gamergate as one early reaction against so-called political correctness, part of a broad panoply of nativist, chauvinist currents which were then capitalized on by the Trump campaign (Maiberg 2017). Still others see his governing style as an extension of "trolling culture," characterized by informational misdirection and open hostility towards experts and Others alike (Cross 2017).

It is beyond the scope of this introduction to offer a comprehensive map of these associations, and the multiple and sometime competing causalities they engender; we make note of them here to demonstrate that gaming constitutes one, key site in a broader apparatus of contemporary governmentality reconstituting and reconfiguring our (ever-precarious) understandings of masculinity and manliness. In her examination of player identity at the margins of games culture, Adrienne Shaw (2014) builds from Judith Butler's theorization of performativity to argue that "performances [of identity] must draw on a broader system of meaning that helps render those utterances, those performances, intelligible. Media representations and connections with them via identification are deeply connected with this process" (67). Indeed, this echoes Butler's (1993) own claim that the performance of gender (and other aspects of self) is a "citational practice" that must constantly reiterate its adherence to conventions in order to maintain "cultural intelligibility," much less aspire to be valued (2; 16). As a communication technology that employs both representation and performance, games and the cultural practices that have emerged around them, in the main, help to maintain existing power relations and reroute them to adapt to historical circumstances.

To wit, one of the key aims of this volume, the first of its kind on the topic, is to organize and advance our nascent understandings of the co-constitutive relations between gaming, masculinities, and the wider cultural and political landscapes in which games and their players move. We believe that it is only through such a programmatic and rigorous approach that we can begin the challenging work of imagining how games might envision and enact ways of doing masculinities *differently*—that is, providing male-identified subjects with modes of expression and experience not rooted in domination. In what follows, we survey the current work in this area, provide two crucial theoretical interventions for continued research, and offer our own conceptualization of how we might productively frame masculinity and gaming in a time of ubiquitous mediatization. We then turn to an overview of the volume's chapter organization.

Boys' Toys?

Video games have historically been the domain of men and boys; decades of research on gender and digital gameplay have established this as an epistemic foundation for research examining, and at times intervening into, the marginalized status of girls (Jenson and de Castell 2011; Kafai et al. 2009), women (Kennedy 2006; Taylor 2006), and other gender identities that trouble heteronormativity (Shaw 2014; Lauteria 2012) in video game texts, practices, and cultures. As a result, we have robust accounts of how patriarchal hierarchies of gender and sexuality continue to be represented in, and reproduced through, the production, marketing, consumption, and critique of digital games.

The conditions of girls' and women's participation in, and exclusions from, gaming cultures have been a consistent lightning rod for game scholars, designers, journalists, cultural critics, and activists for at least the past two decades, if we take the first *Barbie to Mortal Kombat* volume as one starting point—not for the problematization of girls' fraught relation to games and gaming contexts, which predates that volume, but for efforts to programmatically address the exclusionary gender politics of games. Perhaps best epitomized by Fron et al. (2007), this work generally proceeds from the position that game play and production are male-dominated domains, into or against which interventions must be made in order to create more equitable conditions for female participation. Another volume in this series, *Women in Games, Feminism in Play*, continues forward on this path, as well as marking out potential futures for feminist game criticism and women-centered gameplay.

The study of masculinity in relation to games is, by comparison, underdeveloped and fairly *ad hoc*. Existing work in this area can be categorized into two broad trajectories. The first aims to understand how patriarchal ideologies are embedded in gaming media: that is, how games and their attendant texts and artifacts communicate and mediate masculinities. The second, arguably less clearly defined trajectory explores how masculine subjects are recruited via games (alongside other media industries), to support the neoliberal state's projects of political, economic, and environmental subjugation.

With regard to the first trajectory, we are deeply indebted to scholarship that has begun articulating the vital role games play in the representation and concretization of hierarchical divisions along axes of gender, sexuality, class, and race. This includes scholarship on the representation of masculinity alongside other categories of difference, particularly race (Brock 2011; Leonard 2006; Everett and Watkins 2008) and (post)colonial identities (Mukherjee 2017). We see this as well in work on the cultural, economic, and technological mechanisms through which gaming became "naturalized" as the domain of men and boys (Kocurek 2015; Jenson and de Castell 2010). And of course, we see it in accounts of the decades-long attempts to preserve masculine privilege, whether via eSports and other male-dominated domains of elite play (Taylor et al. 2009; Witkowski 2013; Harper 2014), or online hate campaigns (Consalvo 2012; Salter and Blodgett 2012; Chess and Shaw 2015).

Constituting the second trajectory is scholarship that explores how games mobilize the industry's historically privileged base—cisgendered men, mostly straight, and mostly white—towards supporting the neoliberal state's projects of economic, political, and military domination. We see this perhaps most clearly in work that critically addresses the games industry's collusion with the "militainment" industry (Huntemann and Payne 2009; Stahl 2010). It is also present in research that connects eSports to contemporary forms of neoliberal governance (Voorhees 2015; N. Taylor 2016), and that more broadly celebrates the male body's capacity for violence, particularly in the service of colonialist legacies of racial and ethnic discrimination.

We argue that holding these trajectories in productive tension—maintaining critical attention to the ways masculinity is represented and enacted within games and gaming-related communities, on one hand, while also exploring the work games do in priming the masculine subject for support for (and participation in) the overlapping projects of patriarchy, imperialism, and capitalism—is crucial to understanding our present cultural moment. This is a moment in which gaming figures centrally in the vociferous reassertion of masculinity's most regressive, violent, and devastating formations; under these conditions, studying gaming and gender (including, but not limited to, considerations of masculinities) is a fraught undertaking.

Using and Abusing Masculinity

These days, the work of addressing exclusions based on gender, race and sexual identity in digital gaming often involves harassment from ever-aggrieved, always-angry denizens of the "manosphere" that equate freedom of expression with the capacity to discriminate, harass, and intimidate with impunity. And of course, many of the same communities, media platforms, and forms of trolling associated with gaming-related hate campaigns were put to work in the political ascendency of the alt-right. Under such turbulent conditions, we think it necessary to make two clarifications regarding the study of masculinity and gaming. Both of these clarifications draw from key debates in masculinity studies from the mid-1990s onward, and it is here that our volume is most indebted to, and in dialogue with, this productive but often controversial offshoot of feminism.

The Study of Men?

As Raewyn Connell reminds us, the study of masculinities flows from the work of feminism and queer studies in documenting the subjugation, oppression, and marginalization of non-male, non-straight, and non-cis bodies (2014). Masculinity studies "arose from the feminist breakthrough that created women's studies and gender studies," Connell asserts; it is "part of the feminist revolution in knowledge" (6). Without this historical and theoretical context, masculinity studies can too easily become an examination of "men's issues" shorn from an acknowledgment of men's continued position of privilege within matrices of gender relations. This leads to formulations like "masculinity is the obstacles men face," which Nick overheard in a presentation at a major communication studies conference some years ago. More problematically, masculinity studies can become "a vehicle for masculine backlash against women and feminism" (Connell 2014, 6), which finds current expression in the reactionary politics and ideologies of the online manosphere (Ging 2017; Gotell and Dutton 2016).

In a similar vein, thinking of masculinity studies as somehow interchangeable with "the study of men" does disservice to the contributions made by queer theorists, particularly via Jack Halberstam's groundbreaking work on "female masculinity" (1998) that disentangle discourses of masculinity and femininity from their (powerful but often tenuous) connections to biologically sexed male and female bodies. With regard to gaming, these disentanglements can help us identify and account for more nuanced enactments of gendered play—such as "feminized male play or masculinized female play" (Jenson and de Castell 2010, 63).

Ideological Reasoning

Our second clarification builds on the first, and similarly looks to some of the earliest debates in the field of masculinity studies. In a good portion of the critical, cultural scholarship on gaming, sustained analysis of masculinity is often dismissed as low hanging fruit, as an obvious and therefore too-easy target for critique, a position that relies on two dated, troubled premises. First, it is grounded in a construct of masculinity as singular and more or less immutable, rather than as historically and regionally contingent, competing (and cooperating) *masculinities*. Second, this position treats masculinity as something that has an existence prior to and quite apart from its enactment within the specific context of games, and that can then be applied with little modification to the analysis of games and gaming practices. While this position is seldom a problem in the handful of works that do closely interrogate masculinity in games and game cultures, it is an all too familiar trope, or commonplace, in critical studies of games generally to treat masculinity as a static condition, a constant that works a certain way and produces certain effects consistent across contexts, communities, and time periods. In this (im)mobilization of masculinity (and relatedly, "hypermasculinity" and "hegemonic masculinity"), masculinity serves as a convenient heuristic tool to contextualize more novel events, practices, and artifacts.

Dorothy Smith, in formulating her critique of normative social scientific research, referred to this mode of working with theory as "ideological reasoning"—presuming the existence of an abstract concept separate from its instantiation in everyday contexts (2005). In our view, numerous studies of gender and gaming, and cultural studies of games generally, deploy a preformed and monadic concept of masculinity in order to explain games, rather than see masculinity itself as something that is multiple, malleable, contingent, and, crucially, *reconstituted and reconfigured through* games, including their play, spectatorship, production, and so on. Due in large part to the foundational work of scholars who have helped theorize masculinity (Raewyn Connell, Jack Halberstam, Michael Kimmell, Michael Messner, and Eve Sedgwick, to name a few), we can apply the concept to games and gaming because we already know what masculinity is and how it works. But while deploying a monadic understanding of masculinity has been productive for game scholars, one that has helped us begin to understand the central role games play in valorizing contemporary discourses of masculinity and manliness, it tends to *black box* masculinity itself.

In her own revisitation of "hegemonic masculinity," Raewyn Connell (with Messerschmidt 2005) pointed to this very issue: the danger in reifying the term, rather than seeking to understand how arrangements and performances of gender in local settings may or may not work to produce relations of privilege and oppression. In Connell and Messerschmidt's words, "masculinity is not a fixed entity;" rather, "masculinities are configurations of practice that are accomplished in social action and, therefore, can differ according to the gender relations in a particular social setting" (2005, 836). Applying Connell and Messerschmidt's insight to existing research on masculinity and games, we would argue that we have excellent accounts of how masculinity works on, and in, games, towards the exclusion of non-cis, non-male bodies. But we have much less robust appreciation of what games *do to* masculinities, plural; how digital play elicits transformations in the meanings, practices, and possibilities of masculinities, understood as modes of subjectivization that are historically oriented towards gender-based domination.

One of the goals of this volume, then, is to offer points of entry into an appreciation for the co-constitutive interplay between masculinities and gaming media—to understand that while gaming certainly reflects the ideologies and aims of hegemonic masculinity, it is also agential in transforming how hegemonic masculinity operates. If we understand hegemonic masculinity as not simply the ascendant model of masculinity in a given society or period, but as ascendant *precisely because* it enlists subjects in patterns of gendered relations that support hegemony, then we can see better understand why gaming constitutes a key concern for scholars of masculinity. That is, gaming is central to understanding contemporary hegemonic masculinity *because gaming is itself has historically been an extension of hegemony* (Dyer-Witheford and de Peuter 2009; Fron et al. 2007; Miller 2012).

We turn now to our own theoretical framework for the collected works in this volume, which we think allows for productive explorations of the role of gaming (and media more generally) in shaping masculine subjectivities, while also allowing for the malleability and dynamism of hegemonic masculinity as a historical project of gender-based subjugation.

Theorizing Masculinity as Apparatus

Masculinity is always in flux. Its paradigmatic expressions change—the Marlboro Man gave way to the Dos Equis guy, the rugged frontiersman and stalwart blue-collar worker give way to the manboy and his toys, the gym-buffed bod, the techbro, and so on—but what stays the same is hegemonic masculinity's dual investments in sex-based hierarchies and state-sponsored violence. What we need, arguably, is a theorization of masculinity that acknowledges its protean characteristics (albeit always in the service of maintaining a profoundly conservative hierarchical sex-based organization of humans); its multiple manifestations, particularly with regard to how masculinities intersect with age, class, nationhood, race, and other systems of differentiation; and the fundamental role played by media texts, technologies, and industries, to buttress what Connell long ago called "the patriarchal dividend" (2005). Such a theorization would situate the various texts, techniques, and contexts examined in this volume not as sporadic instances of an (ongoing or emergent) masculinization of games, but as separate points of articulation within a shifting, ever-becoming matrix in which masculinity is not simply *expressed*, but rather through which its participants are *constituted* as masculine subjects, and in which the very contours of masculinity are contested.

Foucault's notion of the *apparatus (dispositif)* may prove a useful starting point here. While Foucault had only scant references to masculinity in his work, his insights into the ways historical institutions shape and make possible certain subject formations have proven tremendously productive for scholars of gender, media, and cultural studies. For our present purposes, we find the "apparatus"—introduced by Michel Foucault in "Confessions of the

Flesh" (1980) and then expanded upon by (among others) Giorgio Agamben and Jeremy Packer—to be productive in helping us orient and ground a consideration of contemporary masculinity, particularly in relation to media. Foucault describes an apparatus as "a network" or "system of relations" that connects particular "discourses, institutions, architectural forms, regulatory decisions, laws, administrative measures, scientific statements, philosophical, moral, and philanthropic propositions." As a network of heterogeneous elements, an apparatus functions as "the response to an urgency," and serves as "a set of strategies of the relations of forces supporting, and supported by, certain types of knowledge" (Foucault, in Agamben 2009, 2).

Further articulated by Agamben, an apparatus is "a set of practices, bodies of knowledge, measures, and institutions that aim to manage, govern, control, and orient—in a way that purports to be useful—the behaviors, gestures, and thoughts of human beings" (Agamben 2009, 19). It is, as such, "a machine that produces subjectifications ... a machine of governance" (23). Voorhees (2012) took this figuration most literally in his analysis of the *Mass Effect* series, arguing that "the series operates as a truth game governed by multiculturalist rationality and validates play practices that embrace heterogeneity in response to difference" (262). But, while digital games do indeed perform some of the operations of an apparatus of government, in fact they are mere material instantiations of the largely intangible structures of reasoning and intelligibility of a governing apparatus, one link in a "network of institutions as particular agents [that function] in order to attach a population to a policy" (Greene 1998, 27).

Packer redirects the concept of apparatus towards considerations of media more generally, as a means of better understanding and accounting for the ascendancy of media in contemporary processes of subjectivization. He describes a "media apparatus" as a concatenation of "signs, signifiers, and technologies of inscription, collection, and processing" that have as their goal the maintenance or redirection of particular power formations (Packer 2013, 20). According to Packer, this conceptualization allows us to "investigate the necessarily historical production of 'subjectivities' coinciding with the use of specific technologies" and to see "how users become 'objectified' through the accumulation and generation of data/knowledge facilitated by such technologies." As he claims, "this double articulation is central to Foucault's theories of the subject and power" (19).

What, then, would we gain from approaching masculinity as a "media apparatus"? Broadly speaking, such a theorization would call attention to the formative role of media texts, technologies, and institutions in not simply communicating (representing) iterations of manhood conducive to contemporary formations of power/knowledge (showing us how and why to be a techbro, a gamer, a manboy), but also in providing the material and institutional conditions for masculine subjects to be shaped/shape themselves. Understood in terms of a media apparatus, then, masculinity may be seen as a "machine" comprised of and connecting texts (games, advertisements, TV shows), technologies (game platforms, cars, computers and peripherals, power tools), contexts (man caves, sports bars, e-sports tournaments, game development studios), policies (parental leave, "crunch time", etc.), and so on, to its dual projects of (1) concretizing a sex-based hierarchy and (2) directing the energies, desires, and efforts of masculine subjects towards state-sanctioned violence in pursuit of its projects of domination—colonialism, imperialism, and neoliberalism.

This outlines how a masculinity/media apparatus functions in terms of its techniques of *subjectivization*; but as Packer alludes to, media apparatuses also carry out the work of *objectification*, "through the accumulation and generation of data/knowledge facilitated by such technologies" (19), recording, storing, processing, and transmitting information about subjects for the purposes of prediction and control (Andrejevic 2016). In this sense, contemporary games are instruments of the masculinity/media apparatus *par excellence*, as they excel at recording, processing, and transmitting the inputs, preferences, and accomplishments of players, communicating these back to players as quantified truth claims regarding their embodied/cybernetic abilities, particularly as compared to others, constituting a "toxic meritocracy" (Paul 2018). Such is the object of achievements, trophies, elo ratings, gamerscores, upvotes, and (as Hanford notes, in this volume), difficulty settings: they are cultural technologies for status-building, operating within a narrowly instrumentalist calculus of competition and one-upmanship (Paul 2013). And of course they enable the extensive work of "audiencing" players (Bratich 2008; Taylor 2016), of converting their activity and affects into aggregated data sets for purposes of further subjectivization and interpellation.

And this completes the circle. All of this game data—these inputs into the machine of mediated masculinity—enables the development of new knowledges, technologies of domination, and techniques of the self. As Foucault's *History of Sexuality* (1990) illustrates by tracing the proliferation of "perversions," once sexuality became an object of study, power adapted to changing historical and social conditions by domesticating otherwise unintelligible or agential practices. In creating new categories to account for novel or even resistant practices, discursive formations evolve to redirect and redistribute power relations. It is through this means that power relations come into their shape, as "stable mechanisms replace the free play of antagonistic reactions.

Through such mechanisms one can direct, in a fairly constant manner and with reasonable certainty, the conduct of others" (Foucault 1982, 794).

The games industry thus constitutes a key site in the "machine" of mediated masculinity by dint of its capacity to produce copious *inputs* (data, capital, attention) and generate culturally intelligible and agential *outputs*. By *outputs*, we mean the reproduction of gaming's persistent "core" demographic, one that is fundamentally rooted in hegemony in both its endless appetite for technological innovation and in its deep investments in patriarchal ideologies.

Book Structure

Like the other books in the trilogy, this volume is organized into three sections that examine how gender is represented in games, how gender is constructed in and through the cultural and material apparatuses that constitute game cultures, and the emerging contexts for future research and possibilities for feminist intervention in and around games.

Section I, *Act Like a Man: Representations of Masculinity*, includes considerations of how contemporary masculinity is portrayed in games, as conveyed through the appearances and behaviors of their playable characters, interactions with non-playable characters, the narrative worlds in which these games take place, and the intertextual connections to historically masculinized media that render these experiences intelligible. These chapters employ various forms of discourse analysis to highlight themes that operate across different titles and genres, explicate close readings of iconic game franchises, and explore the multimodal representational systems that together constitute a gamic performance of masculinity. Collectively, they examine how particular games and game genres invite players to explore themes germane to the modern project of masculine subject formation: violence (Burrill), militarism (Blackburn), economic success (Moody), fatherhood (Cruea), relations with women and other men (Waldie), and sports (Ouellette and Conway).

The first two chapters examine militarism and state-sanctioned violence against the Other. We begin with Derek Burrill's timely and provocative consideration of the ways in which games portray torture, in which Burrill manages to connect gamic enactments of torture to its invocation in contemporary political ideology as proof of a political candidate's (and by extension, nation's) manly virtue. In both, writes Burrill, masculinity is distilled to a power game between the masculine torturer and the abject, dehumanized Other. Greg Blackburn's thorough examination of the *Call of Duty* series provides a deep dive into how digital games both represent and encourage players to perform militarized masculinity. By tracing the imbrication of masculinity and militarism through several iterations of the series, Blackburn draws our attention to important aspects of this relation, notably the centering of intergenerational (particularly father-son) narratives and the way that technological know-how is incorporated but ultimately subordinated to corporeal domination.

The stakes are brought closer to home, figuratively, in the next set of three chapters. Kyle Moody approaches *Grand Theft Auto V* as a simulation that explores the intersections of economic class and masculinities, ultimately making a spectacle of the impossibility of the American dream. In Moody's analysis, the inevitable failure of masculinity is reflected in both the story arc and the limited actional palette when playing as Michael, a character that aspires to a bourgeois masculinity. Waldie's chapter explores similar tropes in the highly narrative-driven indie survival horror game *Until Dawn*, in which a group of teenagers must survive the entanglements—romantic, homosocial, and monstrous—of a weekend at a cabin in the woods. By considering the inventory of possible actions for each of the playable characters, and mapping how different player choices produce different narrative outcomes, Waldie musters considerable evidence to support her reading of the game. Mark Cruea takes a different route in his study of players' responses to themes of fatherhood in *The Last of Us*, focusing on how players themselves describe their experiences with the game. This chapter provides a grounded illustration of how players inhabiting different subject positions actively make meaning of their play experiences. Beyond Cruea's efforts to illuminate the contours of fatherhood as it is represented in *The Last of Us*, his chapter should also be understood as a reminder that any effort to discuss a generalized gameplay experience must always bear qualification.

In the final chapter in this section, Marc Ouellette and Steven Conway consider the role of hockey games in both reifying and reconfiguring the sport's emphasis on the male body—and its capacity for feats of athleticism and violence—as the locus of hypermasculine subjectivity. Ouellette and Conway contextualize hockey games like *NHL Hitz* and EA Sports' *NHL* series within an ecology of hockey-related media (films like *Slapshot*, NHL broadcasts, and sports journalism) that take an ambivalent view towards the effects of digitization on the game. This work reminds us that games are always ensconced within networks of consumption and biopolitical production that include multiple texts, artifacts, and practices—key themes for the following sections.

Section II, *Now You're Playing with Power Tools: Gendering Assemblages*, looks beyond textual representations to other elements of the masculinity/media apparatus, in order to understand the myriad of ways gaming subjectivates and interpellates the male body (or fails in these tasks). These elements include the gendered discourses attached to rulesets (Trammell), difficulty settings (Hanford), music (Austin), and specialized gaming peripherals (Srauy and Palmer-Mehta). Taken together, these chapters expand our understanding of how masculinity is communicated in and remediated by digital gaming, particularly when understood as an assemblage of texts, devices, objects, bodies, and so on.

The first two chapters in this section center the mutually constitutive relationship between games and their communities of players in the making of gaming masculinities. Digging into tabletop gaming's not-too-distant past, Aaron Trammell opens the section by tracing the controversies surrounding early *Dungeons & Dragons* rulesets governing the mechanics of female characters and monsters. Trammell's work reminds us that far from a bygone conclusion, the exclusion of women from gaming communities happened—and continues to happen—through specific communicative acts (in this case, design decisions, letters to the editors of *Dragon Magazine*, and so on). Similarly focusing on game mechanics, Nicholas Hanford provides an innovative look at the gendering of difficulty settings in contemporary digital games. Drawing on specific examples from games ranging from *Viewtiful Joe* to *Metal Gear Solid V*, Hanford provides a categorization of "gender offense punishments" that effectively aim at feminizing and/or dehumanizing the (presumed) male player, and connects this to certain exclusionary constructs of "gamer" identity.

The second set of chapters in this section look at discourses that are both (literally and figuratively) typically considered peripheral to games. Michael Austin's chapter takes us on a historical overview of the various gendered meanings attached to orchestral music, showing us that the sonic themes associated with particular game characters, events, and settings communicate—whether advertently or inadvertently—deeply conservative notions of masculinity and femininity. Austin's work shows us that music can work to either disrupt or underscore (pun intended) the gendered politics associated with other more visually driven game elements. In their chapter concluding the section, Sam Srauy and Valerie Palmer-Mehta turn to the masculinized discourses at work in the marketing of specialized gaming peripherals. Focusing on the website for Razer, a manufacturer of mice, keyboards, and other devices, the authors detail the various themes the company deploys (including mastery, competition, and militarism) in order to construct its masculine audience.

Section III, *The Right Man for the Job: Gaming and Social Futures*, looks at gaming as a site in which male bodies are employed towards regimes of economic, biopolitical, and affective production. These chapters approach different sites—eSports, game studios, and LAN parties—and employ an array of methodologies, but they are fairly uniform in their pessimistic assessment of the potential futures for masculinities. That is, while some of these chapters look at seemingly progressive phenomena and others start from problematic formations, all are united in illustrating how gaming and masculinity are not only co-constitutive, but also how the resultant dynamics are intensely (re)generative. They produce subject positions, capital, and affect, which may alter, to some small extent, the organization of patriarchy but do not challenge it, and in fact help re-entrench patriarchy by making it more resilient.

The two chapters opening the section examine the opportunities afforded to traditionally subordinate formations of masculinity within the context of eSports. Gerald Voorhees and Alexandra Orlando's chapter is a sort of "tropology" of masculinities enacted in competitive gaming, looking at major e-sports clan "Cloud 9" as a case study. Voorhees and Orlando illustrate the ways that conventional binaries around geek and jock masculinity get subverted, retooled, and transformed by the members of Cloud 9, but always in the service of creating a more competitive and marketable eSports commodity: seemingly counter-hegemonic enactments of masculinity are permitted, so long as they make bank. Lily Zhu's chapter also looks at eSports, this time with an emphasis on the intersections of nationalism and masculinity in international tournaments. Specifically, she draws our attention to North American eSports fans and their traffic in stereotypes that demasculinize and dehumanize Asian players, reminding us that the sportive masculinities associated with professional gaming (Witkowski 2012) are unevenly distributed and always intersectional. Zhu's chapter considers the global reach (and implications) of eSports and its associated fandoms, a refreshing perspective as scholarship in this area is too often siloed by regional and national borders.

The next two chapters, and the final chapters of this book, start from equally compelling and problematic premises, the displacement of militarized masculinities for technomasculinities in the game industry, and the plethora of homoeretic play between men in game cultures.

Robin Johnson's chapter contributes a perspective, studio studies, that is underrepresented in game studies and reports on an ethnographic inquiry of the work of masculinization in a AAA gaming studio. In-depth interviews with male game developers provide ample evidence that technomasculinity, a construction of masculinity premised in and around technological mastery, is not only critical to accessing the game industry but is also further enculturated in it. Concluding the section and the book, Nick Taylor and Shira Chess' chapter questions how we might account for incidences of homoerotic aggression between straight white male players—from teabagging in *Halo* to after-hours goings-on at LAN parties. Interweaving theories of homosociality, posthumanism, and cyberfeminism, they argue that these incidences speak to the mix of techno-erotic and homo-erotic pleasures afforded by playing with other men. Such pleasures invoke a gaming body that is vulnerable and penetrated, pointing once again to the fragility of heteronormative masculinity—and illustrating how homoereticism is incorporated into the structure of patriarchal relations.

Taken together, these chapters sketch out a number of pathways for scholars to continue exploring the ways masculinity is reproduced and reiterated through gaming, starting with and moving beyond games' textual and representational aspects into the discursive and material contexts of the production and circulation of games and game cultures. They represent a broad array of approaches, with their attendant methodological particularities, and take on a wide range of texts, discourses, performances, and patterns of practice. That said, this volume stops short of a comprehensive coverage of the intersections between masculinities and gaming. Leaving aside the probability that such a comprehensive look is possible, we want to point to two areas in particular that this collection does not engage.

The first concerns a more robust international and cross-cultural perspective on masculinities and games. As we noted above, following the insights of critical masculinities scholars, masculinities are often regionally and even locally specific. They are also co-constitutive with other systems of differentiation that vary across ethnicities, nations, languages, and so on. We are excited by Lily Zhu's account of how North American and European eSports players and fans stereotype players from Asia, but even this international perspective on the masculinized culture of eSports offers a *unidirectional* account of cultural difference, from the perspective of Western and predominantly English-speaking (i.e., culturally and linguistically hegemonic) players and fans. Asking how eSports players and fan communities from other areas of the world read Western, English-speaking and/or white players is but one among many questions posed by her work. Questions like this are imperative, especially in light of the lack of attention to masculinities in the emerging areas of regional game studies (Wolf 2015; Liboriussen and Martin 2016; Lee and Pulos 2016; Szablewicz 2016; Penix-Tadson 2016) and in most considerations of globalization and (post)coloniality that are otherwise cognizant of the transnational inequities of the human, material, and environmental costs of gaming and the production of racially and culturally situated identities (Lugo et al. 2002; Huntemann and Aslinger 2013; Consalvo 2016; Mukherjee 2017). While some of the chapters in the works noted here look to how women are implicated in theses transnational processes, only Murray's (2017) study of *Spec Ops* and Dyer-Witheford and de Pueter's *Games of Empire* address masculinity (and here, as with Zhu's chapter, the analysis is focused on Western perceptions and constructions of gender).

Also missing from these chapters, even those in the last section ostensibly concerned with "social futures," are considerations of how we might *do* gaming masculinities differently; that is whether and how gaming might provide masculine subjects (male or otherwise) at least a temporary way out of hegemonic masculinity's investments in dominance and subjugation. Is it too pessimistic to suggest that there is no positive future for gaming masculinities? That every permutation of masculinity, definitionally, will produce an iteration—a repetition with some small difference—of inequitable relations of power? So be it. If there is a masculinity that escapes this trap emerging from games or game cultures, it has not been captured in this volume.

By way of conclusion, it should be noted that this *lack* of articulation of what a more progressive, less pathologically inclined masculinity might look like is somewhat endemic to the field of masculinity studies more broadly. That is, the project of fleshing out a masculinity less centered around subjugation, hierarchy, and violence is, as we understand, a challenge since—as foremost scholars from Connell, to Kimmell, to Messner have attested—masculinity *is precisely* the gendering of subordination.

Bibliography

Agamben, G. 2009. *What is an Apparatus?* Palo Alto, CA: Stanford University Press.

Althusser, Louis. 1969. *For Marx*. New York City: Penguin Press.

Andrejevic, Mark. 2016. Theorizing Drones and Droning Theory. In *Drones and Unmanned Aerial Systems: Legal and Social Implications for Security and Surveillance*, ed. Alex Zavrsnik, 21–43. Zurich: Springer International.

Bratich, Jack Z. 2008. Activating the Multitude: Audience Powers and Cultural Studies. In *New Directions in American Reception Study*, ed. Philip Goldstein and James Machor, 33–56. Oxford: Oxford University Press.

Brock, Andre. 2011. 'When Keepin it Real Goes Wrong': *Resident Evil 5*, Racial Representation, and Gamers. *Games and Culture* 6 (5): 429–452.

Butler, Judith. 1993. *Bodies that Matter*. New York: Routledge.

Chess, Shira, and Adrienne Shaw. 2015. A Conspiracy of Fishes, or, How We Learned to Stop Worrying about #GamerGate and Embrace Hegemonic Masculinity. *Journal of Broadcasting & Electronic Media* 59 (1): 208–220.

Connell, Raewyn. 2005. *Masculinities.* 2nd ed. Cambridge: Polity Press.

———. 2014. The Study of Masculinities. *Qualitative Research Journal* 14 (1): 5–15.

Connell, Raewyn, and James Messerschmidt. 2005. Hegemonic Masculinity: Rethinking the Concept. *Gender & Society* 19 (6): 829–859.

Consalvo, Mia. 2012. Confronting Toxic Gamer Culture: A Challenge for Feminist Game Studies Scholars. *Ada: A Journal of Gender, New Media, and Technology* 1. https://doi.org/10.7264/N33X84KH.

———. 2016. *Atari to Zelda: Japan's Videogames in Global Contexts.* Cambridge, MA: MIT Press.

Cross, Katherine. 2017. How Trump Is Trying to Govern America Like an Internet Troll. *Rolling Stone*, February 23. http://www.rollingstone.com/politics/features/how-trump-is-trying-to-govern-america-like-an-internet-troll-w468518.

Deterding, Sebastian. 2009. Living Room Wars: Remediation, Boardgames, and the Early History of Video Wargaming. In *Joystick Soldiers, The Politics of Play in Military Video Games*, ed. Nina Huntemann and Matthew Thomas Payne, 1–16. New York: Routledge.

Dyer-Witheford, Nick, and Greig de Peuter. 2009. *Games of Empire: Global Capitalism and Video Games.* Minneapolis, MN: University of Minnesota Press.

Everett, Anna, and S. Craig Watkins. 2008. The Power of Play: The Portrayal and Performance of Race in Video Games. In *The Ecology of Games: Connecting Youth, Games, and Learning*, ed. Katie Salen, 141–166. Cambridge, MA: The MIT Press.

Foucault, Michel. 1980. Confessions of the Flesh. In *Power/Knowledge Selected Interviews and Other Writings*, ed. Colin Gordon, 194–228. New York: Pantheon Books.

———. 1982. The Subject and Power. *Critical Inquiry* 8 (4): 777–795.

———. 1990. *The History of Sexuality.* Vol. 1. New York: Vintage Books.

Fron, Janine, Tracy Fullerton, and Celia Pearce. 2007. *The Hegemony of Play.* Situated Play, Proceedings of DiGRA 2007 Conference.

Ging, Debbie. 2017. Alphas, Betas, and Incels: Theorizing the Masculinities of the Monosphere. *Men and Masculinities.* https://doi.org/10.1177/1097184X17706401.

Gotell, Lise, and Emily Dutton. 2016. "Sexual Violence in the 'Manosphere'": Antifeminist Men's Rights Discourses on Rape. *International Journal for Crime, Justice, and Social Democracy* 5 (2): 65–80.

Greene, Ronald W. 1998. Another Materialist Rhetoric. *Critical Studies in Mass Communication* 15 (1): 21–41.

Halberstam, Jack. 1998. *Female Masculinity.* Durham, NC: Duke University Press.

Harper, Todd. 2014. *The Culture of Digital Fighting Games: Performance and Practice.* New York: Routledge.

hooks, bell. 2003. *We Real Cool: Black Men and Masculinity.* New York: Routledge.

Huntemann, Nina, and Ben Aslinger, eds. 2013. *Global Games: Production, Play, and Place.* New York: Palgrave Macmillan.

Huntemann, Nina, and Thomas Payne. 2009. *Joystick Soldiers*. New York: Routledge.

Jenson, Jennifer, and Suzanne de Castell. 2010. Gender, Simulation, and Gaming: Research Review and Directions. *Simulation & Gaming* 41 (1): 51–71.

———. 2011. Girls @ Play. *Feminist Media Studies* 11: 167–179. https://doi.org/10. 1080/14680777.2010.521625.

Kafai, Yasmin B., Deborah Fields, and Michael T. Giang. 2009. *Transgressive Gender Play: Profiles and Portraits of Girl Players in a Tween Virtual World*. Breaking New Ground: Proceedings of the Digital Games Research Association (DiGRA), Brunel University, West London.

Kendall, Lori. 1998. Meaning and' Identity in "Cyberspace": The Performance of Gender, Class, and Race Online. *Symbolic Interaction* 21 (2): 129–153.

Kennedy, Helen. 2006. Illegitimate, Monstrous and Out There: Female 'Quake' Players and Inappropriate Pleasures. In *Feminism in Popular Culture*, ed. Joanne Hollows and Rachel Mosely, 183–201. London: Berg.

Kocurek, Carley. 2015. *Coin Operated Americans*. Minneapolis, MN: University of Minnesota Press.

Lagomarsino, John. 2017. Brianna Wu Says the Gamergate Playbook Poisoned the Election. *The Outline*, February 1. https://theoutline.com/post/983/brianna-wu-says-the-gamergate-playbook-poisoned-the-election.

Lauteria, Evan. 2012. _Ga(y)mer Theory_: Queer Modding as Resistance. *Reconstruction* 12 (2). http://reconstruction.eserver.org/122/Lauteria_Evan.shtml.

Lee, S. Austin, and Alexis Pulos, eds. 2016. *Video Games in East Asia*. New York: Palgrave Macmillan.

Leonard, David. 2006. Not a Hater, Just Keepin' It Real. The Importance of Race and Gender Based Game Studies. *Games and Culture* 1 (1): 83–88.

Liboriussen, Bjarke, and Paul Martin. 2016. Regional Game Studies. *Game Studies* 16 (1). http://gamestudies.org/1601/articles/liboriussen.

Lugo, Jairo, Tony Sampson, and Merlyn Lossada. 2002. Latin America's New Culture Industries Still Play Old Games. *Game Studies* 2 (2). http://www.gamestudies. org/0202/lugo/.

Maiberg, Emanuel. 2017. Under Trump, Gamergate Can Stop Pretending It Was About Games. *Motherboard*, February 9. https://motherboard.vice.com/en_us/article/bm5wd4/under-trump-gamergate-can-stop-pretending-it-was-about-games.

Marcotte, Amanda. 2016. Donald Trump's Campaign Really is Gamergate Being Played Out on a National Scale. *Salon*, September 15. http://www.salon. com/2016/09/15/gamergater/.

Miller, Toby. 2012. The Shameful Trinity: Game Studies, Empire, and the Cognitariot. In *Guns, Grenades, and Grunts: The First Person Shooter Game*, ed. Gerald Voorhees, Josh Call, and Katie Whitlock, 113–130. New York: Bloomsbury Academic.

Mukherjee, Souvik. 2017. *Videogames and Postcolonialism: Empire Plays Back*. Basingstoke: Palgrave Macmillan.

Murray, Soroya. 2017. The Rubble and the Ruin: Race, Gender and Sites of Inglorious Conflict in *Spec Ops: The Line*. In *Gaming Representation*, ed. J. Malkowski and T.M. Russworm, 147–163. Bloomington, IN: Indiana University Press.

Packer, Jeremy. 2013. The Conditions of Media's Possibility: A Foucauldian Approach to Media History. In *Media History and the Foundations of Media Studies*, ed. John Nerone, 1–34. New York: Blackwell.

Paul, Christopher A. 2013. *Resisting Meritocracy and Reappropriating Games: Rhetorically Rethinking Game Design*. Selected Papers of Internet Research. https://spir.aoir.org/index.php/spir/article/view/810.

Paul, Christopher A. 2018. *The Toxic Meritocracy of Video Games: Why Gaming Culture is the Worst*. Minneapolis, MN: University of Minnesota Press.

Penix-Tadson, Philip. 2016. *Cultural Codes: Videogames and Latin America*. Cambridge, MA: MIT Press.

Salter, Anastasia, and Bridget Blodgett. 2012. Hypermasculinity and Dickwolves: The Contentious Role of Women in the New Gaming Public. *Journal of Electronic Media* 56 (3): 401–416.

Shaw, Adrienne. 2014. *Gaming at the Edge*. Minneapolis, MN: University of Minnesota Press.

Smith, Dorothy E. 2005. *Institutional Ethnography: A Sociology for People*. Toronto, ON: Altamira Press.

Stahl, Roger. 2010. *Militainment, Inc. War, Media, and Popular Culture*. New York: Routledge.

Szablewicz, Marcella. 2016. A Realm of Mere Representation? 'Live' E-Sports Spectacles and the Crafting of China's Digital Gaming Image. *Games and Culture* 11 (3): 256–274.

Taylor, T.L. 2006. *Play Between Worlds: Exploring Online Game Culture*. Cambridge, MA: MIT Press.

Taylor, Nicholas. 2016. Now You're Playing with Audience Power: The Work of Watching Games. *Critical Studies in Media Communication* 33 (4): 293–307.

Taylor, Nicholas, Jennifer Jenson, and Suzanne de Castell. 2009. Cheerleaders, Booth Babes, Halo Hoes: Pro-gaming, Gender, and Jobs for the Boys. *Digital Creativity* 20 (9): 239–252.

Turkle, Sherry. 1997. *Life on the Screen: Identity in the Age of the Internet*. New York: Simon & Schuster.

Voorhees, Gerald. 2012. Neoliberal Multiculturalism in *Mass Effect*: The Government of Difference in Digital Role-Playing Games. In *Dungeons, Dragons and Digital Denizens: Digital Role-Playing Games*, ed. Gerald Voorhees, Josh Call, and Katie Whitlock, 259–277. New York City: Continuum International Publishing.

———. 2015. Neoliberal Masculinity: The Government of Play and Masculinity in E-Sports. In *Playing to Win: Sports, Video Games, and the Culture of Play*, ed. Thomas Oates and Robert Brookey, 63–91. Bloomington, IN: Indiana University Press.

Witkowski, Emma. 2012. On the Digital Playing Field: How We "Do Sport" with Networked Computer Games. *Games and Culture* 7 (5): 349–374.

———. 2013. Eventful Masculinities: Negotiations of Hegemonic Sporting Masculinities at LANs. In *Sports Videogames*, ed. Mia Consalvo, Konstantin Mitgutsch, and Abe Stein, 217–235. New York: Routledge.

Wolf, Mark J.P., ed. 2015. *Video Games Around the World*. Cambridge, MA: MIT Press.

Part I

Act Like a Man: Representations of Masculinity

2

"We're Going to Have to Do Things That Are Unthinkable": Masculinity/Games/Torture

Derek Burrill

To introduce into the philosophy of War itself a principle
of moderation would be an absurdity.
Carl von Clausewitz

Sometimes war dreams of itself.
Werner Herzog paraphrasing Clausewitz

During the GOP Presidential Primary Debate on Feb. 6, 2016, an ABC moderator asked, "Senator Cruz, some of the other candidates say they don't think waterboarding is torture. If elected President would you bring it back?" Cruz replied: "Um, I would not bring it back in any sort of widespread use, but when it comes to keeping this country safe, you can rest assured that as Commander in Chief, I would use whatever enhanced ter … (corrects himself) interrogation techniques we could to keep this country safe." Donald Trump, when posed with the same question, answers, "I would bring back waterboarding. And I'd bring back a helluva lot worse than waterboarding." The topic of torture on the campaign trail then became a game of one-upsmanship between Trump, himself and his supporters. On February 8th, Trump declared, "The other night at the debate they asked Ted Cruz … serious question, 'Well what do you think of waterboarding, is it ok?' And I, honestly, I thought he'd say 'absolutely' and he didn't!" At which point, one of his supporters in the front yelled, "pussy!" to which Trump responded, like an

D. Burrill (✉)
University of California, Riverside, CA, USA

© The Author(s) 2018
N. Taylor, G. Voorhees (eds.), *Masculinities in Play*, Palgrave Games in Context,
https://doi.org/10.1007/978-3-319-90581-5_2

attorney in a courtroom drama, "She just said a terrible thing. You know what she said? Shout it out cause I don't want to …" "PUSSY! She said he's a pussy … that's terrible. Terrible!" Trump says this with mock disgust, perhaps disappointed that he didn't come up with it himself. The crowd went wild.

In this scenario, Trump's insecure, immature and over-performative masculinity is contrasted with Cruz's hyper-pious, wonky and rhetorical masculinity. This exchange mirrors how men think and *perform* how and what they think about torture. For these two men who have not engaged in torture (and I think we can assume neither Cruz nor Trump have tortured anyone, in a strict sense at least), talking about torture as a bragging point when these two men are in front of the cameras, is a rhetorical device, a mode of proving and competition. Torture, to these two hegemonic, misogynist masculinities, operates within this debate as a force that impugns, a force that places the lesser male (Cruz) in the position, within the hierarchy of torture, as the tortured, the captive, the detained, regardless of whether it is acknowledged that Cruz did in fact (and does in fact) say that he is willing to use torture were he to become President. What places Trump as the Top and Cruz as the Bottom here is Trump's cooptation of one of his supporter's use of the term 'pussy', and in male-coded discourse, 'pussy' signifies the 'weakness' of femininity, and in turn, the penetrated, the queer, the subaltern. The one that 'takes it.' How then does this 'pussy-effect' relate to real torture? And how, for the purposes of this chapter, is this mirrored in the myriad representations of torture in videogames?

Masculinities in the digital imaginary are so often defined by the prevalent, historically situated modes of production, the cultural products and practices that are an expression of one's manhood; think here of the Atari joystick cowboy of the 1980s, or Bobo culture of the San Francisco Bay Area during the Dot Com boom of the late 1990s.[1] These masculine formations and identities are in many ways reactions to, and celebrations of, a particular form (and state) of technology and the cultural practices that surround them.[2] In a similar sense, I would argue that the gamer identity of the late 2000s and 2010s—the identity most commonly associated with the trolls and bullies behind Gamergate—is produced and reproduced through normative associations between gender and technology, cultural practices and the public sphere, as well as result of the ubiquity and normalization of war and battle videogames. At core, male bodies as discursive forces tend to overdetermine what is considered 'acceptable' and therefore, normative behavior.

In the U.S., from the multiplayer melee of the *Call of Duty* franchise, to the blatant military recruitment game *America's Army*, war games serve, in a larger sense, as a reflection and sublimation of the concept of 'militainment' as a direct product of the Constant State of War under George W. Bush's presidency, itself an extension of the continuing war on terror through drone attacks and the maintenance of Guantanamo Bay Prison by the Obama administration (Huntemann and Payne 2009; Voorhees et al. 2012). This will, most likely, continue under the authoritarian and reactionary Trump debacle (although it is early in his reign at the time of this writing) Torture is an increasingly troubling strategy utilized by government and military leaders, particularly after the 9/11 attacks, a practice that has become so omnipresent throughout Iraq, Afghanistan and at CIA Black-sites, that the CIA itself found that it had become functionally mundane. (Senate Select Committee 2014) Part of this normalization is due to it being euphemistically rebranded as 'enhanced interrogation', a term invented by the US military and CIA leaders in order to work around the US Army Field Handbook and the Geneva Conventions on Torture and Inhuman Treatment.

However, for this essay, my central argument is—of substantial importance to the US Military and Government's War of Attrition on public opinion in regards to torture—that there has been an increased normalization and ubiquity of representations of torture throughout the media. Hardt and Negri, in their probing study *Empire* (2000), identify this as "banalized" war, where the culture becomes so anesthetized to war and combat, that global conflicts are relegated to the status of media events. Similarly, Nick Dyer-Witheford and Grieg de Peuter identify a mutually-constative war-machine generated by the US military and the games industry;

> A newly frugal military began not only to adopt or adapt civilian games for training purposes, but also to directly collaborate with private-sector studios to create customized war games. The attacks of September 11, 2001, gave this rapprochement a major boost. The military poured funds into codesigned simulations to anticipate the new challenges of the war on terror. (Dyer-Witheford and de Peuter 2009)

The purpose behind this relationship is arguably, on the surface, to better train, recruit and empower soldiers. Ideologically, however, it seems reasonable to say that this is a means of controlling and molding public opinion in order to create a stultified and passive spectatorial public, a hypermasculinized virtual combat community, as well as an enriched military-industrial, global corporate apparatus. Thus, representations of torture in video games can be classified as examples of ideological inflection (discursive and performative moments of ideological enactment that serve to buttress that self-same ideology) as well as whatever narrative and pleasurable purposes they fulfill. What I am particularly interested in for the purposes of this work is how torture and masculinity are intimately intertwined, as well as how real masculinities and represented torture in the media, particularly video games, work together as an expression of repressed misogyny and homosocial desire, as well as nationalistic and ideological fantasies of imperialism and xenophobia. I take my title from one of Donald Trump's many near-erotic declarations of his nationalistic, masculinist-sadistic credentials as a means of framing the danger of these spiraling performances—and perverse celebrations—both in the virtual and the real.

Games of Torture

Representations of torture in the media are generally media-specific in their use, intent and structure; representations of torture on film are posed as a largely ethical/moral conundrum (*Zero Dark Thirty* being the most obvious recent case), while torture on TV is chiefly narrative and exploitive. On TV, torture scenes serve to move the plot along (a lazy writer's crutch, in many ways) and to compete, as far as violent/adult content, with shows on premium cable networks that don't have the same violent content limitations as network channels. However, torture in games is a hybrid of film and TV, with particular additions; these scenarios, in both cut-scenes and interactive segments, are both exploitive and pleasurable, working to support the U.S. ideological conceptions of torture as both efficacious and necessary, while also allowing the player to pretend they have the 'choice' to participate or not. Thus, an extension of my general argument is that representations of torture in videogames place the player in the position of moral superiority (as an extension of US national power), and through the illusion of choice and control, the player is positioned on the side in power, while also contradictorily being allowed to reject those same moral dimensions in order to act out their basest desires. The player, when they torture in games, can have it both ways; they inhabit a position of superiority (as the torturer) while enacting one of the most vile of human behaviors. To be clear, these torture scenes are where one character or avatar is being purposefully hurt while unable to respond or evade the violence, as opposed to scenes where the player simply watches an NPC get tortured as part of a cut-scene or the like. Often, this is in the context of an interrogation, but occasionally, the scene is framed as purely sadistic.

Torture scenes feature regularly in indie, AA and AAA games; examples exist in, to name a few: *Bioshock, Far Cry, LA Noire, Quake 4, Dead Space 2, Call of Duty: Black Ops, Far Cry 3, Wolfenstein, Battlefield 4, Splinter Cell, Silent Hill: Homecoming, Euphoria, Rampage, Sails of Glory, Tash-Kalar: Arena, Metal Gear Solid: Ground Zero, Manhunt* and *Manhunt 2*, and, of course, *24: The Game*. There are also countless websites like *torturegames.net, 666games.*

Fig. 2.1 Image of the player's avatar smashing a 'terrorist's' head in a grill, *The Torture Game 2*

net and *playragdollgames.com* that feature crude, yet exceedingly violent mini-games and more substantial games like *The Torture Game 2* (with over a million users) (Fig. 2.1).

Their popularity, while disturbing, isn't surprising as they clearly belong within the locus of online, fantasy and real-world activities that can be described as the masculine strategy I have termed "boyhood" in previous works, where the male figure is able to escape any real-world consequences by engaging in regressive, immature and unacceptable behaviors in virtual spaces.[3]

But what of the more narrative, interactive and sustained torture scenes in games like *LA Noire* or *24: The Game*? This brings me to another facet of my argument: that torture scenes in games are metaphorically and literally expressions of the masculine desire for domination through violence. However, for the purposes of this study, I am not as interested in discrete torture scenes within games as I am the interrogation of masculine desire and its expression in torture as personal, national and ideological statement. It can be argued, after all, that interrogation and torture are inherently game-like: there are essentially two players, both with ostensible strategies, order of play, and outcomes.[4] There are time limits, particularly if the ticking time bomb scenario is present;[5] there are limited areas of play, usually the interrogation room; and there are in-game objects: recording technologies, torture devices, information packets, pictures, etc. Additionally, there are 'results', usually in the form of winners and losers and 'information' gained through the use of intimidation, pain and mutilation, but also in player satisfaction and gameplay rewards. So, how to theorize torture within games as masculine expression and desire?

While it is hardly surprising that there is not a great deal of work done on masculinity and torture, there is even less work done on torture in video games. Mark Sample's excellent, "Virtual Torture: Videogames and the War on Terror," stands as the most substantial, if not the only (to my knowledge), example of a probing analysis of how torture works in videogames, as well as how torture is proposed as an efficacious form of player engagement. In analyzing *Splinter Cell* (2002), Sample writes:

> The player knows by virtue of the game interface that the apprenticeship in torture will always have a pay-off. The information is always useful, and always useful immediately. Here the intel is a five-digit key code that opens a door in the room. There is a proximity, then, between the site of torture and the site of information efficacy, where the intel is put to use. Such proximity reinforces the notion that not only does torture work well, it works well now. Put simply, *Splinter Cell* presents the fantasy that perfect information is always the outcome of coercive interrogation. (Sample 2008)

Sample then turns his attention to *24: The Game*, finding that the game mechanics and play have been constructed to further enhance the realism and necessity of techniques of torture:

> The player decides which tactic to use—and he may use several within the space of a few seconds—based on the current position of the cooperation zone. The stress graph is thus a biofeedback system, transforming internal psychological states into external data, which allows the player to hone his or her interrogation technique on the spot. (Sample)[6]

Sample completes his analysis with a call to resist, "fetishization of verisimilitude or a desire to meet or exceed the game's arbitrary scoring rubric," in favor of a critical praxis involving "thoughtful deliberation" where the relations of power laid bare by torture can be more thoroughly inspected. Needless to say, masculinities are not a crucial nexus in Sample's argument, but I find that his investigation of power and violence assumes a masculine subject as both player and character. This is logical, as nearly all of the avatars portrayed in interrogation and torture scenes are male and players of war and combat adventure games are almost exclusively boys and men.[7]

Embodied Torture

As per the above definition of torture within games, an interesting rhetorical problem within arguments surrounding torture often sparks calls for a more inclusive, expansive definition of torture. Here is where the aforementioned term, the 'pussy-effect', comes in. Now while this may be a problematic term for many academics and human rights activists, for everyday men, broadening the definition of torture to include solitary confinement, or saying that enhanced interrogation is both ethical and justified, is to let the edifice of heteronormative tough-guy masculinity weaken and dilute. And if for a moment the reader doesn't think educated men in power—politicians, legislators, bureaucrats—don't believe this at least at the subconscious level, then they are kidding themselves. Masculinity, no matter how it is formed or developed, operates as a bank does, through accumulation and investment. To assail ones assets—and this means all cultural codes pertaining to all other male 'investors'—is to assail each and every man's edifice. Redefining what constitutes torture risks treating the 'enemy' with kindness and therefore weakens the U.S. stance on foreign combatants, terrorists and any others considered enemies of the state. Also, more significantly, it erodes masculine standards of physical control and power (and therefore psychological coping and management strategies). Since masculinity and the hierarchy of male domination and submission is, at root, based on physical size—height, weight, fitness and technique—any 'lowering of the standards' risks destabilizing the hierarchy and therefore, all inter-masculine (and by extension, male-female and all other gendered/sexual) relations. Here, I argue that depictions of torture in videogames are more than just representations, they are *symptoms* of our collective discomfort, anxiety, desire and confusion over substantial changes in U.S. culture and politics, particularly the post-9/11 War on Terror waged by the U.S. military and government on a multitude of fronts, as well as the waning political and economic power of the middle-class (particularly white, middle-class males). In a sense, this is the objectification of white masculinity. Bib Brecher writes in *Torture and the Ticking Bomb*:

> So what sort of act is torture? What sort of intention is an intention to inflict 'severe pain or suffering' on a person? ... Pain itself is not enough: it has to be of a sort and of an intensity to achieve something very specific. The intention is to destroy the victim's normative relation to the torturer, and thus to themselves as a person: to make the victim into something that is no longer a person. Alone with their torturers, treated by them not as a person but as an object, human beings cease to be persons. (Brecher, 76)

Brecher's central assertion is that by erasing the victim's relationship, *as a subject*, to the torturer, the victim is transformed into an object. Thus, the male torturer is attempting to, with each blow and shock, to evacuate the affective qualities and control of the victim, to devalue them into a state of pure abjection. In gamespace and during gameplay, this desire to evacuate the affective is posed as pleasure, for many of these scenes are clearly not essential to the narrative. We can then ask, does a torture objective in a game frame the event the same way that other media do? Is it possible this abject, affectless object then exists outside of ideology? Can a real body be so de-corporealized that it can no longer be identified, located, felt? What of a digital body, one that ostensibly doesn't feel pain, but still reacts to the player's violence?

If we look to Kristeva's use of *abjection*, a body's locus between subject and object, an entity that exists in purely liminal and figurative terms, we begin to see another key component of the masculine acts of torture: competition (Kristeva 1982). A main goal of masculine torture then, whether stated or not, is to thrust the victim outside of *himself* (for it is nearly always a male being tortured), outside the *symbolic order*, so that the dominant can achieve complete submission, so as to comingle food and shit, water and piss, force and pain. This stands as the central goal of torture: the complete abjection of the other. Of course, this has homoerotic and sadist dimensions, but in this case, abjection and total control are fundamental.[8]

On the abject, Judith Butler writes:

> We see this most clearly in the examples of those abjected beings who do not appear properly gendered; it is their very humanness that comes into question. Indeed, the construction of gender operates through exclusionary means, such that the human is not only produced over and against the inhuman, but through a set of foreclosures, radical erasures, that are, strictly speaking, refused the possibility of cultural articulation. Hence, it is not enough to claim that human subjects are constructed, for the construction of the human is a differential operation that produces the more and less "human," the inhuman, the humanly unthinkable. (Butler, 8, 1993).

For Butler, then, there is no way to *know* ourselves, our bodies, and by extension our gender. We must constantly say that we are not, a) inhuman, and b) the *other* gender. What then happens to the male when he is tortured? As I have argued earlier, if we are to accept that gender is built, acculturated through dynamic, discursive processes—and that this process is necessarily maintained (and instigated) by Butler's sense of enunciation of the self and the body, its boundaries and its differences—then the self and the body can certainly be 'undone'. In this sense, a body is undone by the removal of the boundaries between the tortured body and the torturer's tools. Even in skin-to-skin contact, the fist is a tool; for the attacker it is an extension, but for the victim the fist is just another machine in a disembodying arsenal. If the the body is broken, the self follows. But, sometimes, the opposite is pursued, where the self is beset upon by lies, exaggerations, threats and steady, constant stimulus, so that the victim no longer is able to judge with his perceptive apparatus what is real and what is not. In this way, the self can fall out of the Symbolic; it can be said to exist outside of discourse. Not forever banished, but when subjected to gross amounts of pain and even the removal of body parts (so one is left to make sense of a palimpsest of one's own body), the idea of self-containment is shattered. Thus, game torture scenes become a fantasy space where masculinity can witness it's own annihilation first-hand, arguably placing the player in the position of 'those that give orders'—higher ups in the chain of command at, say, Guantanamo Bay or Abu Gharib—those that use the hierarchy to avoid responsibility and the ugly truth of broken bodies. This is, again, boyhood, rebooted, with pliers in hand.

So, it seems that in real torture as well as in simulated torture, the aim is to ensure that the body's boundary is undone. Essentially, the player is able to safely experience this dissolution through the tortured avatar while also enjoying the inherent power that accompanies torture through the torturing avatar. The body can also be abjected through the removal or dissolution of common signifiers and materiality of gender: the penis and testicles, most obviously.[9] But, there are other pieces of gender that are exploited—autonomy is key to masculinity, from others (especially women) as well as from one's own emotions. So, to confiscate autonomy (often mistakenly referred to as agency), as well as the ability to prove one's masculinity (crucial to embodied masculinity as well as psychological narratives of heroism and self-sufficiency), is to also take away gender itself. Additionally, taking away the temporal anchors of the self—through endless noise, cold, boredom, nothingness—as well as evacuating the spatial power ensured by the male physique (the inability to move in space, close confinement, proximity to hostile others, drowning, entombing, etc.), both of these strategies work through the process of removal. Finally, the attainment of this state for the torturer, the state of having undone a self and body, to render it ungendered and desexed, is to attain not just mastery and abjection of the other, it is also to witness one's own power articulated and enacted through a kind of iteration, so that the torturer takes over the process of gendering itself.

Serious Games: Torture as Competition

When it comes to violence, particularly torture, every conflict or event that finds two men squaring off against each other acts as a hypothetical scenario that I call the mytho-hypothetical. If one of these hypotheticals is posed, the masculine urge is to prove themselves up to the challenge, or not (see the film

Force Majeure for an excellent example of this in a family setting; for a more literal example, see the game *L.A. Noire*, particularly the interrogation scenes). Hence torture for the masculine viewer/consumer is often about divining whether the viewer himself would 'break'. "I could get him to talk," or, "I wouldn't break," are the equivalent of the enactment of the masculine mytho-hypothetical; this is a performed example of the Great Chain of Masculine Being, a constantly produced and reproduced embodied masculine hierarchy.

Thus the mytho-hypothetical relies on the mythos of machoness and classical, antiquated masculinities, that 'might makes right'. The mytho-hypothetical takes many forms, but is essentially, "will I be able to use my body, my masculinity, to win and overcome another male-as-obstacle." A familiar form of the masculine mytho-hypothetical is the hero's journey, first identified by Joseph Campbell in *The Hero With a Thousand Faces* and famously played out in Star Wars and throughout the always-cooptive work of George Lucas. The mytho-hypothetical is historically and culturally situated, so the specifics of a black teenager's hypothetical may differ from a 65 year-old gay white male, but the larger structure is always the same: the body must be tested and prevail. A common product of the mytho-hypothetical is the 'versus' trope, perfectly realized in the sensationalized and epic violence of *Batman vs. Superman: Dawn of Justice* (2016), and any of the mash-up Marvel video-games or head-to-head combat games like the *Mortal Kombat* franchise. The 'versus' mytho-hypothetical is, essentially, pontificating about which person, hero, character—friend, even—would win in a fight. This is at the root of all masculinities; it is its basic common denominator.[10] Building on this 'logic', the nucleus of pleasure and desire in torture scenes found in 24: *The Game* or *Manhunt* as well as in the horror genre (the *Resident Evil* films and games, for example), is composed of bodies damaging other bodies in the hopes of identifying a winner—either the one who succeeds in the interrogation, or the one who holds out and doesn't break. Thus, it can be said that all forms of screened torture are linked to the greater ideological matrix of masculine nationalism through their competitive structure, clearly defined players and purposeful outcomes. It should come as no surprise that torture 'works'—is productive—within narrative, interactive and cut-scene segments of videogames, and that its competitive core serves as a reflection of masculine cultural desires and anxieties over the War on Terror, the Great Recession and the general malaise and fascism that seems to be withering Western democracies.

Of course, competitive masculinities are tied to Timothy Beneke's "proving" masculinity, as well as Connell's "hegemonic masculinity" in that a performance of power must be enacted in order for the male identity to be legitimized (Beneke 1997; Connell 2005). In the case of torture, however, the power dynamic has been collapsed; one man enters the torture chamber with the power to kill another. And yet, in narrative (and often non-narrative) game scenes, we are always left to believe that the tortured still retains *some* power, however small. This could be the power to resist, the power of knowledge that they will not disclose, the power of time in the case of a 'ticking time bomb scenario'. However, it is patently false to declare that the tortured has any power in a real interrogation; again, the central purpose of torture is to annihilate the victim's self. If someone argues that torture in the real is a means of acquiring intelligence or information, they are performing the fallacy of narrativizing torture, revealing their own stakes in supporting (and therefore answering the interpolation of) the masculine mytho-hypothetical.[11] Games as torture and torture within games serve to illustrate one of the most debilitating and profoundly self-destructive facets of masculinity: the need to inhabit all positions at once, to speak and stand in for all others, to control, own and dominate all bodies and selves within their grasp. Could it be that the very foundation of democracy—representation—is itself that which ensures its own collapse? And if so, is the ubiquitous representation of torture in the media one of the most telling symptoms of this collapse?

Torture, as an act, is the opposite of possibility. It is monological, bounded, delimiting and fixed. Rhetorically, torture destroys collaboration, it disrupts empathy and affective flow; it is always a monologue, no matter how much the victim speaks or screams. It is manned in the same way a drone attack is unmanned. Its ends are its means. Torture is hegemonic masculinity *ne plus ultra*, a violent performance that ensures and guarantees its own logic. And when we play through games of torture, our bodies are the losers, devalued both psychically and ideologically. The players are left in an abject state, evacuated of empathy, all the better to serve as puppets of a capitalist, nationalistic, and colonialist project.

Notes

1. See Carly Kocurek's Coin-Operated Americans: Rebooting Boyhood at the Video Game Arcade for an excellent history and study of young masculinities and games; (Minneapolis, Minnesota: U of Minnesota Press, 2015).
2. For a more complete discussion of this conception, I pursue this type of techno-masculinity in detail in *Die Tryin': Videogames, Masculinity, Culture* (New York: Peter Lang, 2008).
3. See *Die Tryin': Videogames, Masculinity, Culture*, New York: Peter Lang, 2008.
4. Miguel Sicart, in *Play Matters*, proposes a theory of play that understands play as deeply entrenched in reality, not separate from it. In many ways, for Sicart, play is a strategy, a ontological tactic akin to my notion of boyhood I lay out

in *Die Tryin*; play is a way to navigate the increasingly technological world, but is also a behavioral response to increased competition, logics of accumulation and antagonistic modes of being. His notion of 'dark play' is particularly useful for framing activities that while 'fun' to some, are dangerous, illegal or immoral to many.

5. This is a familiar scenario: information must be 'acquired' from a suspect in order to prevent the explosion of a bomb, with a definitive time limit in which to obtain the information. This is also the most common scenario that those who are pro-torture use to justify either 'enhanced interrogation' or outright torture.

6. Sample likens this to the relationship between Walter Benjamin's division of types of experience into *Erfahrung*, lived, continuous experience, and *Erlebnis*, momentary and disconnected experience, that the sudden, repetitive and demonstrable actions required in a torture game sequence shift knowledge and experience from the more positive and reflective *Erfahrung* to *Erlebnis*. He writes, "So much rides on performing the immediate action that the larger framing experience dissipates, leaving only the shock of the present moment, and that too is fragmented. As such, the game conceals the full experience of torture-interrogation from the player, imparting instead a stylized distillation that focuses only on the next goal". Here, although Sample doesn't quite enunciate it, he seems to clearly favor Erfahrung as a means of understanding and perceiving the world, particularly in relation to what are potentially demoralizing, degrading and sadistic interactive enactments. In this sense, his reading of Benjamin generally follows my own, in particular when it comes to performative masculinity. Benjamin's conception of the loss of aura and the politicization of art as entwined effects of the age of mechanical reproduction work here to highlight both the necessity of modern masculinities to find an authentic root in the built, macho body (and a traditional, stalwart masculinity), as well as how a natural outcome of the War on Terror is to digitize moral and ethical demonstrations of national fervor and duty in the form of discrete, violent performances under the guise of in-game progress and narrative closure (and triumph).

7. See *Generation M2: Media in the Lives of 8–18-Year-Olds*, Victoria J. Rideout, M.A., Ulla G. Foehr, Ph.D. and Donald F. Roberts, Ph.D., A Kaiser Family Foundation Study, (2010) pp. 25–27, www.kaiserfamilyfoundation.com, and two of my essays, "There's a Soldier in All of Us": Choreographing Virtual Recruitment in Choreographies of 21st Century War, edited by Gay Morris and Jens Geirdorf (Oxford: Oxford University Press, 2016), and "Value Theory and Online Video Gaming," *Advances in Journalism and Communication*, (Vol 2, 3, Sept., 2014).

8. See Leo Bersani's compelling essay "Is the Rectum a Grave?".

9. One of the most memorable of these sexualized, sadistic scenes in film is the rope-testicle torture of James Bond by Le Chiffre in *Casino Royale* (2006).

This scene is commonly placed at the top of Top 10 Bond torture scenes lists. Presumably, this scene would have been included in the *Casino Royale* video game, but the game was canceled early in its production by Electronic Arts. However, many of the scenes from the film did find their way into the game *007: Quantum of Solace* (Activision, 2008), and yet this infamous torture scene was not included, presumably to garner a lower classification rating. Or perhaps because the developer thought the player wouldn't be able to stomach something so emasculating, to both the avatar and player?

10. It is also at the basis of pleasure in the *Saw* films—and of the entire torture porn genre—the viewer is asked, 'Would you survive? Are you smart or tough enough?' It would seem that the blood and gore of torture porn would be the center of interest for the viewer, and in a sense it is, much like other horror and slasher genres and films.Yet, the way the torture events are staged, so often between an anonymous torturer (Jigsaw for the *Saw* franchise) and what seems like a randomly chosen victim, illustrates that torture, as the heart of the narrative, is actually an elaborate game for the torturer, as well as an elaborate manipulation of audience expectations and identification. The audience is interpolated relentlessly; What would you do? Would you escape? Saw off another victim's limb to break free? As there is not room to discuss the torture porn phenomenon in more detail in this work, this study focuses on torture that is framed as politically motivated or socially contextualized, instead of upon torture for it's own visual and auditory pleasures (like torture porn).

11. In this sense, a TV and game character like *24*s Jack Bauer serves an a unique vessel for masculine desire as he is both the torturer and the tortured over the course of the show's 7 seasons and films (excepting the 2016–2017 reboot), and throughout the game's multiple levels and chapters. He tortures both men and women, and is himself tortured on many occasions, and yet is never broken. Bauer is, in effect, the Platonic masculine figure within the game of torture, always the winner, by any means necessary.

Bibliography

Beneke, Timothy. 1997. *Proving Manhood: Reflections on Men and Sexism*. Berkeley, CA: University of California Press.

Bogost, Ian. 2008. Simulating Torture. watercoolergames.org. Accessed 8 Jan 2017.

Brecher, Bob. 2007. *Torture and the Ticking Bomb*. Malden, MA: Blackwell.

Connell, Raewyn. 2005. *Masculinities*. 2nd ed. Berkeley, CA: U. of California Press.

Dyer-Witheford, Nick, and Greig de Peuter. 2009. *Games of Empire: Global Capitalism and Video Games*. Minneapolis, MN: University of Minnesota Press.

Hardt, Michael, and Antonio Negri. 2000. *Empire*. Cambridge, MA: Harvard University Press.

Huntemann, Nina B., and Matthew Thomas Payne, eds. 2009. *Joystick Soldiers: The Politics of Play in Military Video Games*. New York: Routledge.

Kristeva, Julia. 1982. *Powers of Horror: An Essay on Abjection*. New York: Columbia University Press.

Sample, Mark L. 2008. Virtual Torture: Videogames and the War on Terror. *gamestudies.org*, 8 (2).

Senate Select Committee on Intelligence, and Diane Feinstein. 2014. *The Senate Intelligence Committee Report on Torture: Committee Study of the Central Intelligence Agency's Detention and Interrogation Program*. New York: Melville Press.

Voorhees, Gerald, Joshua Call, and Katie Whitlock. 2012. *Guns, Grenades and Grunts: First-Person Shooter Games*. New York: Bloomsbury.

Games/Films/TV

25: Quantum of Solace
26
27: The Game
America's Army
Bioshock
Battlefield 4
Casino Royale
Dead Space 2
Call of Duty: Black Ops
Euphoria
Far Cry
Far Cry 3
Hostel 1 & 2
LA Noire
Metal Gear Solid: Ground Zero
Manhunt
Manhunt 2
Quake 4
Rampage
Sails of Glory
Saw franchise
Splinter Cell
Silent Hill: Homecoming
Tash-Kalar: Arena
The Shield
Wolfenstein
Zero Dark Thirty

3

Army Men: Military Masculinity in *Call of Duty*

Gregory Blackburn

In 1961, a group of young programmers at a Department of Defense–funded MIT research lab created *Spacewar!*, a simple yet revolutionary representation of space combat (Halter 2006). As the video game industry developed, this initial influence from the US military persisted, as branches of the military have both adapted commercial game technology for training purposes (Nichols 2010; Stahl 2010) and offered support and guidance in the development of commercially available games (Leonard 2004; Mirrless 2009; Power 2007). In this way, video games began their contribution to the world of "militainment," the long-standing tradition of cultural artifacts that turn warfare into a consumable entertainment product (Stahl 2010, 6). The decades following the development of *Spacewar!* have seen the release of hundreds of military-themed video games (Breuer et al. 2011; Hitchens et al. 2014), many produced in association with the US military (Nichols 2010), constituting a distinct genre in gaming (Huntemann and Payne 2010). As an interactive medium, these military-themed video games provide civilians with an "invitation to cross over and try on a soldier identity" (Stahl 2010, 91), an invitation that carries the potential to "normalize certain practices, habits, and dispositions toward war" (15). The particular construction of the soldier identity offered in these games has attracted criticism for its bias toward a Western perspective (Breuer et al. 2011; Neiborg 2010; Smicker 2010), its reliance on violence and aggression (Gagnon 2010; Mirrless 2009; Stahl 2010), and its oppositional relationship to a heavily stereotyped violent and exotic Middle

G. Blackburn (✉)
University of Massachusetts, Amherst, MA, USA

© The Author(s) 2018
N. Taylor, G. Voorhees (eds.), *Masculinities in Play*, Palgrave Games in Context,
https://doi.org/10.1007/978-3-319-90581-5_3

East (Cassar 2013; Höglund 2008; King and Leonard 2010). What has remained underexplored is the ways in which this soldier identity is constructed in highly gendered ways, situated in our cultural understanding of militarized masculinity.

Military Masculinity

Masculinity is not a single fixed, biologically determined set of attitudes, thoughts, and behaviors enacted by men (Pleck 1981), as race, class, sexuality, and other components of identity intersect to produce many distinct and constantly shifting forms of masculinities (Connell and Messerschmidt 2005). While these many forms of masculinities exist in society, they are not all granted equal standing, but exist within a hierarchy (Connell 2005). At the top of this hierarchy exists hegemonic masculinity, a particular assemblage of traits and behaviors that reflects and reinforces patriarchal structures, both through the structural advantaging of men over women and through privileging certain forms of masculinity while marginalizing others. In this formulation, hegemonic masculinity is not to be understood as the typical behavior of most, if any, men. Rather, it is a constructed ideal that serves to naturalize the economic and social control men wield within a patriarchal structure. Though aspects of this ideal can shift to preserve its hegemonic position, some qualities have remained entrenched and relatively stable over time.

Historically, the military has played an important role in cultural conceptions of the hegemonic masculine ideal. Coercing a large population into participating in war requires significant social pressure, and masculinity has been co-opted by military institutions worldwide as an effective means of socializing men into roles that support the aims of militarization (Ashe 2013; Hale 2012; Higate 2003; Hopton 2003; Kovitz 2003). This has resulted in the cultural valorization of those traditional aspects of hegemonic masculinity deemed useful in the socializing of soldiers, including but not limited to an emphasis on physical strength, aggression, emotional stoicism, and normalized heterosexuality (Arkin and Dobrofsky 1978; Barrett 1996; Duncanson 2015; Higate 2003; Hockey 2003). As such, an insuperable overlapping of the cultural ideals of the warrior and the masculine man is one of the most persistent and universal cultural formations of gender (Basham 2016; Hale 2012; Hutchings 2008; Morgan 1994). Even as women have increased their presence within the armed forces, this coding of military service as fundamentally masculine has remained largely in place within mediated representations of the military (Brown 2007; Tasker 2002) and within military institutions themselves (Hale 2012; Kronsell 2016).

But just as hegemonic masculinity is not a fixed construction, new facets of masculinity are grafted onto the soldier identity as it shifts in response to changes in social reality. The increasing importance of managerial roles within the military, alongside the rising importance of technological mastery, reinforced the qualities of intelligence and professionalism as key aspects of masculinity, if still subordinate to the traditional image of combat masculinity (Brown 2007; Duncanson 2015). As Western militaries became increasingly occupied with peacekeeping and nation-building missions in recent decades, softer aspects of masculinity that emphasized a soldier's role as a protector, civilizing force, and harbinger of democratic values were emphasized alongside the traditional warrior ideal (Duncanson 2015; Khalili 2011; Niva 1998; Whitworth 2004). This has resulted in multiple military masculinities, all constructed in relation to the traditional hegemonic formation (Brown 2007; Higate 2003).

Military masculinity is constantly reproduced within military institutions through recruitment, enlistment, training, and service (Arkin and Dobrofsky 1978; Brown 2007; Hale 2012; Hockey 2003). However, only an estimated 7.3% of living Americans have ever taken part in military service (Chalabi 2015). While most people lack this direct experience, the military masculine ideal still circulates throughout society, represented in mediated images of the soldier identity. Connell and Messerschmidt (2005) argue for the significance of these mediated models of masculinity, as "such models refer to, but also in various ways distort, the everyday realities of social practice" (838). These models may not reflect the day-to-day lived experience of most men, just as most men are not directly involved with the military or exposed to active combat. Instead, they function at a symbolic level, demonstrating ideals of masculinity that can be translated "as on-hand material to be actualized, altered, or challenged through practice in a range of different local circumstances … provid[ing] a cultural framework that may be materialized in daily practices and interactions" (849–850). In the case of military masculinities, the practices of the relatively small percentage of the population are distilled into selected media representations, which provide a framework for understanding masculinity in the everyday lives of people, thus "contribut[ing] to hegemony in the society-wide gender order as a whole" (838). These models appear throughout society, in film, television, advertisements, and even children's toys (Furia and Bielby 2009; Stahl 2010). The consequences of the dissemination of military masculinity are numerous, from affirming masculinized aggressive foreign policies (Cockburn 2010), to encouraging sexual violence (Eriksson Baaz and Stern 2009; Higate 2007), to maintaining the cultural subordination of feminine qualities (Duncanson 2015).

It is into this landscape that military-themed video games now contribute to the social construction of gendered identity, led most prominently by the *Call of Duty* series. Composed of over 20 entries, *Call of Duty* has been the top-selling video game franchise in North America for seven consecutive years, with publisher Activision reporting sales exceeding a quarter of a billion units across the life of the series (Knight 2016). As the industry leader, it is an exemplar of the military games genre, a significant potential source of representations of masculinity, and a suitable entry point for exploring military masculinity in video games. In this analysis, I examine how militarized masculinity is constructed within *Call of Duty*, how this construction reinforces the default conflation between military and masculine ideals, and how traditionally entrenched aspects of masculinity are in turn reinforced and challenged throughout the series. I focus my analysis on the single-player campaign modes of the games. This is not to discount the importance of the series' popular multiplayer modes, as the social and ludic elements of those modes can yield considerable insight (e.g. Höglund 2014; Payne 2010). Rather, as authored experiences featuring cutscenes, dialogue, and highly scripted set pieces, the single-player campaigns provide reasonably fixed ideological representations that frame the more dynamic multiplayer experiences (Höglund 2014), providing for an initial inquiry into the question of military masculinity in gaming. Additionally, to maintain a focus on current, shifting constructions of masculinity, I restrict my analysis to the entries in the series set in either modern or near-future time frames.

Men at War

First and foremost, *Call of Duty* marks the military as a predominantly male space, where war is a contest primarily instigated, waged, and resolved by men. This is most visible in the deeply skewed patterns of gender representation apparent in the series. The story campaign of *Black Ops 2* provides a typical example of these male-dominated narratives, featuring two playable protagonists, the father-son team of Alex and David Mason, battling their principal antagonist, Raul Menendez. All but three named characters in the game are male. There are no women in the squads of soldiers who accompany the player, nor are there women present within the entire command structure of the military, from the player's immediate commanding officer to the Secretary of Defense. This imbalance extends beyond the main cast, as both the friendly and enemy armies are rendered with exclusively male avatars. With few exceptions, this lack of representation for women can be found throughout the series.

The military is further marked as a male domain by the repeated appearance of a thematic link between fatherhood and war. Throughout the series, fathers are responsible for bringing their sons into the military sphere. In *Black Ops 2*, Alex Mason trains his son David for military service from a young age; the game later follows David as he continues to fight his father's old enemies. *Advanced Warfare* begins with protagonist Jack Mitchell and his friend discussing how their choice to enroll was determined by their fathers' roles as military men. *Ghosts* centers on the Walker family, a father and two brothers who are all in the service. Mothers are conspicuously absent in these stories, either briefly mentioned as deceased or not acknowledged at all. In this recurring trope, military service becomes an almost genetically inherited trait passed down from father to son, naturalizing the myth of a biological, inborn militaristic character in masculinity. Even in the absence of such biological ties, a patriarchal family dynamic is recreated symbolically through the repeated appearance of older commanding officers instructing and directing their younger charges. The *Modern Warfare* series conflates the process of military training and mentoring with a sort of surrogate fatherhood, as Captain Price inherits command of the unit from his mentor and previous captain, Macmillan, and later initiates the game's protagonist McTavish into the unit. These relationships are portrayed as significant to the men, with Macmillan affectionately referring to Price as "son," and Price later referring to McTavish the same way. This symbolic conflation of military structure and family is literalized in *Ghosts*, where Elias Walker is both the father and commanding officer of the protagonist. By marrying the military with this father-son dynamic, access to the power and prestige of military command becomes a familial birthright, a mantle handed down from father to son.

The player is implicated in this dynamic through the campaign structure of an alternating sequence of playable missions and non-interactive cutscenes. These interstitial cutscenes typically take the form of a virtualized mission briefing, voiced by a male superior officer. Whether ordering the player on to the next mission, or providing the definitive account of the circumstances of the last, the game lends a predominantly male authorial voice to these sections. A reinforcing and repeating pattern emerges. During play, a cast of younger men enact war, while during breaks, an assemblage of older men narrativize and validate their actions.

Men and Women in the Military

Of course, despite the heavily gendered images of militaries, they are not exclusively male institutions. Women play a prominent role in the US military, comprising 15.3% of all active-duty personnel (Johnson and Stamp 2015). Recent years have seen greater opportunity for female representation in the armed forces, including the opening of all combat roles to women soldiers and the introduction of the first female Army Rangers (Rosenberg and Phillips 2015). Yet, even as regulations explicitly favoring men break down, the long-standing implicit norms in the military continue to favor traditionally masculine traits and disparage traditionally feminine traits (Kovitz 2003; Kronsell 2016; Rosenberg and Phillips 2015). Hegemonic masculinity is a relational concept, and remains constructed against femininity to support the continued existence of patriarchal social structures (Connell 2005). The integration of women into the armed services thus becomes dependent upon their embodiment of preexisting masculine ideals, rather than a necessary acceptance or validation of the feminine (Hale 2012; Hopton 2003). This pattern is reflected in mediated representations as well, as analyses of both film and military recruiting ads largely continue to place femininity and military service in opposition to each other (Brown 2007; Furia and Bielby 2009).

These larger social conditions inform *Call of Duty*'s recent attempts to integrate women into the series. Developers added the ability to select a female avatar in the game's multiplayer to *Ghosts* in 2013. The following year's *Advanced Warfare* featured Ilona, a female soldier who fights alongside the player throughout much of the game. In 2015's *Black Ops 3*, players were first granted the option to select a female avatar for the campaign. This entry in the series also featured several notable female antagonists and included women among the common enemy combatants. These changes earned critical praise for expanding the limited portrayals of women in games, and for supporting the cultural visibility of female soldiers (Riendeau 2014). However, this inclusion comes only in the form of women who adhere strictly to the masculinized soldier identity. Apart from her appearance, which is coded as typically feminine, *Advanced Warfare*'s presentation of Ilona is absent any other identifiable feminine markers. Her presence as the only woman shown in a military role goes unremarked upon, and her personality—stoic, tough, aggressive—is indistinguishable from any number of the game's male characters who embody the typical masculine warrior ideal. In *Black Ops 3*, regardless of the selection of a male or female avatar, the player experiences the same story, events, and dialogue in what the developers' label a "gender neutral script" (Makuch 2015, n.p.). These reductions of gender to its purely aesthetic qualities strip it of its larger social significance, ignoring the degree to which the soldier identity arrives pre-coded as masculine. Through its omission, the feminine remains positioned as incompatible with military masculinity, further enforcing masculinity's hegemonic subordination of femininity.

Due to the oppositional relationship of military masculinity to femininity, military practices often discursively marry the feminine to the image of a vulnerable civilian in need of military protection (Kronsell 2016). Likewise, outside of the examples discussed above, *Call of Duty* typically presents women as victims, liabilities to be either rescued or revenged by the male protagonists. While the waves of enemies faced by the player are almost exclusively male, the crowds of civilians routinely caught in harm's way, such as in *Modern Warfare 2*'s airport massacre, are composed of an equal mix of genders. In *Modern Warfare 3*, the human cost of a terrorist attack is demonstrated through an extended sequence that culminates in the player witnessing the death of a civilian mother and her daughter. Even women who occupy positions of potential power see their agency removed as they are placed in danger, dependent upon rescue by men. In the first *Modern Warfare*, the only female soldier depicted in the campaign is the pilot of a crashed helicopter who the player must rescue and carry from the wreckage. *Black Ops 2*'s President Marion Bosworth's presence within the game is reduced to the subject of an escort mission, as the player leads her to safety following an attack on her motorcade.

The *Black Ops 2* mission "Time and Fate" demonstrates the strength of this male protector–female victim dichotomy, as the player controls the principal antagonist Raul Menendez in his attempt to reach his captured sister. Placed in this perspective, the player is asked to identify with the a narco-terrorist and torturer. The strength of the motivation to protect his innocent sister provides the rationale for the player to empathize with a character such as Menendez. The entire mission is structured to lean heavily into the emotional valence of this dynamic, as the player encounters enemy soldiers attacking female villagers in a manner strongly implying sexual violence. Combat is designed to be uncharacteristically up close and graphic in this sequence, with the player provided close-quarters weapons and enemies programmed to directly charge close rather than seek cover. As such, kills during this scene take place quite close to the player's perspective, with many being accompanied by a time-slowing mechanic that emphasizes the violence and gore. Taken together, the mission connects the player to Menendez on a visceral, emotional level in a way that supersedes the moral and political motivations defining the character elsewhere in the game, further normalizing and universalizing the protector quality of the masculine military ideal.

Heteronormativity

Hegemonic masculinity does not simply place men above women, but functions in part by creating a hierarchy of masculinities. The most problematic aspect of this hierarchy is the subordination of gay masculinities to a dominant heterosexual masculinity, wherein "[g]ayness, in patriarchal ideology, is the repository of whatever is symbolically expelled from hegemonic masculinity" (Connell 2005, 78). This has traditionally been evidenced in military attitudes toward homosexuality, where "the insecurities brought about by a homosocial culture have at times engendered an acute homophobia" (Duncanson 2015, 235). This homophobia drove the long-standing ban on gay service members and the institutional belief that homosexuality was a deviant trait that could undermine troop morale and unit cohesion (Arkin and Dobrofsky 1978). These attitudes were made manifest in discursive practices of military training, where failure to adhere to masculine standards of physical toughness and endurance was equated with homosexuality and emasculation, typically through homophobic and misogynistic slurs from instructors and fellow soldiers (Higate 2003; Hockey 2003; Woodward 1998). In recent years, attitudes have shifted; since the repeal of Don't Ask Don't Tell in 2011, gay men and women have been allowed to serve openly, and studies show military personnel to be generally accepting of the new policy (Belkin et al. 2013). While the presence of gay service members is tolerated, there still exists a cultural pressure to keep homosexuality private and discreet (Bulmer 2013).

Call of Duty reinforces this subordination of gay masculinities largely through a tacit heteronormativity. For the most part, questions of sex and sexuality are simply avoided; the focus of these games is war, and the majority of time spent playing is preoccupied with the acts of warfare. In the rare moments that the series steps outside the battlefield and into a setting where elements of sexuality have an opportunity to appear, they do so within a heterosexual framework. This happens in small moments, such as a cutscene where the protagonist's (and thus the player's) eyes linger over a stereotypically sexualized secretary while touring the Pentagon in Black Ops, when the character Harper catcalls women at a tropical resort in Black Ops 2, or elsewhere in that same game when a group of soldiers gather prior to a mission to discuss their wives' inability to refrain from gossip. In this, Call of Duty is in line with most mainstream video games, which with rare exception operate from a default heteronormative stance (Krobova et al. 2015; Shaw 2009). While sexuality is not a particularly salient element of the series, this assumed heterosexual perspective, coupled with a total lack of any identifiably gay characters, still conforms to the hegemonic masculine ideal.

Aggression and Obedience

Many of the primary traditional attributes of the soldiering identity correspond closely with traditionally valued masculine attributes, such as an emphasis on physical strength and fitness, aggressive and dominating behavior, and an orientation toward action and competition (Basham 2016; Hockey 2003; Duncanson 2015). It is these characteristics of militarized masculinity which the moment-to-moment gameplay of the *Call of Duty* series most emphasizes. The majority of gameplay consists of standard first-person shooter elements. The range of actions available to the player is relatively restricted, allowing for movement, selecting weapons, and firing them. Level design and mission structure are built to accommodate these actions, and thus emphasize a straightforward, aggressive playstyle. Enemies will spawn in infinite waves until the player passes predetermined checkpoints. At other times, the player's progress will be blocked until a set number of enemies have been killed. In either case, gameplay is dependent upon killing and moving forward. If the player resists these impulses, the world quickly settles into a static equilibrium, where squadmates will repeatedly urge the player forward to the next objective. In the world of *Call of Duty*, war is represented as a place of perpetual action, ceaseless motion, and limitless killing. The game does not so much reward action and aggression as normalize it, allowing it as the only available option.

Hegemonic masculinity can be complex and contradictory (Connell 2005), and one of the central contradiction in the masculine military ideal is the tension between aggression and obedience. As much as aggressive tendencies are encouraged to acclimate soldiers to the violence of war (Hopton 2003), unit cohesion and a soldier's survival are often dependent upon prudence, rationality, and obedience to command (Hockey 2003). The design of a *Call of Duty* campaign embodies this tension as it encourages the player to enact aggression and violence within a tightly controlled framework. Most levels present a linear corridor through which the player is directed, with options for exploration or choice almost entirely absent. The player is invariably accompanied by a fellow soldier, often a commanding officer, who provides step-by-step instructions on how to proceed through the path laid out by the developers. This obedience is further reinforced by the game's user interface, which features waypoints that direct the player more explicitly. At its most narrow, the game will assume control of the player character and relegate player interaction to a series of quick time event button presses. In these cases, the game curtails any deviation from the developers' planned experience through the frequent use of fail-states. Killing the wrong person, killing the correct person at the wrong time, straying from the mission directives, and other deviations result in the game stopping and resetting to a previously saved checkpoint, where the player is allowed to proceed in the intended fashion. In this way, the violence and aggression in the game is controlled and limited by the player's obedience to the game design.

Toughness and Stoicism

One of the foundational elements of the traditional masculine-feminine dichotomy is the assignment of rationality and reason to the masculine sphere, and the relegation of emotion to the feminine (Connell 2005). The military has capitalized on this dichotomy in its construction of the soldiering identity. Military service is physically demanding and requires tolerating extended periods of discomfort, and by goading soldiers with the gendered expectation of stoicism, militaries enforce an expectation that soldiers will tolerate willingly the physical and mental stresses of war (Hockey 2003). While emotion cannot be entirely excised from a soldier, it remains carefully policed. Even in cases of extreme trauma, such as the death of a fellow soldier, the natural response of grief is expected to be sublimated, as the continued function of the military unit is given paramount priority (Hockey 2003). For much of the nineteenth and twentieth centuries, soldiers failing to control their temperament in the face of wartime trauma were derided, and succumbing to "shell shock" served as evidence of a deficient masculinity (Chamberlin and Sheena 2012). Now understood to be posttraumatic stress disorder (PTSD), the emotional manifestations of PTSD still bear a stigma among military men, resulting in low levels of treatment-seeking among men suffering from the condition (Garcia et al. 2011).

Call of Duty offers an exaggerated portrait of the emotionally stoic soldier. Within a given mission, the player character may kill dozens of men, survive a helicopter crash, or witness civilian massacres without any indication of an emotional response, continuing along with dispassionate regard. Ghosts provides an extreme example of such stoicism, wherein the main characters are forced to witness the execution of their father. While the killing is met initially with anger, gameplay soon resumes, and within moments the characters revert to an emotionless, professional mode of operation while attempting to escape from capture. Attempts to grapple with the emotional consequences of war expose the game design's unsuitability toward the topic. Advanced Warfare features a military funeral, and as with other moments where gameplay extends to actions beyond movement and shooting, the game elects to offer the chance to express emotion through quick-time event. The player is invited to pay their respects through the press of a button, at which point the game's scripting halts until the player complies, a design choice that was widely derided as clunky and undercutting the potential for real emotional expression (Fahey 2014). In a reflection of the military itself, both the narrative and the mechanics provide no outlet for emotional expression.

Masculinity and Technology

Men and technology are intimately linked in the formation of hegemonic masculinity. This is not only rooted in long-standing cultural definition of science as a masculine field (Morse 1997) but heightened by the economic structures of modern-day capitalism (Connell 2005). In early industrial labor, men's economic value was derived from their strength and endurance as the engaged in physical work (Connell 2005). In the later part of the twentieth century, advancements in technology led to a labor market that increasingly valued knowledge and technical skill over raw physical power. Accordingly, the hegemonic construction of masculinity shifted to incorporate technological mastery as a key component (Cockburn 1985). At the same time, the military has increasingly integrated advanced technology into its operations, and mastery of technology has become even more central to the soldier identity (Brown 2007; Der Derian 2001; Higate 2003).

As a genre, military games have been noted for the degree to which they fetishize military hardware and technology, fastidiously recreating the look and sound of real weapons and reveling in the spectacle of their use (Neiborg 2010; Stahl 2010). *Call of Duty* continues this representation of technology as an extension of masculine military might. This relationship is sown into the mission structure of many levels, which are designed to lead the player through a series of combat encounters, all resolved through traditional first-person shooter gameplay until encountering a situation that can only be overcome through the employment of advanced technology. In *Modern Warfare*, waves of human enemies are repeatedly capped by the arrival of heavily armored vehicles which are impervious to standard weaponry. At those moments, the player is directed toward the advanced armaments needed to overcome these opponents, functionally rewarding the player for their success with the presentation of high-tech weaponry.

As central as technology is to the characterization of military masculinity in *Call of Duty*, the series continually reinforces the hierarchy of a dominant, brawn-based masculinity and the subordination of a technical, intelligence-based masculinity. Echoing the dynamic present in modern militaries where the masculinity of support roles remains subordinate to the combat masculinity of soldiers on the frontlines (Higate 2003; Brown 2007), those who are smart enough to design the technology are placed in secondary positions. This includes the timid support officer Farid, who is repeatedly referred to as "egghead," and the hacker Chloe Lynch, whose primary role is that of a target to be protected. Meanwhile, soldiers in the field may utilize and rely upon advanced technology, but are not required to understand it. This is demonstrated in *Black Ops 2*, where following the player's failed attempts to repair a drone through traditional means, the stereotypically masculine soldier Harper restores it to working order simply by kicking it. This dichotomy extends to the act of playing the game itself. The series often turns to advanced technologies—armored vehicles, high-tech drones, electromagnetic pulse generators (EMPs), and explosives—to provide moments of spectacle. Since these moments are often brief and occur within the larger flow of the game, the developers dedicate very little time to tutorializing their use. This results in simplified control schemes, as when an aircraft's controls are mapped to the standard first-person shooter (FPS) control scheme, or in the reduction of complex actions, like infiltrating a computer system, to a single button prompt. The game emphasizes the pleasures of the use and mastery of these technologies while subordinating the value of understanding them.

The link between masculinity and industrial technology was historically situated in the material mastery over technological objects through the perceived physical strength of the male body (Cockburn 1985). In the technologies that drive post-industrial capitalism, this dynamic of "man over machine" is being replaced, through the disappearance of the body in virtual spaces, or through the integration of technology into the body itself (Braidotti 2011; Hayles 1999). These sexless new formations of technology and body bring tremendous potential to upset gender dynamics rooted in physical sexual differences. Optimistic visions construe these "cyborg" formations as a route past masculine-feminine dichotomies, even as the ideologies of white capitalist patriarchy persist in contemporary examples of this fusion (Braidotti 2011; Haraway 2006). In short, this changing dynamic is a source of anxiety for traditional masculine norms, an anxiety evidenced by the entries in *Call of Duty* set in near-future time periods. Here, drones, nanomachines, and other advanced devices are increasingly positioned as the source of military dominance, and the pleasures of playing are heavily dependent upon the mastery of this technology. As technology becomes more central within the series, it becomes more closely integrated into the body, with cybernetic implants and prosthetics granting the characters increased strength, endurance, mobility, and power. This move away from masculine bodily strength to a sexless technological source of power has been accompanied by the aforementioned increased representation of women in these games. Yet this positive development is undercut by the frequency with which a dependence on technology ultimately undermines the security of the state. The terrorists of *Black Ops 2* commandeer the US drone force to attack the homeland, while *Ghosts* finds America attacked by its own orbital defense network. In *Black Ops 3*, a computer virus corrupts American soldiers by targeting their cybernetic implants, while in *Advanced Warfare*, the exosuits worn by the protagonists are eventually disabled by enemy forces. These storylines make salient the perceived threat of technology that exists outside the physical control of bodies, articulating contemporary fears regarding the potential for algorithms and artificial intelligence to upset the existing patriarchal economic structure, just as automation in the manufacturing sphere once disrupted the relationship between masculine strength and economic power.

Modern Warfare, Traditional Masculinity

When reflecting on the social realism of military games, Galloway (2006) concludes that it is dependent not upon realistic aesthetic representation, but hinges upon "a true congruence between the real political reality of the gamer and the ability of the game to mimic and extend that political reality" (83). He examines *America's Army*, the Department of Defense funded recruitment game, finding its realist qualities emerge through the intended audience's participation in its articulation of America as a dominant global military power. Likewise, the significance of *Call of Duty*'s articulations of masculinity does not rest in realistic representations of masculine models, as the fantastic narratives in these games are divorced from the reality of actual military service, let alone the reality of a typical gamer. Rather, these games can be considered realist in that they grant players the opportunity to step into a soldier identity and identify with one of the most powerful mythic symbols of hegemonic masculinity. In this, the games primarily reflect the preexisting forms of hegemonic masculinity that have become deeply entrenched in the military itself, circulate models of the traditionally masculine ideal soldier, and serve to reinforce the deeply patriarchal system military masculinity reflects.

Bibliography

Arkin, William, and Lynne R. Dobrofsky. 1978. Military Socialization and Masculinity. *Journal of Social Issues* 34 (1): 151–168.

Ashe, Fidelma. 2013. Gendering War and Peace: Militarized Masculinities in Northern Ireland. *Men and Masculinities* 15 (3): 230–248.

Barrett, Frank J. 1996. The Organizational Construction of Hegemonic Masculinity: The Case of the US Navy. *Gender, Work, and Organization* 3 (3): 129–142.

Basham, Victoria M. 2016. Gender and Militaries: The Importance of Military Masculinities for the Conduct of State Sanctioned Violence. In *Handbook on Gender and War*, ed. Simona Sharoni, Julia Welland, Linda Steiner, and Jennifer Pederson, 29–41. Cambridge, MA: Harvard University Press.

Belkin, Aaron, Morten G. Ender, Nathaniel Frank, Stacie R. Furia, George Lucas, Gary Packard, Steven M. Samuels, Tammy Schultz, and David R. Segal. 2013. Readiness and DADT Repeal Has the New Policy of Open Service Undermined the Military? *Armed Forces & Society* 39: 587–601.

Braidotti, Rosi. 2011. *Nomadic Theory: The Portable Rosi Braidotti*. New York: Columbia University Press.

Breuer, Johannes, Ruth Festl, and Thorsten Quandt. 2011. *In the Army Now— Narrative Elements and Realism in Military First-Person Shooters*. Proceedings of DiGRA 2011 Conference: Think Design Play.

Brown, Melissa Tracey. 2007. *Enlisting Masculinity: Gender and the Recruitment of the All-Volunteer Force*. Ph.D. Diss., Rutgers.

Bulmer, Sarah. 2013. Patriarchal Confusion? Making Sense of Gay and Lesbian Military Identity. *International Feminist Journal of Politics* 15: 137–156.

Cassar, Robert. 2013. Gramsci and Games. *Games and Culture* 8 (5): 330–353.

Chalabi, Mona. 2015. What Percentage Of Americans Have Served In The Military? *FiveThirtyEight*, March 19. http://fivethirtyeight.com/datalab/what-percentage-of-americans-have-served-in-the-military/. Accessed 1 Apr 2016.

Chamberlin, Eagan, and M. Sheena. 2012. Emasculated by Trauma: A Social History of Post-Traumatic Stress Disorder, Stigma, and Masculinity. *The Journal of American Culture* 35 (4): 358–365.

Cockburn, Cynthia. 1985. *Machinery of Dominance: Women, Men and Technical Know-How*. London: Pluto.

———. 2010. Gender Relations as Causal in Militarization and War. *International Feminist Journal of Politics* 12: 139–157.

Connell, R.W. 2005. *Masculinities*. Berkley: University of California Press.

Connell, R.W., and James W. Messerschmidt. 2005. Hegemonic Masculinity: Rethinking the Concept. *Gender & Society* 19 (6): 829–859.

Der Derian, J. 2001. *Virtuous War: Mapping the Military-Industrial-Entertainment Network*. Boulder, CO: Westview Press.

Duncanson, Claire. 2015. Hegemonic Masculinity and the Possibility of Change in Gender Relations. *Men and Masculinities* 18 (2): 231–248.

Eriksson Baaz, Maria, and Maria Stern. 2009. Why Do Soldiers Rape? Masculinity, Violence and Sexuality in the Armed Forces in the Congo. *International Studies Quarterly* 53: 495–518.

Fahey, Mike. 2014. Nothing Says Funeral Like a Quick Time Event. *Kotaku*, November 3. http://kotaku.com/nothing-says-funeral-like-a-quick-time-event-1653938147. Accessed 1 Apr 2016.

Furia, Stacie R., and Denise D. Bielby. 2009. Bombshells on Film: Women, Military Films, and Hegemonic Gender Ideologies. *Popular Communication* 7: 208–224.

Gagnon, Frédérick. 2010. "Invading Your Hearts and Minds": Call of Duty and the (Re)Writing of Militarism in U.S. Digital Games and Popular Culture. *European Journal of American Studies* 2: 2–17.

Galloway, Alexander R. 2006. *Gaming: Essays on Algorithmic Culture*. Minneapolis: University of Minnesota Press.

Garcia, Hector A., Erin P. Finley, William Lorber, and Matthew Jakupcak. 2011. A Preliminary Study of the Association Between Traditional Masculine Behavioral Norms and PTSD Symptoms in Iraq and Afghanistan Veterans. *Psychology of Men & Masculinity* 12 (1): 55–63.

Hale, Hannah C. 2012. The Role of Practice in the Development of Military Masculinities. *Gender, Work and Organization* 19 (6): 699–722.

Halter, Ed. 2006. *From Sun Tsu to Xbox: War and Video Games*. New York: Thunder's Mouth Press.

Haraway, Donna. 2006. A Cyborg Manifesto: Science, Technology, and Socialist-Feminism in the Late 20th Century. In *The International Handbook of Virtual Learning Environments*, ed. Joel Weiss, Jason Nolan, Jeremy Hunsinger, and Peter Trifonas, 117–158. Dordrecht: Springer.

Hayles, N. Katherine. 1999. *How We Became Posthuman: Virtual Bodies in Cybernetics, Literature, and Informatics*. Chicago: University of Chicago Press.

Higate, Paul R. 2003. 'Soft Clerks' and 'Hard Civvies': Pluralizing Military Masculinities. In *Military Masculinities*, ed. Paul R. Higate, 27–42. Westport, CT: Praeger.

Higate, Paul. 2007. Peacekeepers, Masculinities, and Sexual Exploitation. *Men and Masculinities* 10 (1): 99–119.

Hitchens, Michael, Bronwin Patrickson, and Sherman Young. 2014. Reality and Terror, the First-Person Shooter in Current Day Settings. *Games and Culture* 9 (1): 3–29.

Hockey, John. 2003. No More Heroes: Masculinity in the Infantry. In *Military Masculinities*, ed. Paul R. Higate, 15–25. Westport, CT: Praeger.

Höglund, Johan. 2008. Electronic Empire: Orientalism Revisited in the First Person Shooter. *Game Studies* 8 (1). http://gamestudies.org/0801/articles/hoeglund. Accessed 10 Nov 2011.

————. 2014. Magic Nodes and Proleptic Warfare in the Multiplayer Component of Battlefield 3. *Game Studies* 14 (1). http://gamestudies.org/1401/articles/jhoeglund. Accessed 1 Nov 2016.

Hopton, John. 2003. The State and Military Masculinity. In *Military Masculinities*, ed. Paul R. Higate, 111–123. Westport, CT: Praeger.

Huntemann, Nina B., and Matthew Thomas Payne. 2010. In *Introduction to Joystick Soldiers. The Politics of Play in Military Video Games*, ed. Nina B. Huntemann and Matthew Thomas Payne, 1–18. New York and London: Routledge.

Hutchings, Kimberly. 2008. Making Sense of Masculinity and War. *Men and Masculinities* 10 (4): 389–404.

Johnson, David, and Bronson Stamp. 2015. See Women's Progress in the U.S. Military. *Time Labs.* http://labs.time.com/story/women-in-military/. Accessed 1 Nov 2016.

Khalili, Laleh. 2011. Gendered Practices of Counterinsurgency. *Review of International Studies* 37: 1471–1491.

King, C. Richard, and David J. Leonard. 2010. Wargames as a New Frontier: Securing American Empire in Virtual Space. In *Joystick Soldiers. The Politics of Play in Military Video Games*, ed. Nina B. Huntemann and Matthew Thomas Payne, 91–105. New York and London: Routledge.

Knight, Shawn. 2016. 'Call of Duty: Black Ops III' was the Best-Selling Game of 2015. *Techspot*, January 15. http://www.techspot.com/news/63496-call-duty-black-ops-iii-best-selling-game.html. Accessed 1 Apr 2016.

Kovitz, Marcia. 2003. The Roots of Military Masculinity. In *Military Masculinities*, ed. Paul R. Higate, 1–14. Westport, CT: Praeger.

Krobova, Tereza, Ondrej Moravec, and Jaroslav Svelch. 2015. Dressing Commander Shepard in Pink: Queer Playing in a Heteronormative Game Culture. *Cyberpsychology: Journal of Psychosocial Research on Cyberspace* 9 (3). http://www.cyberpsychology.eu/view.php?cisloclanku=2015081905. Accessed 1 Nov 2016.

Kronsell, Annica. 2016. Sexed Bodies and Military Masculinities: Gender Path Dependence in EU's Common Security and Defense Policy. *Men and Masculinities* 19 (3): 311–336.

Leonard, David. 2004. Unsettling the Military Entertainment Complex: Video Games and a Pedagogy of Peace. *Studies in Media & Information Literacy Education* 4 (4): 1–8.

Makuch, Eddie. 2015. Call of Duty Gets First Playable Female Lead With Black Ops 3. *Gamespot*, April 27. http://www.gamespot.com/articles/call-of-duty-gets-first-playable-female-lead-with-/1100-6426927/. Accessed 1 Nov 2016.

Mirrless, Tanner. 2009. Digital Militainment by Design: Producing and Playing SOCOM: U.S. Navy SEALs. *International Journal of Media and Cultural Politics* 5 (3): 161–181.

Morgan, David H.J. 1994. Theater of War: Combat, the Military, and Masculinities. In *Theorizing Masculinities*, ed. Harry Brod and Michael Kaufman. Thousand Oaks, CA: Sage.

Morse, Margaret. 1997. Virtually Female: Body and Code. In *Processed Lives: Gender and Technology in Everyday Life*, ed. Jennifer Terry and Melodie Calvert, 23–36. London: Routledge.

Nichols, Randy. 2010. Target Acquired: America's Army and the Video Game Industry. In *Joystick Soldiers. The Politics of Play in Military Video Games*, ed. Nina B. Huntemann and Matthew Thomas Payne, 39–52. New York and London: Routledge.

Nieborg, David B. 2010. Training Recruits and Conditioning Youth: The Soft Power of Military Games. In *Joystick Soldiers: The Political Play in Military Video Games*, ed. Nina B. Huntemann and Matthew Thomas Payne, 53–66. New York and London: Routledge.

Niva, Steve. 1998. Tough and Tender: New World Order, Masculinity and the Gulf War. In *The 'Man Question' in International Relations*, ed. Marysia Zalewski and Jane Parpart, 109–128. Boulder, CO: Westview.

Payne, Matthew Thomas. 2010. F*ck You, Noob Tube!: Learning the Art of Ludic LAN War. In *Joystick Soldiers. The Politics of Play in Military Video Games*, ed. Nina B. Huntemann and Matthew Thomas Payne, 206–222. New York and London: Routledge.

Pleck, Joseph H. 1981. *The Myth of Masculinity*. Cambridge, MA: MIT Press.

Power, Marcus. 2007. Digitized Virtuosity: Video War Games and Post-9/11 Cyber-Deterrence. *Security Dialogue* 38 (2): 271–288.

Riendeau, Danielle. 2014. Call of Duty: Advanced Warfare Does Right by Women Warriors. *Polygon*, November 26. http://www.polygon.com/2014/11/26/7295887/call-of-duty-advanced-warfare-women-combat-warriors. Accessed 1 Nov 2016.

Rosenberg, Mathew, and Dave Phillips. 2015. Pentagon Opens All Combat Roles to Women: 'No Exceptions.' *New York Times*, December 4, sec A.

Shaw, Adrienne. 2009. Putting the Gay in Games: Cultural Production and GLBT Content in Video Games. *Games and Culture* 4 (3): 228–253.

Smicker, Josh. 2010. Future Combat, Combating Futures. Temporalities of War Video Games and the Performance of Proleptic Histories. In *Joystick Soldiers. The Politics of Play in Military Video Games*, ed. Nina B. Huntemann and Matthew Thomas Payne, 106–121. New York and London: Routledge.

Stahl, Roger. 2010. *Militainment, Inc: War, Media, and Popular Culture*. New York: Routledge.

Tasker, Yvonne. 2002. Soldiers' Stories: Women and Military Masculinities in Courage Under Fire. *Quarterly Review of Film & Video* 19: 209–222.

Whitworth, Sandra. 2004. *Men, Militarism and UN Peacekeeping: A Gendered Analysis*. Boulder, CO: Lynne Rienner.

Woodward, Rachel. 1998. 'It's a Man's Life': Soldiers, Masculinity, and the Countryside. *Gender, Place, and Culture* 5 (3): 277–300.

4

The End of the Dream: How *Grand Theft Auto V* Simulates and Subverts Its Male Player-Character Dynamics

Kyle Moody

Introduction

When Dan Houser, the co-founder and vice president of creativity for Rockstar Games, was asked about their latest game *Grand Theft Auto V* (*GTA V*)—earning sales of US$1 billion American in three days after its retail release (Sliwinski 2013)—and what it represented, he answered in a direct reflection of his game's principles: "This is the endpoint of the American dream" (Hill 2013).

But the game itself promises new beginnings. As virtual reality games, augmented reality titles, and other deeply immersive gaming technologies become more practical, the promise of emergent, thriving virtual worlds is one many companies and players desire. Houser's company emerged with its own spin on this with *Grand Theft Auto Online* (Hill 2013). This player-driven virtual open space allows users to commit in-game virtual crimes and heists with their peers outside of the title's campaign mode.

GTA V forces players to engage with the game via the perspective of its playable male characters, drawing its players who play the structured experience of the story campaign into the world of a game. This allows players and reviewers to examine the context of narrative-based play through the lens of masculine studies. Moreover, given its popularity and ubiquity within popular culture, it stands as an iconic franchise of the industry and a reference point of the video game culture it both references and lampoons.

K. Moody (✉)
Fitchburg State University, Fitchburg, MA, USA

© The Author(s) 2018
N. Taylor, G. Voorhees (eds.), *Masculinities in Play*, Palgrave Games in Context,
https://doi.org/10.1007/978-3-319-90581-5_4

My aim in this chapter is to suggest that *GTA V*'s systems of play further make these men inadequate agents of change within the progression of the narrative, and thus highlight a subversion of masculinity as defined by Burrill (2008) as a performative act done by the writers and programmers of the story structure.

Defining *Grand Theft Auto*

GTA V can be classified as a third-person action and driving game with an open world environment. *GTA V* takes place in the virtual environment of Los Santos, a simulacrum (Baudrillard 1983) of Los Angeles and its surrounding area. The game has three playable male characters in its story campaign: Michael De Santa (nee Townley), Franklin Clinton, and Trevor Phillips. The story offers a central narrative and forms of character development to its three playable characters in the story campaign. The player controls their character in the virtual environment of Los Santos, but is prompted to travel to specific locations in order to progress the story, most of which the player may do at their whim, or even ignore completely. Once the player reaches one of these markers—highlighted by a glowing yellow halo on the floor of the game environment—the game shifts and triggers an in-engine event. This usually cuts off the flow of gameplay via a cutscene sequence, often used to explain the present progression of the story campaign.

After the cutscene, the game returns control to the player with a new, clearly indicated objective to complete within specific parameters. This is referred to as an in-game mission, and its purpose also focuses on progressing the story. However, these missions require the player to be the driver of the in-game experience, unlike the cutscenes that portray complex interactions not available to the player due to the limitations of the interface and story parameters. When the player completes the mission, they then have full control to travel through the environment freely until the next mission is triggered, either by them or by the computer.

The remainder of this study will be focused on the single-player narrative portion of *GTA V*, focusing on the available story missions and campaign as opposed to the player-controlled ludic dimensions. *Grand Theft Auto Online* will not be covered beyond cursory mentions and smaller links.

Literature Review

The purpose of studying masculinity as a form of identity is to reach a deeper understanding of its elemental pieces and their myriad forms. This can be achieved by classifying character traits and modes of expression that appear to be culturally related to any form of masculinity, as well as the possible sort of social implications they foster. One must study the sources used by people to create these social norms, and this can be done by understanding those traits associated with masculine identity.

One view of masculinity, as defined by Wil Coleman (1990), and applied to video games by Derek A. Burrill (2008), takes two forms: structural and dramaturgical acts. The first states that masculinity is an ongoing set of internal sociological and psychological processes and redefinitions that are explicated by the outward actions of the subject. The second states that masculinity is a performative state, focused on managing a presentation of self. Since *GTA V* encourages players to engage with the single-player campaign and virtual environment as one of its three male playable characters, it is worth examining its contribution to masculine identities via textual play of the story campaign. The masculine identities in question are formed through the performative state of play, which occurs through in-game actions and cutscenes. While the masculine identities of the player-controlled characters are thusly determined by the programmers of *GTA V*, the performative actions of the players contribute to the collaborative creation of player-controlled character empathy, which makes the players complicit in the final determination of masculine identities as performative states.

Therefore, masculinity as studied within this chapter can be defined as a *performative state of intertextuality that requires repetition to maintain authenticity within the world of the game.* The masculinity of the characters and the player(s) is formed through in-game dialogue and actions, which also requires a basic understanding of the in-game rules and world. The parallels of the in-game world of *GTA V* to our own reflect a social and cultural hybrid of the American culture circa 2013 (when the game was released), along with existing moral and ethical cues. Masculinity in the game must therefore reflect the performative concept of masculinity within the "real world," or representations of the world outside of the game, as an intertextual reading of *GTA V* would require this for comparative analysis.

Defining masculinity and subversion requires a stronger understanding of how the two are linked. The seminal scholar Judith Butler discussed gender in terms of performativity, highlighting gender as an effect of the subject it is trying to express (1991). By creating masculine and feminine content through linguistic reinforcement, masculinity is a gendered expression of activity that is meant to represent authenticity via repetition. This linguistic interpellation helps define masculinity as a performative function instead of a singular, inborn trait (Butler 1991). Particular constructions of gender are systematically taken as more authentic, which means that subversions of these linguistic and performative norms require an examination of how they strip away perceptions of privilege (Butler 1991; Brickell 2005).

Ewan Kirkland (2009) examines how machismo and representations of masculinity in *Silent Hill* are considered problematic when contrasted against the actions of the main male character. Even though the game is a survival horror title with elements of combat and fighting, *Silent Hill* complicates such aspects by dint of the avatars' unremarkable abilities, limiting supplies, poor combat methods, obtuse progress through the game space, representations of entrapment, and the potential for all-encroaching inability to win (Kirkland 2009). These are exemplified by the games' predetermined linear structures, which limits the player's ability to directly impact the events of the game in terms of the supposed nature of play in an open world setting.

Kirkland supposes that the problematic nature of video-game interactivity and identity are also mixed with the potential gendering of video game activity, much like DeVane and Squire (2008). By encouraging a necessary distance from the controllable male game characters, the designers of *Silent Hill* were attempting to make the players recognize the futility of the rescue missions they are doomed to fail, the grotesque caricatures of femininity they encounter, and the voyeuristic practices in which they engage (Kirkland 2009). The stripping of the machismo characteristics of the genre and setting allows for a designer-crafted narrative subversion to occur, which in fact enhances the message of a subverted masculinity.

The subversion of masculinity is made possible through *GTA*'s fictional setting of Los Santos, which is a hyperreal representation of Los Angeles. Neither real nor wholly disconnected from the real, Los Santos contains a mixture of real and fictitious landmarks (Hill 2013) to create its own form of iconography. While part of the pleasure of playing games like *GTA* has been their attempts to create hybridized worlds and semiotic systems using the agents of the real and the creations of the digital façade, the game worlds of *GTA* soon create their own versions of landmarks, which then show up within the game world as more real than the iconic symbols pulled from reality. Los Santos is the latest iteration on this idea, a new world that is reflective of the iconography associated with Los Angeles, California. Since the performative nature of masculinity takes place in this game environment, it creates a natural link between the gameplay and the real world since Los Santos is a fictional representation of Los Angeles.

Furthermore, the links between the real and the hyperreal are meant to illustrate the exaggerated qualities of the game. The player-controlled characters can be seen as agents of subversion simply because they represent extensions of player agency within the game world.

In her 2013 review of *GTA V*, Nora N. Khan claimed that her play of the title was rooted in an empathetic understanding of masculinity. When she cited the possibility that the alienation and dysfunction experienced by the main characters is linked to the identifiable performative qualities of masculinity, she also stated that her understanding of those men illustrated how she recognized the game as a subversive text. By highlighting how little control the male characters had over their fate, and how the game and its narrative overrode the masculine performances of power and control, Khan illustrates how *GTA V* uses a level of possibility that makes the empathetic masculinity of these men shift from traditional masculinity of domination (Khan 2013). In this, the game's male characters take on stunted and reactionary forms of agency typically reserved for female game characters.

When Khan reviewed the game, she admitted that her interaction with its male protagonists was a form of counter-play that enhanced her empathetic understanding (Khan 2013). This structural subversion marks a subtle shift from Rockstar's previous installment of the franchise, which aimed instead at narrative subversion. In the earlier game, Niko Bellic, its playable protagonist, is a soldier from Eastern Europe who comes to Liberty City to find salvation from the sins of his past life through the American Dream. But through the course of the game, Niko develops a hatred of American culture, finding its materialism and false advertising to be horrific. This is different from the narrative of *GTA V*, where Franklin quickly becomes disillusioned with every member of his various crews and yearns for a respect that only Michael grants. The narrative of the game constantly works to provide a seeming semblance of reality through the mediated form of the game.

The subversion of the game's story is complemented by the title's in-game actions. Niko's frustration with the American Dream is expressed through the game's predetermined narrative, yet the crimes he commits are at the behest of the player controlling him. This tension is what Clint Hocking refers to as "ludonarrative dissonance" (Hocking 2007), a term which helps illustrate the potential for subversion within *GTA V*.

Methodology

Using an approach to textual analysis that encompasses both structural and semiotic game elements, I studied *GTA V* as a technological artifact with a focus on the intertwined systems of play and enactments of masculinity. Espen Aarseth claims that any game features three elements: (1) rules, (2) a game space or world setup through material or semiotic systems, and (3) gameplay that emerges when the player engages the rules in the world of the game (Aarseth 2004). Therefore, I focused on how the in-game actions of the characters reflect the intentional limitations of the game.

By finding points where the game and the player meet, gameplay can be studied (Arsenault and Perron 2008). Game structures are meant to be the skeletons upon which players create activities and gain some control, henceforth engaging in play. In that sense, *GTA V* is exemplary; in popular user-created gameplay videos, we can see how car chases utilize filmic camera angles, hand-tossed grenades that explode police cruisers, and powerful electronic music to emphasize the hyperbolic actions of the game system.

My analysis requires an understanding of how the game's interface operates in conjunction with the narrative thrust of the title. After examining the textual play and subversive politics underlying the boundary data for players of *Grand Theft Auto IV*, Marc Ouellette (2010) found that the checks and balances of the rules and semiotic game world covered up a system that was not wholly subversive. Likewise, it is also possible to read any subversion in the subsequent game as simply textual traits embedded by its creators, design without direction. In this manner, *GTA V* comes closest to realizing what Ouellette concluded with regard to the previous iteration of the series, released to similar fanfare: that its alleged subversive nature was ultimately tied to its status as a mass media product (Ouellette 2010).

The issue at hand with *GTA V* is exactly what Ouellette (2010) defines as the main tension with its predecessor: the structured gameplay versus the player-driven actions. It is crucial to analyze the predetermined narrative elements of the game alongside the possibility spaces for player agency that are opened up through its rule set and interface (Ouellette 2010). I suggest that the narrative devices of *GTA V* are illustrative of thematic and semiotic cohesion.

I argue that the game's rule sets, when explored alongside the game's narrative campaign and the limitations of its controller and interface, work together to enact a masculinity heavily bound by strictures.

Textual Analysis

My textual reading follows the set of intertextual methodologies laid out by Carr (2009). The game was played once through for pleasure when it was released. It was then replayed in preparation for this analysis, with particular set pieces and early in-game cutscenes played for context and representation. Notes were taken regarding the interface. I utilized my play of the game to understand how the systems of the interface and the scripted narrative were tied together, and I engaged in a textual analysis of the in-game situations and scripting of the non-playable scenes to illustrate how the progress of the narrative was linked to the character progression of the player-controlled characters.

Analyzing in-game situations and dialogue to locate coded themes, this chapter explores how the player-controlled characters of the game are limited by the game systems and narrative thrusts, thereby subverting the male-player-controlled character agency. This is an inversion of the normative power relationship between the player and the game in typical gaming texts. As such, the player-controlled characters of Michael, Franklin, and Trevor are explored in terms of how they trouble these normative relationships.

Of course, since games are not created in a vacuum, their reflection of these social and cultural norms requires us to understand their place in shaping these for audiences (Leonard 2006). Although this study proceeds by examining my own engagement with *GTA V*, it is important to acknowledge that players' individual interpretations of the game, including how it pertains to masculinity and to their own gendered identity, depend largely on their own social position and experiences.

The virtual space of *GTA V*'s story campaign is fixated on a breakdown of the player-controlled character's narrative masculine identity, which subverts the normal power accumulation dynamics of traditional open-world games like *Grand Theft Auto*. Therefore, its play environment may be considered a subversion of this intent through its plethora of interactive potential and lack of reactive structural inputs. This lack of control mirrors the characters' failure to live up to normative masculinity, while the game's control scheme exemplifies the limited expressive vocabulary of masculinity.

Observations

GTA as a series has often been seen as a more "adult" game series among the popular press, and this is often due to its subject matter of crime and vice. Its player-controlled characters are involved in systemic crime across a wide swath of social domains. The entirety of the experience of *GTA V* takes place through the eyes of male playable characters, and their progression is displayed onscreen via the in-game economy of dollars. Players can measure their success based on their accrual of in-game dollars and economic commodities, like stocks, boats, and vehicles. These symbols of capitalist power and social status reflect a similarly masculine focus for the player, as mimetic expressions of how masculinity is often assessed in Western societies. Capitalist accumulation thus becomes the bellwether of the playable character's masculine status.

Tying masculine identity to economic fortune means that the character (and by extension, the player) is expected to succeed in the game by becoming a more active participant in the game's often illegal and frequently anarchic systems of accumulation. The goals of each player-controlled character are also based on financial and classist success, and measured as well by the respect they are given from other non-playable characters. Michael yearns for his family to respect their opulence and his role as provider and father, while Franklin wants out of a life of gang-related violence, his dysfunctional family and friendship with his partner-in-crime Lamar.

Nonetheless, in *GTA V*, the capacity of Michael, Trevor, and Franklin to embody these ideals—to be rich and respected—is frequently undermined through in-game actions and cutscenes involving the characters. In one instance, Michael's boat is destroyed by thieves, illustrating the powerlessness of Michael as Franklin watches on. In another instance, one side mission has Michael challenging a female jogger to a run, and the jogger continuously emasculates Michael as she triumphs over him in the initial stages. Even after eventually winning the challenge, Michael receives no congratulations or shows of respect. These actions are paralleled throughout the game in other story and side missions.

Michael and Trevor represent levels of binary white maleness in their respective storylines during the campaign (Franklin is an African American male with ties to local gangs). Michael begins the game with a modicum of respect and success. He has a wife, two children, and an opulent house in Rockford Hills (Los Santos' version of LA's real Beverly Hills). But Michael is a former gangster who is in witness protection after a botched heist, and his family explicitly despises him. Whether it is his wife engaging in an affair with her tennis instructor, or his two media-obsessed children who have no concept of a work ethic, Michael's life reveals a rotten core at the center of the opulence. He seeks therapy, but even his therapist is largely uninterested in his problems and treats him as a commodity. During his initial presentation, Michael's therapy session seems to be building to a breakthrough when the therapist immediately cuts him off, stating that they are out of time. This indicates the constant inarticulate frustration that consumes the character of Michael throughout the game, and shows how ill-equipped he is to deal with his new role as a law-abiding citizen. Even as a wealthy man hiding out among the people he once robbed, he embodies impotence, subverting the performance of masculinity as seen in most video games.

Trevor is his partner in crime and his polar opposite. He lives in Sandy Shores, a simulacrum of American squalor filled with trailer parks and laboratories for cooking methamphetamines. He has concentric lines tattooed across his neck that are accompanied by a message of "Cut here." He represents a player's unchained id, filled with psychoses that he elaborates upon during scenes where he tortures his victims. If Michael desires respect, Trevor desires pure chaos.

Yet there is a distinct set of identity politics at play here, flipped from its apparent real-world inspiration. The true power for the player comes most clearly through playing as Trevor, in spite—or because of—his refutation of the social dynamics that Michael desires. Trevor presents himself as a force of violent masculinity, and the fear he elicits from others reinforces his place in the social circle of the three playable characters. His psychopathy engenders power, while Michael and Franklin only receive pity. This is a subversion of traditional norms of gaming and masculinity, in which those characters who uphold and enforce the law are afforded vaunted masculine status.

Therefore, the character of Michael is put into much sharper relief of his narrative embodiment as frustrated male and trapped game avatar, with Trevor as his unhinged id self. Michael enjoys older films as a relief from his life, while Trevor falls asleep during the screening. The narrative of the game reflects Michael's lack of agency with his family as well. Early missions in the game force Michael to protect his son from criminals who steal Michael's boat, and his daughter from pornographic filmmakers and reality TV moguls. Everyone in the game eventually tries to go after Michael, which is how the semiotic systems in the game disempower him as a male. By making the player-controlled character Michael for these story missions, his agency via the game's ludic systems is repeatedly robbed. He can only work within limited confines, never really changing his own story. Even after he rescues his children on these missions, they still openly despise him.

In addition to being a cuckold after his wife engages in an illicit affair with her tennis coach, Michael soon finds himself deep into debt with a Mexican crime lord after pulling down the house of his temperamental wife. Michael and Franklin thus begin their partnership in crime as a way of reducing Michael's debt. More story missions open up, and as the game progresses, soon Trevor is introduced as a playable character. But it must take time to unlock him as a possible character identity, and even the first set of story missions does not allow the player to exercise any agency and continued play of the game beyond the story parameters. The open world is lost, beholden to the narrative, and the agency of masculinity (both the characters and the player's) comes into question.

Through its three protagonists, *GTA V* is a simulation of the modern male identity as depicted by Houser and Rockstar Games. It posits itself as a violent power fantasy, but the virtual play space operates in such a way that one cannot actually dominate the space, only be dominated by its rules. For example, only after completing certain missions and story directives will players have access to the full range of the game's mapped play space environment. Much like the original Borges map that became the thing it originally simulated in

Baudrillard's (1983) original text, the simulacrum of Los Santos suggests a power that is instead hidden behind the curtain of ludic achievements. It guides the player through these spots, refusing to allow them to discover these spaces on their own.

Subversions and Rules

Ultimately, the rules and semiotic structures of the play environment do not change. Therefore, the characters of Michael, Trevor, and Franklin are unable to overcome the performative masculinities and accompanying problems that face their financial success. For example, Michael's status as a white male criminal allowed him access to opulence via the witness protection program. This is in direct contrast to Franklin's poverty-stricken smaller home. Both of the houses are available to the player early in the game, setting up an expectation for the players. Michael and Franklin's story missions will shift regularly before they converge and allow players to unlock the character of Trevor, the psychopathic third playable figure.

This isn't true of *GTA V*, not at its outset. After an initial tutorial story mission, the game forces the players into the roles of Franklin and Michael, with Franklin as the initial player character in the larger world of San Andreas. No matter which character the person with the controller chooses to be, they are trapped by the game in terms of how to proceed. Unlike what Ouellette (2010) says about the state of *GTA* titles as relatively freeform, *GTA V* does not initially allow idiosyncratic negotiations away from the preferred reading of the text. It is not until the initial jewelry store heist with Franklin and Michael that the player can unlock Trevor and further modes of play. The player's capacity for agential exploration and action, hallmarks of earlier titles in the franchise, is undermined by a ludic structure that insists on a narrative progression showcasing its characters' shortcomings.

Moreover, the idea of earning power through play and shaping the world never truly occurs due to the myriad systems at work within *GTA V*. For example, during mission play and free play, death is a possible fail state for the players. When this occurs, the player-controlled character respawns at a hospital within Los Santos or San Andreas, and the system restarts with the player having no wanted stars to indicate criminal activity or any weapons on their person. This suggests that the symbol system of the world repeats, and that it remains unconquerable to the players. Therefore, the gameplay of *GTA V* is actively working to create a regressive state for its intentional subversion of masculinity as performative, regressive action.

This regression is also shown in the game narrative. As much as Michael craves a new purpose in his narrative and character, he can never have one outside of the frustrations of the life that was forced upon him. His simulation of imprisonment within a virtual environment and false façade of the happy, successful home indicates his flawed existence as a playable character. No matter what actions the player takes, Michael is trapped in an endless feedback loop.

Though Ouellette found the fourth *GTA* game wanting in terms of the substance of the novelty and the governed anarchy of the gameplay (2010), the subversion of gameplay and semiotic structure may not be the bigger point of *GTA V*. Instead, the true subversion may be Rockstar Games' marketing of a modern male identity crisis to a hungry audience of young gamers, earning the company more than a billion dollars.

This representation of the protagonists' identity crisis is also reflected in the game's non-playable character interactions. In spite of the player having the ability (later on in the game) to manipulate the world to create vivid situations in a bricolage of chaos and lawlessness, Michael is the player's truest avatar due to his impotence and inability to control the world around him. No matter how much players may want to remain at home and provide for the De Santa family, their in-game actions cannot stop the narrative progress and possible downfall of Michael. The play space around Michael remains the same in spite of all the chaos he creates and achievements he earns, and since that play space of Los Santos is a construction for the player, it remains an unconquerable object due to the rule set of play. Subversion in the truest sense is not possible; the game may offer the illusion of choice and direction, but Michael's character arc most closely reflects the idea of a hyperreal world that has replaced our own when the player-controlled character is beholden to remain a cuckold and powerless in his state-sanctioned witness protection program life style, apart from his own potential for criminality and control.

This occurs through the principle of intersectionality, a theory that systems of oppression—including racism, sexism, classism, ableism, homophobia, and transphobia—are interlinked with each other to compound the effects of the other (Allen 2013). Most intersectionality studies are focused on discussions of how the myriad social and cultural issues facing minority populations and oppressed classes of people are connected in a schema of problematic ways. However, if applied to the lens of this particular iteration of the game series, the player will be able to experience variations of intersectionality that could make them better understand how the existing structures of the game are forcing users to grapple with these concepts through the narrative and play. These intersections will center on masculine identity, classism, and economic stratification.

Intersectional analysis does not place emphasis on one aspect of social or cultural differences; instead, it relies on mutual constitution of said differences (Yuval-Davis 2011). This includes emphasizing how social and cultural differences are predicated upon schedules of interactions and iterative processes of identity creation, including—but not limited to—gender, self, and group identity. Theories of intersectionality often focus on myriad identities and their situatedness as varied social agents, which builds the ways they impact and are impacted by different social, economic, and political projects (Yuval-Davis 2011)

Using intersectionality as a lens applied to the character of Michael, one sees how the construction of his social identity as an escaped criminal and wealthy white man affects his personal life when situated in the game's portrayals of his personal and familial interactions. Despite the privileges afforded to him by his social position, his status as an escaped means he never really enjoys the opulence placed in front of him. No matter what he does in the game, he will still be regarded as a soft criminal, a rough man with the edges sanded off due to his past as a paid heel. His status as a lowered male has already been shown to us at the beginning when the therapist Michael sees as a way of negotiating the mundane boredom of his life is slow to provide any real help to address the vacuum and anxiety at the center of his world, and he cannot reach any real breakthrough during this performative act. The notion of a criminal seeking analysis for the vacuity of his life illustrates how his seeming success masks a lack of measurable, legitimated accomplishments in his personal view.

The game further remonstrates male social upheaval when Michael takes on a job for a friend that requires infiltrating Lifeinvader, a Facebook analogue. The clash of ideologies is illustrated by Michael's inability to communicate with the pivotal actor in question, who arguably has more agency as a narrative construct in this interaction. In order to sneak into the company's building, Michael must learn how to pass as a programmer for an elite technological firm, including how to dress. When he takes on the mission, he must first head to a clothing store and seek out new attire that will help camouflage him as he makes his way inside. The store clerk asks him whether he has lost himself and is trying to start a new career as a way of addressing the fears of being middle-aged and directionless. This scene cuts to the heart of Michael's potential dissolution with himself as he is confronted with the verbal explication of his potential crisis, which is that his social and cultural identity is now in flux due to his situational actions.

When he enters into the firm, Michael meets Devin, a "brogrammer" that has eyes on other criminal enterprises. Devin speaks only in technocratic, systemic phrases that are aimed to push away those who do not understand him, and Michael's responses regarding union laws are rooted in older classist systems. Even though Michael makes it inside the office and to his destination for the mission, he never truly belongs as a member of this society. The intersectionality of age and social caste remains clear, along with a technological dimension that also pokes fun at the impenetrability of certain game developments.

But Michael's comfortable life in witness protection is not an idealized fantasy world like Niko dreams of in *GTA IV*. Instead, his angry family and escalating tensions betray his unhappiness with his situation, which is escalated because he most acutely speaks about the American Dream in the narrative. The entitlement to financial and social success derived from his background as a white man who oversaw multiple robberies, always in charge, is undermined by his own masculine shortcomings and the game's ludic and narrative construction of his impotency. He sees himself as inadequate at the beginning of the game, and that translates into anger as his wife cheats on him, his son becomes an antisocial media consumer, and his daughter engages in illicit practices to gain fame as a reality star. His status as a white male is threatened by making him a joke according to the beginning of the narrative, and his maleness is consistently called into question by his wife and his family through their actions. Eventually, his world falls apart.

The intersectionality of the oppressive systems presented by the gaming narrative collides here in this segment. No matter how much the player tries to reverse the downfall of Michael's family, the agency of the player only extends to the criminal and aggressive actions possible through the game's input. It is through the intersectionality of the narrative and the lack of inputs that the truest subversion is revealed: Rockstar Games found a way to make people pay a premium price to witness the undoing of its main white male protagonist. What has been marketed as an escapist fantasy subverts player expectations, and challenges us to understand how Michael could become the embittered ex-criminal that is suffering throughout the game. It is, if anything, a parable of the fragility of white masculinity.

Conclusion

Games are loose structures that enable players to push their simulated rules and codes to the breaking point, yet the characters of Michael and Trevor are narratively confined to fit within their predefined narrative roles, and the players are meant to empathize with this restricted performance of masculinity. Trevor is an agent of chaos, one who has no narrative drive and structure, while Michael has no actual accomplishments to be proud of during his play.

When Khan was finished with the game, she deeply empathized with his narrative arc, claiming that Michael's lack of character progression through his life meant that he would never truly change toward a more human perspective (Khan 2013). The structures of the gameplay make such change impossible to occur, and the performative nature of masculinity is thus forced to concede to the structural forces that tear it apart and subvert it throughout the game.

The subversion of *GTA V* is not found solely in its play, but largely in its story and identity politics. It is not the audiences who become powerful when we inhabit Michael while playing; it is Michael who becomes more whole when we give him meaning and purpose. Trevor may be a representation of the player's intentions, but Michael is a real creation of failed identity development. He is incomplete in the virtual world of Los Santos, unable to come together without the help of the player-agent responsible for his actions. The virtual space of Los Santos is used as a subversion of the player's narrative identity in terms of power and agency through Michael and Trevor. The intersectionality presented in the game is not solely one of race or sexuality. It is more one of social class as it intersects with masculinity's affinity for violence, filtered through a set of inputs that promises chaos but is too neatly structured to make drastic changes.

Therefore, the game succeeds at taking the realm of a power fantasy and subverting it through its rules and corresponding gameplay interactions. By illustrating its masculine heroes as powerless amidst a criminal network that is too vast and spreads across illegal and legal organizations, the characters of Michael, Franklin, and Trevor become pawns, not agents of change or drivers of progression. Their fates are determined by others, and thus their masculine identities as criminals and lawbreakers are regulated by other systems that subvert and overwrite the performative states of masculinity. Both the systems of power in the criminal networks surrounding them and the systems that command their actions via button inputs and game interfaces rob them of their agencies and abilities. Ultimately, they are puppets controlled to some degree by players, but even more by the game's prescripted representations of social class and the confines of capitalism.

Bibliography

Aarseth, Espen. 2004. Genre Trouble: Narrativism and the Art of Simulation. In *First Person: New Media as Story, Performance, and Game*, ed. Noah Wardrip-Fruin and Pat Harrigan. Cambridge, MA: The MIT Press.

Allen, Samantha. 2013. Wrath of the Gods: Teaching Intersectionality Through Bastion|. *The Border House*, October 2. http://borderhouseblog.com/?p=11456.

Arsenault, Dominic, and Bernard Perron. 2008. In the Frame of the Magic Cycle: The Circle(s) of Gameplay. In *The Video Game Theory Reader 2*, ed. Bernard Perron and Mark J.P. Wolf. New York: Routledge.

Baudrillard, Jean. 1983. *Simulations*. New York: Semiotext (e), Inc.

Brickell, Chris. 2005. Masculinities, Performativity, and Subversion: A Sociological Reappraisal. *Men and Masculinities* 8 (1): 24–43. https://doi.org/10.1177/10971 84X03257515.

Burrill, Derek A. 2008. *Die Tryin': Videogames, Masculinity, Culture*. New York: Peter Lang.

Butler, Judith. 1991. Imitation and Gender Insubordination. In *Inside/Out: Lesbian Theories, Gay Theories*, ed. Diana Fuss, 13–31. London: Routledge.

Carr, Diane. 2009. Textual Analysis, Digital Games, Zombies. http://homes.lmc.gat-ech.edu/~cpearce3/DiGRA09/Tuesday%201%20September/306%20 Textual%20Analysis,%20Games,%20Zombies.pdf.

Coleman, Wil. 1990. Doing Masculinity/Doing Theory. In *Men, Masculinities, and Social Theory*, ed. Jeff Hearn and David Morgan, 2nd ed., 186–202. London: Routledge.

DeVane, Ben, and Kurt D. Squire. 2008. The Meaning of Race and Violence in Grand Theft Auto San Andreas. *Games and Culture* 3 (3–4): 264–285. https://doi.org/10.1177/1555412008317308.

Hill, Matt. 2013. Grand Theft Auto V: Meet Dan Houser, Architect of a Gaming Phenomenon. *The Guardian*. http://www.theguardian.com/technology/2013/sep/07/grand-theft-auto-dan-houser. Accessed 28 Nov.

Hocking, Cliff. 2007. Ludonarrative Dissonance in Bioshock. *Click Nothing*, October 7. http://clicknothing.typepad.com/click_nothing/2007/10/ludonarrative-d.html.

Khan, Nora. 2013. Grand Theft Auto 5 Channels the Violent, Lonely Minds of Men, Especially Mine. *Kill Screen*. http://killscreendaily.com/articles/reviews/grand-theft-auto-5-review/. Accessed 28 Nov.

Kirkland, Ewan. 2009. Masculinity in Video Games: The Gendered Gameplay of Silent Hill. *Camera Obscura* 24 (2): 161–183. https://doi.org/10.1215/02705346-2009-006.

Leonard, David J. 2006. Not a Hater, Just Keepin' It Real The Importance of Race- and Gender-Based Game Studies. *Games and Culture* 1 (1): 83–88. https://doi.org/10.1177/1555412005281910.

Ouellette, Marc. 2010. Removing the Checks and Balances That Hamper Democracy: Play and the Counter-Hegemonic Contradictions of Grand Theft Auto IV. *Eludamos. Journal for Computer Game Culture* 4 (2): 197–213.

Sliwinski, Alexander. 2013. Grand Theft Auto 5 Sales Surpass $1 Billion. *Joystiq*, September 20. http://www.joystiq.com/2013/09/20/grand-theft-auto-5-sales-surpass-1-billion/.

Yuval-Davis, Nira. 2011. *The Politics of Belonging*. London: SAGE Publications. https://us.sagepub.com/en-us/nam/the-politics-of-belonging/book229032.

5

"You're a Hunter, Bro": Representations of Masculinity in *Until Dawn*

Rebecca Waldie

Video games occupy a large space in the consumable media landscape necessitating the critical analysis of how video game content informs and reinforces societal norms. As the traditional target audience for video games is male gamers between ages 18 and 35, the construction of masculinity in the medium is especially important to consider. *Until Dawn* (Supermassive Games 2015), like many horror genre media, relies on the use of specific character archetypes. Built into these archetypes are clear references to hegemonic gender conventions (Benshoff 1997). Significant research on the representation of women in video games overall has been conducted (Sundén and Sveningsson 2012; Shaw 2014), yet in-depth focus on horror media specifically is substantially lacking, with the past majority of research into horror video games avoiding discussion of societal hierarchies and marginalization. Due to the often problematic and harmful stereotypes utilized in horror media, it is essential to critically analyse horror video games to the same degree as other video game genres. This chapter seeks to do so using an intersectional (Crenshaw 1991) lens to consider the impact of hegemonic power dynamics on the representations of masculinity.

In the horror genre, male characters are regularly categorized as protectors, while ascribing to specific stereotypes such as "the jock" or "the nice guy". I will be addressing these conventional archetypes as they relate to the representations of hegemonic masculinity in *Until Dawn*. Character tropes are defined

R. Waldie (✉)
Concordia University, Montreal, QC, Canada

N. Taylor, G. Voorhees (eds.), *Masculinities in Play*, Palgrave Games in Context,
https://doi.org/10.1007/978-3-319-90581-5_5

along many characteristics, including physicality, sexuality, and intelligence (Steele and Shores 2015). As the male characters within *Until Dawn* share relatively similar levels of intellect, it is not a suitable trait to consider in this research. I will instead focus on the permeation of white male dominance, sexual prowess, and protector imagery to demonstrate the ubiquitous nature of hegemonic masculinity in the game.

Hegemony and Horror

Any stereotype has some relationship to the hegemonic social structures from which it is born (Och 2015), and often the stereotype perpetuates a specific constructed perception of a subgroup of people (King 2013). Within horror media, several conventional stereotypes have developed, spanning a variety of marginalized categories (King 2013). A major delineation in horror media archetypes is that of masculine and feminine roles (Lorber 1998). Rarely will the horror archetypes engage in gender role reversal (Godwin 2013) unless in a direct attempt to subvert the hegemonic representations that permeate the conventional dynamics (McCann 2008). Some of the many horror tropes include "the jock", "the nerd", or "the hero" for men (Klepek 2015). Although these do not represent an exhaustive list of character stereotypes, each of the above are examples of frequent character types that are also present in *Until Dawn*.

Male archetypes are usually tied to the hegemonic perception of masculinity as the role of the protector, or the dominant (Steele and Shores 2015), as well as sexual prowess (Coulthard and Birks 2015). The jock or the hero is usually perceived as capable of protecting those weaker than himself (King 2009) and also as possessing the confidence to dominate women without the use of violence (Dill and Thill 2007). Violence not used for self-defence or the protection of others is a trait reserved for the anti-hero, the deviant, the monster (Consalvo 2003). The nerd characterization relies mostly on its lack of hegemonic masculinity either by appearing physically weaker and therefore failing as a potential protector (Luyt et al. 2015), or by demonstrating submissive tendencies to other males or females (King 2009). Although the level of intelligence is often a trait that is considered in these categories, it is generally not tied to their perceived ability to succeed, as the nerd and the hero may both be smart, though decidedly separate on the masculinity spectrum. As Kendall observes, "Most depictions continue to reinscribe the nerd as marginalized and undesirable" (2011). Intelligence is not overtly linked to the degree of perceived masculinity (Steele and Shores 2015), even if it may contribute to a character's ability to survive in a given situation.

Methodology

My methodological approach consisted of detailed content analysis of *Until Dawn*. I chose to stick solely to the content of the game rather than the discussions of players and the community in order to read the game design.

Data collection for this research spanned several completions of the game, each with different intent, to maximize the contact with all aspects of the game. Some playthroughs involved keeping all characters alive to understand impact of survival on their storylines and on the overarching plot of the game. Others focused on deteriorating relationships and early on-screen deaths to assess character reactions when relationships had soured.

One playthrough was dedicated to measuring active and passive screen time of all primary characters.[1] During active screen time, the character was player-controlled, whereas passive screen time was when a character was visibly a part of the scene on-screen, but the player did not have control of him/her. After multiple game completions, it became clear that certain characters had a substantial influence in the story through interactions with the player while not expressly being controlled by the player. As the data inevitably showed, the passive screen time in fact illuminated a larger disparity in screen time between corresponding male and female protagonists (see Table 5.1).

Due to the flexibility of gameplay styles and goals, this time-gathering playthrough did not involve any secondary collection items unless vital to keeping a main character alive. Exploration for exploration's sake was also avoided. Where possible, the "speed walk" function was utilized during active screen time for all characters. The reasons for these decisions were to avoid artificially inflating a specific character's time on screen, ensuring that every character's storyline was realized fully and that no character was killed prior to the game's completion. While the times presented, detailed to the millisecond from my data, would vary slightly based on the playstyle of the individual player if replicated, they represent a fair approximation of the minimum potential

Table 5.1 Screen time by character

Character	Gender	Active time	Passive time	Total time
Ashley	Female	37:53.63	23:44.98	1:01:38.61
Chris	Male	34:48.79	1:02:22.58	1:37:11.37
Emily	Female	23:46.22	30:49.64	57:35.86
Jessica	Female	5:38.16	36:33.68	42:11.84
Josh	Male	3:52.03	36:53.61	40:45.64
Matt	Male	22:58.80	10:55.45	33:54.25
Mike	Male	1:14:22.65	33:24.53	1:47:47.18
Sam	Female	43:15.59	33:04.10	1:16:19.69

screen time of each character if all survive until the end of the game. Any deaths would change the results drastically in many cases, which is why I chose to dedicate one playthrough exclusively to timing.

The content gathering during the other playthroughs involved considering the dialogue of characters, clothing throughout the game, individual story arcs, role in the overall plotline, and the objects with which each character may interact. To gather information on the latter, a separate playthrough was dedicated to maximizing exploration and object interaction, sometimes returning to the same object multiple times as different characters, to determine which objects had limited access and to assess if the access privileged one gender.

Although most objects only served to illuminate one of the several backstories of the narrative, some objects were able to be picked up and used by the characters. I catalogued those objects based on their intended purpose in the storyline and documented the result of their use or non-use to assess their functionality as determined by the game. All usable objects obtained in the game fall into one of two categories: weapons, both ranged and close combat, and sources of light. It is important to note that an object's usefulness is almost entirely unrelated to a player's skill. Players may influence the potential for a character to obtain a tool, but the storyline will almost always have a set outcome for the impact of that tool.

The notable exception to this general rule is the use of firearms and other ranged weapons. In order to fire a gun, the user must align the crosshair on the screen using the controller's analogue stick within the allotted time (see Fig. 5.1).

Fig. 5.1 Chris and a Wendigo in combat

Failure to do so affects the results of the combat, ranging from a negative relationship development to the death of a character. When considering the effectiveness of a weapon in the game, user error was not included as a failure of the weapon since the potential existed for the weapon to function properly. Only situations where the game forced a weapon to fail were considered in these cases.

The Structure of *Until Dawn*

Until Dawn is a PlayStation4 exclusive horror genre game that utilizes interactive narratives. The video game tells a partially pre-determined storyline across ten chapters where the player's choices influence the relationships, situations, and survival opportunities of the characters. The game refers to this as the "butterfly effect". Decisions that have an influence through this effect are highlighted in the moment through a visual cue. Players may then enter the butterfly effect menu to see the update (see Fig. 5.2). Menu entries do not show upcoming decisions or the ramifications of current decisions until after each step has been completed or the corresponding storyline has ended. Thus, players are not able to ascertain exactly how their decisions will impact the story until they have completed the game at least once. Decisions affecting relationships and characteristics are labelled "status updates" in the game. While character trait changes do not affect the game narrative, they do offer a glimpse into the pre-determined construction of each character's personality.

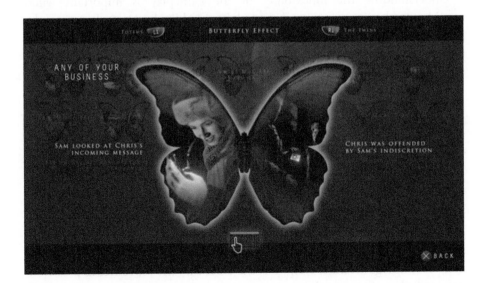

Fig. 5.2 The Butterfly Effect Menu

Relationship changes, however, affect the storyline throughout and often influence situational options that could lead characters to their deaths prematurely. The nuances of these choices are less evident in a first or even second playthrough, but they become clearer as a player becomes familiar with the impacts and the influences of decisions on the plotlines.

Gameplay itself is very fixed since the player does not choose his/her character at any time. The game is designed from a character point-of-view perspective that changes among all the primary characters, often rotating between several in any given chapter. Although there are eight distinct characters in the game, with four women (Ashley, Emily, Jessica, and Sam) and four men (Chris, Josh, Matt, and Mike), certain characters, namely Jessica and Matt, are destined for early, challenging-to-avoid deaths or minimal screen time even if they survive.

User interaction involves selecting from on-screen choices of dialogue options and action options. Action options frequently come with a timer forcing quick decisions. They are intermixed with several quick-time events, where specific buttons are displayed in rapid succession for the user to enter, and the occasional combat scenario involving aiming and shooting a firearm within the allotted time. Player agency outside the above structure is limited to exploring any open space available and interacting with static objects highlighted by the game at a given time. Some objects may only be available to players while a certain character is active or at a certain point in the storyline, and unavailable at all other times, so the player's agency is still fairly limited.

Understanding the inflexibility of the gameplay is important when considering the construction of masculinity within the game. For example, player agency could have significantly influenced character development if players had control over which characters they could play. The lack of character selection agency removes the potential for character preference to be a factor in the analysis. If a weapon is not available until the player has become a certain character, that is due to the game design and not player agency.

The Characters

As the characters are first introduced, the game pauses to provide a brief introduction of each individual, highlighting the primary relationship in the group and three key personality attributes (see Table 5.2). These attributes supposedly dictate the traits found on each character profile page. However, there is such significant overlap in some cases that the attributes as presented do very little to flesh out the characters, and perhaps serve only to pigeonhole each character into a specific horror genre trope.

Table 5.2 Characters and their corresponding relationships and traits

Character	Relationship	Traits		
Ashley	Has a crush on Chris	Academic	Inquisitive	Forthright
Chris	Has a crush on Ashley	Methodical	Protective	Humorous
Emily	Mike's Ex	intelligent	Resourceful	Persuasive
Jessica	Mike's New Girlfriend	Confident	Trusting	Irreverent
Josh	Hannah & Beth's Brother	Complex	Thoughtful	Loving
Matt	Emily's New Boyfriend	Motivated	Ambitious	Active
Mike	Emily's Ex	Intelligent	Driven	Persuasive
Sam	Hannah's Best Friend	Diligent	Considerate	Adventurous

Fig. 5.3 Matt wearing his letterman jacket

The clothing of the characters further serves to categorize them into archetypes such as "the jock" or "the sexy girl." In stark contrast to the women in the game, all the men start out wearing loose-fitting clothing that primarily highlights their rugged, masculine nature. Mike, Josh, and Chris share similar clothing choices of baggy jeans and long-sleeved shirts with vests. The only man whose masculine identity is tied directly to his clothing initially is Matt, the jock (see Fig. 5.3). Not only is he wearing sweatpants and a letter jacket in a freezing Alberta winter on a mountain top, but the game goes out of its way to have a dialogue between him and Emily, highlighting the importance of his jacket as it pertains to his relationship with women:

Emily: Where's my bag?
Matt: Huh?
Emily: My bag! The … the little bag with the pink pattern! The one I got on Rodeo! Matt, are you listening? Oh my god, don't you remember? Next

to the Italian shoe place where I got the stilettos and you knocked over the rack while you were drooling all over that girl at the counter?

Matt: Well, I mean, she was asking about my letter jacket—

Emily: Right. Because she gave a shit about your "designer" letter jacket.

Matt: Why do you hate my jacket?

Emily: MATT, I need MY BAG!

The context of the conversation allows Emily to emasculate Matt by mocking his masculinity directly, by questioning the quality of his clothing and by implying his inability to impress a female sales associate with his masculine identification. Not only did the "girl at the counter" not "[give] a shit" about the jacket, according to Emily, Matt was a "drooling" klutz who embarrassed himself, a very different image than one of a star athlete with a letter jacket. She is discounting his ability to succeed as a man.

It is also important to note here that Matt's role as the only male character of colour and categorical representation as a "meat for brains" jock stereotype reinforces the inherent whiteness in depictions of intelligence within nerd culture (Kendall 2011). Matt's race continues to inform his character in several problematic ways throughout the game, though the foundation is laid at the outset through the design of his character's persona.

As the game progresses, clothing becomes an integral visual component of Mike's identity as well. After Jessica's inevitable kidnapping by the Wendigo, Mike chases after her into the snowy woods at night in nothing but a tank top, jeans, and boots (see Fig. 5.4). Although he makes sure to grab a rifle, he does not grab any additional clothing, while his clothing is right next to him and the gun is in a display case across the room. The length of time he spends wandering the mountaintop in this outfit is significant, over an hour and a half. Eventually, the player is directed to grab an army jacket, an obligatory action in order to advance through the storyline, and Mike's visual persona is transitioned from one masculinized stereotype, to another, a rugged military man (see Fig. 5.5) complete with shotgun, machete, and a handgun, which is provided immediately after donning the army jacket. Within two hours, Mike has evolved through two stereotypical male roles and has been inundated with weaponry.

Fig. 5.4 Mike chasing after Jessica in the woods

Fig. 5.5 Mike's appearance during the second half of the story

Weaponry and Combat

Throughout the game's narrative there are several instances of combat. Except for one optional situation the combat involves weapons, so the weaponry available is extremely important to the overall narrative and to the survival of individual characters.

Here I differentiate between pre-determined narrative developments that do not rely on user ability—there is no crosshair to aim—and actual combat scenes where users must aim to successfully defend themselves. The former, which I label as violent exchanges, are pre-determined and inflexible. They occur through user choices in the story, but once the plotline is established by these choices the outcomes of the scenes are unalterable. The on-screen presentation is combat in the literal sense, but it differs from the in-game combat because the user has no control over the outcome—no opportunity to aim and no ability to ensure the weapon is a success.

These scenes are important to categorize because, while violent exchanges happen for both genders, combat scenarios focus mostly on male characters. The player has actual control of weapons only when playing as a man in all but 3 out of at least 20 combat situations. Of those three scenes, one is a playful snowball fight tutorial and not true combat in defence of the character's life, and a second is an alternate, near inaccessible situation realized only after a long combination of several specific decisions. Otherwise, the combat responsibilities rest solely with the male characters, forcing them to adhere to protector roles. Their exclusive possession of effective weaponry automatically dictates that they are the ones empowered to protect the women.

To be clear, women do gain access to weapons on occasion (see Table 5.3), but almost every instance is in a limited, non-combat capacity. Also, every weapon a woman gains is due to elective user decisions. For Sam to have access to a baseball bat, with which she defends herself while being pursued, the player must make specific choices several chapters earlier so the bat is laid out in advance. Ashley finds a pair of scissors to stab her attacker only if the player wanders into a side room and moves objects off the scissors. Emily's access to the flare gun requires the character to explore the fire tower completely, and even still, upon finding the weapon, she is immediately given the choice to give it to her boyfriend, Matt. All the women, through the player, must actively search out weaponry to use in their individual, potentially fatal situations. Ashley, Sam, and Jessica are never even able to access any form of ranged weaponry.

Table 5.3 Catalogue of weaponry

Character	Weapon	Requirement	Combat use	Outcome	Effective
Ashley	Scissors	Optional	No	Increases violence against her	No
Chris	Pistol	Required	Yes	Affects relationship with Ashley	No
	Revolver	Optional	No	No significance	Not used
	Shotgun	Required	Yes	Kills Wendigo	Yes
	Plank	Required	No	Disarm Mike or injure Josh	Yes
Emily	Flare gun	Optional	Yes	Kills Wendigo	Yes
	Flares	Optional	No	Minimal delay of pursuers	Somewhat
Jessica	Shovel	Optional	Yes	No significance	No
Josh	Josh uses one of two weapons as the antagonist but never while player-controlled				
Matt	Axe	Required	Yes	Kills elk	Yes
	Flare gun	Optional	Yes	Kills attacker	Yes
Mike	Lighter	Required	No	Frees Sam Kills Wendigo	Yes
	Hunting rifle	Required	Yes	Follows Jessica's kidnapper	No
	Machete	Required	Yes	Kills Wendigo	Yes
	Revolver	Required	Yes	Escape chapel Kills Emily (optional)	Yes
	Shotgun	Required	Yes	Kills Wendigo Blocks door from pursuers	Yes
Sam	Baseball bat	Optional	No	Increases violence against her	No
	Shovel/Pipe	Optional	Yes	Disables or kills a Wendigo	Yes

The only guaranteed combat scene wherein a woman actually fights comes immediately before the climax as Mike is escaping the Wendigo of the insane asylum. Sam finds him wrestling with a Wendigo and grabs a nearby shovel to bat it off. It is the only moment that the player is required to fight as a female character, though the result will be the same as Mike is unable to die at this point in the story. This illustrates the disparity of weapon effectiveness in the hands of women versus men in *Until Dawn*.

In all the possible violent situations, the outcomes for the women are predetermined. That is not inherently negative; the game has a narrative to present, so only limited deviation can be accommodated. However, in no instance of a woman utilizing a weapon, with the exception of the one combat scene outlined above, does the weapon actually serve to protect her. In the cases of Sam and Ashley, the baseball bat and the scissors do not stop their attacker but enrage him. In Ashley's case, her retaliation results in physical abuse from her assailant. In both situations, the weapon does not protect them and does not help them escape. The weapon is essentially powerless in the hands of a woman.

Emily's combat situation is the alternate scene mentioned earlier. In order to access the alternate escape from a Wendigo, the player must complete a complicated series of steps and decisions. When compared to the earlier description of the weapons Mike receives in one chapter, the hurdles Emily must overcome to have a functional weapon are significantly challenging. Missing any of these steps results in the standard plot development where she is bitten by the Wendigo and later faces death at the hands of Mike. In fact, the violence that the women face is almost exclusively at the hands of male characters, namely Josh, whose degree of violence escalates when the women fight back. In part, it is his antagonist role that makes him unable to fulfil the role of protector, leading to his vulnerable isolation and subsequent high probability of death.

Comparatively, the other men are given ample opportunities to embrace the protector aspect of their masculinized roles by not only having access to several forms of weapons—most are notably required to advance in the game—but they also fight bare handed. All of their weaponized scenes are actually combat scenes, many left to player agency with the lives of the characters at stake. If Chris does not fire his shotgun fast enough or aim properly, he will die at the hands of the Wendigo, and Matt will be pushed off a cliff to his death if he attacks the elk with his axe. Although Mike technically can't die until the final scene, his inability to perform his role of protector will result in severe injuries and the potential death of Jessica and a companion wolf, both relying on Mike for protection. Mike's future is not hanging in the balance, but others' lives depend on his ability to properly handle his weapons in combat situations. In the end, his capability to be protector is his major defining quality.

The men's weapons are also easily discarded in many instances, further highlighting their overabundance. In the fire tower scene, Emily effortlessly climbs the ladder with a large flashlight in hand, yet Matt discards the axe he has in hand before beginning his ascent. This theme of weaponry abandonment is carried further in the safe room scene where Mike has the opportunity to shoot Emily before she changes into a Wendigo, continuing his role as the group's protector. Whether he does or does not shoot her, he places his handgun on the table before leaving the safe room to find a secure exit for everyone. The group eventually follows him, and all the characters who survive the scene—Ashley, Sam, potentially Emily, and Chris, if he survives the Wendigo—walk past the loaded weapon without stopping to grab it. As a tool of protection, and the role of protector being squarely in the realm of masculinity, the only feasible person to take the weapon would be Chris, but at this point in the storyline he is completely emasculated and relegated to a feminized role through his reliance on Ashley for survival, so he is as excluded from accessing weaponry by virtue of his story arc.

Storylines and the Priority of Masculinity

The accessibility and functionality of weaponry are both heavily dictated by the narrative of the story, specifically pertaining to the character archetypes at a given time. It is impossible to separate the tools from the roles and genders of the characters. Gender roles initially delineate along the lines of male and female but as the story develops, the differentiation is less about the embodied gender of each character and more about the hegemonic gender roles of each character at a given time, as determined by various intersections of marginalization such as race and mental health. Through their storylines, Chris and Matt are emasculated and forced into passive, feminized positions. These transitions directly impact their ability to utilize weapons and to play the role of protector.

Matt's emasculation begins almost immediately at the hands of Emily, as demonstrated in the scene surrounding his jacket. Their interactions often question his intelligence and highlight his physicality, emphasizing his position as the jock archetype in the game. His opportunities to play protector are minimal and occur in only two optional combat scenarios. Of these, one contributes to a premature potential death outcome, and the other relies on the charity of his girlfriend and their relationship status prior to the scene. Matt is also only seemingly protecting Emily in the scene with the axe since, regardless of attacking the elk, and with or without Matt, Emily survives to continue to the fire tower. Matt's protection in both scenarios influences only his own survival, extremely precarious in its own right.

If Matt survives the fire tower's collapse, he is not seen in the game until four chapters later and only then for less than four minutes when he resumes the role of protector for himself, and potentially for Jessica if she also survives. Their interaction is awkwardly indicative of his inability to be a protector in that she is in a near catatonic state, barely able to walk or speak. Having failed in his protection of Emily, a higher-functioning woman, the narrative gives Matt a chance to protect someone who poses less of a challenge to his masculinity. In a way, he is only capable of protecting the weakest of the weak. Prior to her trauma, Jessica also emasculates Matt in a verbal confrontation, demonstrating she can dominate him as much as Emily.

Matt fails to meet the hegemonic expectations of a protector in almost every instance, often relying on Emily's help or guidance even as she berates him as a failure. Once again, Matt's existence as a character of colour informs a major component of this representation. Matt is the most vulnerable of the men, and arguably the hardest to keep alive even with the least amount of screen time, which engages the often overused stereotype of the disposable black character (Brock 2011; Barone 2013) and adheres to the hegemonic convention of limiting the role of protector and protagonist to white males (Dill et al. 2005; Williams et al. 2009).

Yet, as a man, he more easily accesses weaponry throughout the game. He need not go through the cumbersome, seemingly overwhelming, additional steps to obtain weapons as Emily does, and he is required to gain at least one weapon, the axe, in order for the narrative to continue. He also visibly and unnecessarily discards the axe if he survives, again highlighting the disposability of weapons used by men.

A variation on the relationship between storylines and masculinity is Chris' role in the narrative. Chris starts out at a shooting range near the cable car station. Although the player is controlling Sam, as soon as the combat tutorial begins, control changes to Chris who demonstrates his proficiency with firearms as a way to impress Sam, complete with bragging and celebratory strutting. He leads the way for Sam, although she is as familiar with the space as he, solidifying his role as leader from the beginning.

Chris is labelled as "protective" in his introduction, a trait which develops early on as he and Ashley explore the house for clues to the twins' murder. He's given the option to hide evidence from Ashley in order to avoid scaring her. During the investigation, Ashley defers to him, passing leadership, and player control, to him when she feels too scared to continue. She then goes on to serve as the prize for him to save not once, but three times. The first time she is attacked by the kidnapper and he forces the door open to rescue her, although he is unsuccessful. He then pursues her kidnapper across the property to find he must make a fatal choice between saving Ashley and his best friend. The game forces him to save her regardless of the player's choice in order to protect the narrative. Basically, the game requires him to be Ashley's saviour. From that point on, Ashley's dependency on Chris' guidance and protection is reinforced continually as she descends into hysteria while he remains steadfast in his determination to see them survive.

When they are once again captured, Chris was in the middle of trying to save Sam. He wakes up trapped with Ashley in another zero-sum situation risking his life against Ashley's. This is one of two deciding points that determine Chris' masculine identity. He may save himself and shoot Ashley, or he may save her and shoot himself. Throughout the scene, Ashley pleads with Chris to let her save him by giving up her life.

Once the player decides, the story continues. The gun had blanks, no one died, and both Ashley and Chris must live with the decision Chris made. He eventually rushes into the wilderness to save Josh, shotgun in hand, and must fight his way back through several Wendigo attacks. This is the second component in the transition from masculine protector to a subservient feminized role for Chris. If Chris chose to save Ashley earlier, she will open the door to save him, taking on the masculine role of protector and ultimately leading to Chris' emasculation. However, if Chris chose to save himself, Ashley will leave the door closed, condemning Chris to decapitation. In the latter situation, Chris is still stripped of his protector status as he loses the ability to save himself when seconds earlier he successfully survives five combative engagements using a shotgun that is still technically functional at the moment he seeks Ashley's assistance. He goes from the protector to being the protected as his survival is dictated by the girl whom he has protected until this point.

If Chris survives, his emasculation is continually present as he becomes an empty shell. His dialogue is limited to a couple of small, unimportant lines and he often stands off to the side in silence while the group actively discusses survival plans. He no longer participates in protecting the women, instead needing protection and motivation from Ashley to keep going. He receives no further access to weapons and he does not assist Matt with destroying the Wendigo in the final scene, choosing instead to flee the lodge in the same way that Ashley and Emily do. His actions mimic those of the female characters after his emasculation at the hands of Ashley. In a potential ending in the mines, Ashley, not Chris, goes off in search of Jessica, and Chris is only given the option to follow her. Even if he does, he is not able to save her but instead finds her decapitated body shortly before being killed himself. This is a long way from the hero protector he portrays in the beginning.

Mike is the only male character to maintain his masculinized role, repeatedly rushing into dangerous situations and protecting the female characters at any cost. He often takes control of the situation, leading the decision-making and seeking ways to save the female characters at varying points in the narrative, regardless of his feelings for them. First, he rushes after Jessica. Then, after believing her to be dead, he saves Sam from Josh and comes to the aid of Ashley and Chris. He rushes back to the lodge when he sees Emily has returned and protectively holds Ashley if she chooses to let Chris die. In the safe room he has the opportunity to shoot Emily if she is bitten, seeing himself as the protector of the group even if Chris is still alive. Mike is held up as the only true man of the group, even compared to Josh who is also shown as an aggressive male character.

Josh is portrayed in a weakened state once his identity as the antagonist is revealed, and like Chris, he devolves into a shell of himself, needing to be rescued by Mike in the mines. Sam aids in Josh's rescue, further demonstrating his lack of strength in needing to be saved by a woman. Josh's only weapons are his bare fists and his only combat is against abstract hallucinations.

Dialogue

The dialogue in *Until Dawn* presents numerous examples of hegemonic masculine discourse. In all the conversations between two or more male characters, the words "bro", "dude", and "man" form a large portion of the commentary. It became unwieldy to document the frequency of these words, so I selected a pivotal scene between Chris, Josh, and Mike as a case example, not only of the use of these terms, but also of the overtones of sexual dominance being a key component of the masculine identity. Mike confronts Josh when he reveals that he is the one who has been terrorizing the group.

Josh: I don't think there's enough hard drives in China to count all the views we're gonna get, you guys.

Mike: What are you talking about, you ass hat? Jessica IS FUCKING DEAD.

Josh: What?

Mike: Did you hear me?! Jessica is dead … and YOU ARE GONNA FUCKING PAY, YOU DICK!!!!

Mike pistol whips Josh in the side of the head, knocking him out.

Mike ties Josh up and stands watch over him to keep him from harming anyone else. During this time, Mike lectures Josh about his unethical treatment of the women. As this is prior to Chris' emasculation, he joins in, punching Josh in the face if Ashley was assaulted in retaliation for using the scissors.

Chris: Why did ya hit her, man?! Why'd you have to fucking hit her?!

Chris punches Josh in the face.

Josh: What are you talking about?

Chris: You punched Ashley, you piece of shit!

Josh: I got so mad.

Chris: You don't hit a girl. You just don't.

Chris and Mike are not only protecting the women, they're objecting to what they perceive as immoral treatment of Ashley and Jessica by Josh based on their gender. Nowhere does anyone object to a man hitting another man in these scenes, but both object to Josh's violence toward the female characters, referencing the convention that men should never hit women.

This conversation devolves further into the topic of male sexual performance as a defining characteristic of masculinity. Josh questions Chris' masculinity due to his passivity with Ashley and implies that Mike is more of a man because he has more success with women.

Josh: "Ohh … Ashley … I never imagined in my wildest dreams that you liked me …!"

Chris: Stop.

Josh: You know what that sound is? It's the sound of never kissing Ashley, you pussy.

Chris: Stop!

Josh: Yeah, you know? You might as well let Ashley sleep with Mike. I mean, at least he's got some notches on his belt, you know? He'll treat (*thrusts*) her (*thrusts*) right (*thrusts*)! You're fucking pathetic, Christopher.

Sexual prowess is an overarching theme in many of these discussions. Early in the game, Josh is discussing Chris' lack of initiative in trying to have sex with Ashley, drawing a parallel between men as hunters and women as prey.

Josh: Ashley was looking pretty hot today, right? She's like a "sleeper hit" kinda gal, you know?... Now I just want to rip that parka right off her … make some snow angels. Right?

Chris: Cut it out, man.

Josh: When are you gonna take her to the bone zone?

Chris: Sheesh … Like that could ever happen.

Josh: Come on, man. She practically spends her entire life with you as it is.

Chris: Well, yeah, but we're like, friends—

Josh: Listen dude. Look around you. Look at these beautiful mountains. Do you see any parents? I mean can you imagine a more perfect, ripe scenario, just dripping with erotic possibilities? You, and Ashley, alone at last … You've laid all the groundwork … you've been a perfect gentleman. Now you come in for the kill!

Depending on the option the player chooses at this point, two different yet equally masculinized discussion endings take place. If Chris agrees:

Chris: Maybe you're right.
Josh: You're a hunter, bro. No fear. No mercy. I mean she won't even know what hit her.

Whereas if Chris disagrees:

Chris: I don't know, man …
Josh: How can you NOT KNOW!
Chris: But what if it's, like, weird … and what if she might not like, wanna be friends with me anymore if I try something like that.
Josh: I mean, weren't you just listening? You gotta buck up, bro. Grow a pair.

Each conversational option references dominance as masculinity. The man as hunter metaphor, the implication of lacking male genitalia, the implied lack of masculinity in hesitating, all establish a connection to hegemonic masculinity. The dialogue ties masculinity to sexual prowess in undeniable ways regardless of player choice, and this is simply one of several potential examples, including several chapters where Jessica and Mike's sole communication is sexual banter.

Discussion

In exploring the permeation of dominance, sexual prowess, and protector imagery in *Until Dawn*, it is clear that their ubiquitous presence creates strong hegemonic representations of masculinity. Relying on the horror genre stereotypes necessitates the inclusion of certain attributes. The problem persists in most forms of video games, but with the steadfast nature of horror genre media clinging to harmful stereotypes around marginalized groups, the need for a diverse and nuanced approach to character construction and player agency within those characters' stories becomes even more essential. The various areas considered herein demonstrate that much of the masculinized identities within the game fulfil and exceed those of standard horror tropes through heavy-handed dialogue, emasculating storylines, weaponry, and combat. When considering race, gender, and mental trauma, the use of horror tropes only serves to solidify masculinity as a physically capable, white male, serving to uphold the traditional characterization of hegemonic masculinity.

With the extensive academic discussion of female representations in video games, there is a greater need for research considering the impact of hegemonic gender on masculine and non-binary depictions as well. This chapter sought to address the former in a preliminary way by proposing the use of intersectionality as a way to bring nuance and depth to the discussion of masculinity in media. As with any research that engages with power dynamics and social structures, intersectionality is vital. The problematic use of race as lacking ability and mental illness as weakness stand out as significant and ubiquitous patterns in *Until Dawn*. Through an intersectional lens, the impact of race and mental illness as forms of marginalization becomes increasingly clear, highlighting the importance of this tool at the outset of this line of research.

Additionally, this chapter utilized a hybrid approach to content analysis. The interactive nature of the video game opens up the possibility to subvert these archetypes through player agency, but even then the structure of *Until Dawn* enforces a rigidity along gender lines that ensures the maintenance of these conventional masculine and feminine representations. The combination of imagery, dialogue, forms of death, and objects—access and effectiveness— enabled a deeper reading of the video game in terms of both the underlying power structures and the forms of marginalization. Although some of the more troubling depictions existed on the surface, the triangulation of methodologies in this hybrid approach brought to the forefront strong evidence to this chapter's initial premise and to establish a more systemic issue with the forms of representation within the game.

In holding horror video games to the same level of critical analysis of other video game genres, the sub-genre can be pushed to reconsider these stereotypical depictions in lieu of more subversive and complex character development, especially in a genre already so full of potential for alternative storytelling.

Note

1. Secondary characters, such as Dr. Hill, the Stranger, and Josh's alter ego were not included in this chapter due to length requirements.

Bibliography

Barone, Matt. 2013. Fact Check: Do Black Characters Always Die First in Horror Movies? *Complex: Pop Culture.* http://ca.complex.com/pop-culture/2013/10/black-characters-horror-movies/. Accessed 31 Oct.

Benshoff, Harry. 1997. *Monsters in the Closet: Homosexuality and the Horror Film.* New York: Manchester University Press.

Brock, André. 2011. 'When Keeping it Real Goes Wrong': Resident Evil 5, Racial Representation, and Gamers. *Games and Culture* 6 (5): 429–452. https://doi.org/10.1177/1555412011402676.

Consalvo, Mia. 2003. The Monsters Next Door: Media Constructions of Boys and Masculinity. *Feminist Media Studies* 3 (1): 27–45. https://doi.org/10.1080/1468077032000080112.

Coulthard, Lisa, and Chelsea Birks. 2015. Desublimating Monstrous Desire: The Horror of Gender in New Extremist Cinema. *Journal of Gender Studies.* https://doi.org/10.1080/09589236.2015.1011100.

Crenshaw, Kimberle. 1991. Mapping the Margins: Intersectionality, Identity Politics, and Violence Against Women of Color. *Stanford Law Review* 43 (6): 1241–1299. https://doi.org/10.2307/1229039.

Dill, Karen E., and Kathryn P. Thill. 2007. Video Game Characters and the Socialization of Gender Roles: Young People's Perceptions Mirror Sexist Media Depictions. *Sex Roles* 57 (11): 851–864. https://doi.org/10.1007/s11199-007-9278-1.

Dill, Karen E., Douglas A. Gentile, William A. Richter, and Jody C. Dill. 2005. Violence, Sex, Race, and Age in Popular Video Games: A Content Analysis. In *Featuring Females: Feminist Analyses of the Media*, ed. Ellen Cole and Jessica Henderson Daniel, 115–130. Washington, DC: American Psychological Association.

Godwin, Victoria. 2013. *Twilight* Anti-Fans: 'Real' Fans and 'Real' Vampires. In *The Twilight Saga: Exploring the Global Phenomenon*, ed. Claudia Bucciferro, 93–106. New York: Scarecrow Press, Inc.

Kendall, Lori. 2011. 'White and Nerdy': Computers, Race, and the Nerd Stereotype. *The Journal of Popular Culture* 44 (2): 505–524. https://doi.org/10.1111/j.1540-5931.2011.00846.x.

King, Claire Sisco. 2009. It Cuts Both Ways: Fight Club, Masculinity, and Abject Hegemony. *Communication and Critical/Cultural Studies* 6 (4): 366–385. https://doi.org/10.1080/14791420903335135.

———. 2013. A Gendered Shell Game: Masculinity and Race in *District 9*. In *Communicating Marginalized Masculinities: Identity Politics in TV, Film, and New Media*, ed. Ronald L. Jackson II and Jamie E. Moshin, 80–98. New York: Routledge.

Klepek, Patrick. 2015. How Until Dawn Messes With Two Of Horror's Most Overused Tropes. *Kotaku.* http://kotaku.com/how-until-dawn-messes-with-two-of-horror-s-most-overuse-1729817525. Accessed 10 Sept.

Lorber, Judith. 1998. Men's Gender Politics. *Gender & Society* 12 (4): 469–472. http://www.jstor.org/stable/190179.

Luyt, Russell, Christina Welch, and Rosemary Lobban. 2015. Diversity in Gender and Visual Representation: An Introduction. *Journal of Gender Studies* 24 (4): 383–385. https://doi.org/10.1080/09589236.2015.1052641.

McCann, Ben. 2008. Pierced Borders, Punctured Bodies: The Contemporary French Horror Film. *Australian Journal of French Studies* 45 (3): 225–237. https://doi.org/10.3828/AJFS.45.3.225.

Och, Dana. 2015. Beyond Surveillance: Questions of the Real in the Neopostmodern Horror Film. In *Style and Form in the Hollywood Slasher Film*, ed. Wickham Clayton, 195–212. Basingstoke: Palgrave Macmillan.

Shaw, Adrienne. 2014. Representation Matters (?): When, How and if Representation Matters to Marginalized Game Audiences. In *Challenging Communication Research*, ed. Leah Lievrouw. New York: International Communication Association.

Steele, Sarah L., and Tyler Shores. 2015. Real and Unreal Masculinities: The Celebrity image in Anti-Trafficking Campaigns. *Journal of Gender Studies* 24 (4): 383–385. https://doi.org/10.1080/09589236.2014.959477.

Sundén, Jenny, and Malin Sveningsson. 2012. *Gender and Sexuality in Online Game Cultures*. New York: Routledge.

Supermassive Games. 2015. *Until Dawn*. Video Game.

Williams, Dmitri, Nicole Martins, Mia Consalvo, and James D. Ivory. 2009. The Virtual Census: Representations of Gender, Race and Age in Video Games. *New Media & Society* 11 (5): 815–834. https://doi.org/10.1177/1461444809105354.

6

(Re)reading Fatherhood: Applying Reader Response Theory to Joel's Father Role in *The Last of Us*

Mark Cruea

According to *Oxford Dictionaries* (2016), fatherhood is defined as "The state of being a father." Unfortunately, that definition provides no assistance in understanding the varieties of fatherhood that exist or how fatherhood is viewed in real-life relationships or through the lens of popular culture texts. Unlike other forms of popular culture such as television, only recently has fatherhood been portrayed in any depth within video games. For example, consider *BioShock Infinite* (2K Games 2013), *The Walking Dead* (Telltale Games 2012), *Dishonored* (Arkane Studios 2012), and, more recently, *The Witcher 3: The Wild Hunt* (CD Projekt Red 2015). In fact, the popular press and individual bloggers (Brice 2013; Clauson 2015; Joho 2014; Myers 2013; Pollock 2013) have paid more attention to fatherhood as a video game trope than as academe. One game, *The Last of Us* (Naughty Dog 2013), has fatherhood as one of its central themes, and while this chapter does not seek to provide a singular definition of fatherhood, it is interested in understanding how fatherhood is performed, enacted, read, and reread in the context of *The Last of Us* (*TLoU*). As noted, the predominant responses to fatherhood in video games come from popular press and personal blog entries; this chapter engages the latter, and three questions are of interest: First, how can the father-daughter relationship in *TLoU* be read through the lenses of masculinity and fatherhood? Second, from a reader response perspective, how did bloggers

M. Cruea (✉)
Ohio North University, Ada, OH, USA

© The Author(s) 2018
N. Taylor, G. Voorhees (eds.), *Masculinities in Play*, Palgrave Games in Context,
https://doi.org/10.1007/978-3-319-90581-5_6

view the father-daughter dynamic within *TLoU*? Finally, how do the bloggers' readings of TLoU fit the reader-response framework? Following is an overview of the literature on masculinity and fatherhood.

Masculinity

Before proceeding to masculinity, it is salient to acknowledge the work conducted by gender and feminist researchers regarding video games. For example, a range of studies have focused on representation (Dietz 1998; Dill and Thill 2007; Kennedy 2002), factors influencing female motivations to play and play style (Carr 2005; de Castell and Jenson 2003; Jenson and de Castell 2008), and, more recently, gamer culture (Consalvo 2012), among many others. Just as gender and feminist studies have examined a number of areas, so too have studies of masculinity in video games. These include violence in video games (Chess and Shaw 2015; Sims 2014; Thomas and Levant 2012; Tragos 2009), subordinate masculinities such as the nerd/jock dichotomy and geek masculinity (Bell et al. 2015; Consalvo 2003; Nakamura 2012), and non-hypermasculine males or men as caretakers and fathers (Kirkland 2009; Voorhees 2016). In fact, masculinity studies evolved directly from the women's liberation and LGBT (lesbian, gay, bisexual, and transgender movements. Evidence also shows that current Western conceptions of masculinity are outgrowths of the "military, social, and economic history of North Atlantic capitalist states" (Connell 1993, 597). Connell (1993) noted how family, workplace, and state institutions all impact our understanding of masculinity as well as how cultural conceptions of sexuality are intrinsically intertwined. Since Connell's seminal work during the 1990s, the notion of masculinity has been further complicated.

More recently, Milestone and Meyer (2012) have theorized three different discourses of masculinity. The first masculinity discourse is identified as the Old Man. This traditional embodiment of masculinity is characterized by authority, strength of mind and body, aggressiveness, competitiveness, and violence. Moreover, men are primarily defined by their occupations and roles as protectors, while physical attractiveness and enhancing one's appearance is the concern of women. Additional characteristics include a strong heterosexual orientation combined with an emphasis on rationality and lack of emotional expression (Milestone and Meyer 2012). Indeed, the Old Man is considered the least progressive form of masculinity (Edwards 2003; MacKinnon 2003).

Emerging in the 1980s, the New Man developed along two different strands both influenced by feminism and changing gender attitudes. The first strand is the Narcissist. In contrast to the Old Man, the Narcissist is consumed with appearance and fashion. His attention to a sound body is similar to that of the Old Man, but the purpose is different since the Narcissist refines his body to accentuate appearance. Also in a similar vein as the Old Man, the Narcissist is quite career conscious, but his career success helps provide him with entertainment and consumption options. The second strand of the New Man is the Nurturer. This version of the New Man is marked by sensitivity and his ability to care. Furthermore, the Nurturer is likely involved in household chores, and sympathy with the feminist cause is common. Consumerism, on the other hand, is not (Chapman 1988; Milestone and Meyer 2012).

In the early 1990s in Britain and late 1990s in the United States, a third discourse of masculinity emerged. Dubbed the New Lad, this third strand maintains some of the New Man's characteristics, but reintegrates aspects of the Old Man. More specifically, the New Lad retains his focus on style and consumerism while readopting the more macho aspects of the Old Man including aggressiveness and misogyny (Beynon 2002; Milestone and Meyer 2012). Attwood (2005) sees the New Lad as a bricoleur since he blends the two former discourses in new ways. In no way do these discourses describe the full spectrum of masculinity that exists, and while they are presented in sequential fashion, each version can be found today alongside nerd/jock, geek, and non-hypermasculine masculinities (Bell et al. 2015; Consalvo 2003; Nakamura 2012; Voorhees 2016). However, the framework of the Old Man, New Man, and New Lad provides a useful lens through which to view masculinity in *TLoU*. The following discussion on fatherhood builds on these discourses.

Fatherhood

The first variety of fatherhood is referred to as Old or Traditional Fatherhood. The Old Father has its roots in the industrial revolution and is closely tied to the provider role. A father is the breadwinner while the mother is the nurturing caregiver. Since the Old Father is responsible for most of the family income, he is essentially tasked with helping his family survive and ideally thrive. This division of labor also reinforced the father's ability to maintain an emotional distance from his children while simultaneously retaining control over the family (Griswold 1993; Wahlström 2014). Later, as families migrated to the suburbs and fathers spent more time commuting, the time available for children correspondingly diminished (Pleck 1987; Witt n.d.). Indeed, the Old Father is marked by absence rather than presence. Although calls for increased fatherly participation have their roots in the early part of the twentieth century, those calls had little to no impact on the gendered division of labor (Griswold 1993; Wahlström 2014). Instead, a father's involvement "was a 'gift' men granted to women and children" (Griswold 1993, 6). Examples of the Old Father still exist today.

Moreover, as a result of these privileged societal norms, the father role remained relatively unchanged until the growth of feminism in the 1960s. Dubbed the New Father, the resultant changes in fatherhood mirrored the emergence of the New Man as Nurturer. Questions were also raised about a woman's innate disposition to serve as caregiver and keeper of the home—reasons often given to legitimize a father's absence. Indeed, the need for women to work outside of the home during World War II had a strong impact. Having successfully demonstrated their capabilities away from home during World War II, women began to change their expectations regarding their options outside of homemaking and childrearing. Consequently, men faced rising expectations to be more fully involved in childcare. Co-parenting was expected as opposed to occasionally helping around the house. Furthermore, New Fathers were expected to be more emotionally engaged with their children (Griswold 1993; Wahlström 2014; Witt n.d.). As with masculinities, there are other forms of fatherhood not included in this framework. Witt (n.d.) also outlines the Deadbeat Dad, the Visiting Father, the Sperm Father, the Stepfather, the Nearby Guy, and the Good Family Man as additional forms of fatherly involvement.

Reader Response Theory

At a very basic level, reader response theory is concerned with what the reader of a text takes away from that text. The theory asserts that a text cannot be separated from what that text does. In addition, reader response theory maintains that texts are not passively consumed in some objective manner determined by the author. Instead, readers are actively involved in the meaning-making process. As a result, different interpretations of a text may arise among several readers (Tyson 2014). However, critics have pointed out that readers do not have complete control over the meaning created. In all, three approaches exist. First is a privileged approach, which asserts that while a reader has some control over the interpretation, the author's intended meaning strongly influences the reader. Second is a negotiated reading where the reader and the author mutually influence one another. Third is the subjective approach, which has the reader creating unique textual understandings (Bleich 1976; Brooks and Browne 2012; Rabinowitz 1987; Rosenblatt 1982; Sipe 2008).

Important to this chapter is the Brooks and Browne (2012) perspective on culturally situated reader response theory. Here, the authors propose that readers occupy a cultural position when encountering a text that is influenced by family, peers, community, and ethnic group. While the evaluation of these blogs does not engage ethnicity, it is interested in how gender and parental roles might impact the bloggers' interpretations. Not commonly used in video game studies, reader response theory invites new understandings of video games and their impact on the user. A search of academic studies yields few results, which include studies that examine reader response in relation to literature, film, and video games (Mackey 2011), gamer responses and simulation (von Gillern 2016), and narrative experiences in *Silent Hill* (Holmquest 2013). Moreover, Kücklich (2006) advocates for the use of reader response theory to study video games as a method of understanding the impact these games have on the reader. Since the interaction between the player and game occurs in a different way than books and films (Royse et al. 2007; Taylor et al. 2015), understanding the game players' responses can add to our understanding of how players make meaning through video games.

Game Overview

Before proceeding to the analysis, a brief overview of *TLoU* is provided. In *TLoS*, Joel occupies the father role. He is also the primary protagonist in the game. *TLoU* opens by establishing Joel's relationship with his daughter Sarah. After falling asleep while Joel is still home, Sarah awakens to find her father gone as news reports of a viral outbreak flash across the TV screen. Joel returns home, and after an encounter with an infected neighbor, Joel and Sarah attempt to flee from the ensuing chaos with Joel's brother Tommy. Up to this point, the player controls Sarah, but she is essentially helpless. After a car accident in which Sarah's leg is broken, the player assumes control of Joel, and Joel, Sarah, and Tommy work their way through town while being pursued by infected. With Tommy holding back a crowd of infected, Joel and Sarah reach the perimeter of town only to encounter a soldier who is ordered to kill them both. During their attempt to flee, Sarah is shot, and Tommy kills the soldier in time to save Joel. The scene ends with Sarah dying in Joel's arms (*TLoU* 2013).

Twenty years later, Joel is now partnered with Tess. They work as smugglers in the Boston area. In order to recover a shipment of guns, Tess and Joel agree to escort a 14-year-old girl named Ellie across town to a group of freedom fighters called the Fireflies. Ellie is the only known person to be bitten by an infected and subsequently survive. Through her immunity, the Fireflies hope to develop a cure for the infection. Later, Tess dies from a bite, and the group fails to contact the Fireflies; Joel and Ellie then travel across the country encountering a variety of assailants including the leader of a group of cannibals named David. In the end, Joel and Ellie arrive in Utah where the Fireflies are encamped at a hospital. Once Joel discovers that Ellie will die from the surgery needed to develop the cure, he fights his way to Ellie, flees to the hospital parking garage, and kills Marlene (the leader of the Fireflies) to escape the facility. The game ends with the player in control of Ellie as she and Joel walk to an overlook. Joel tells Ellie that the Fireflies were unable to develop a cure and that other immunes were discovered. Even when Ellie questions Joel, he maintains his story in order to shield Ellie from the truth (*TLoU* 2013).

This brief description essentially sums up a large portion of the plot, which is predominantly conveyed through periodic cut scenes. Gameplay largely consists of either Joel or Ellie sneaking by the infected and/or using their weapons to defeat enemies. In addition, the user is in control of Joel for most of the game, and Ellie is largely out of the picture. Early in the game, Joel even instructs Ellie to remain hidden and refuses to provide her with a weapon. While Ellie eventually gains the ability to use weapons, she is never in any real danger. As well, these sequences rely entirely on escort mechanics with Joel serving as Ellie's escort. The only time *TLoU* veers from the escort mechanics is during a sequence when Joel is injured and Ellie must fend for herself. During this segment, the player controls Ellie, but she never escorts Joel because he is unconscious. Once Joel has recovered, the player reverts to Joel and the escort mechanics return. Overall, the cut scenes largely contain the plot elements that communicate Joel's roles as protector and eventual father figure while the escort mechanics serve to reinforce those roles (*TLoU* 2013).

Masculinity and Fatherhood in *TLoU*

The first question asks how the father-daughter relationship in *TLoU* can be read through the chosen masculinity and fatherhood lenses. In many ways, Joel is a complicated character and his life experiences and circumstances shape who he is. During the opening series with his daughter Sarah, Joel most closely embodies the nurturing version of the New Man and correspondingly, the New Father. While this segment of the game is fairly short, we see Joel as a single father who is closely attached to his daughter. There is an emotional connection between the two that is evident as Sarah lovingly gives Joel the gift of a watch, a gift that he keeps as a memento long after it has stopped working. Reflecting the key Nurturing New Man and New Father characteristics, Joel is sensitive, caring, and emotionally engaged with Sarah, and as a single parent, he is responsible for the home and childcare.

Twenty years later, Joel is a changed man. Unfortunately, the change is regressive as his actions are more symbolic of the Old Man and Old Father. He is gruff. He uses violence to solve his issues, and upon meeting Ellie and hearing the request to escort her, he is very reluctant. The only way that Tess convinces Joel to take the job is by convincing him that Ellie is simply cargo; Joel views Ellie as a means to an economic end; she is just another job. He is also unconcerned with his appearance, which is in direct contrast to what he looked like at the beginning of the game. Other characteristics that tie to the Old Man/Father include Joel's strength of body, aggressiveness, strong heterosexuality as evidenced by his relationship with Tess and his emotional distance from others.

However, as the game progresses, the relationship between Joel and Ellie transforms. Eventually, Joel begins to use terms of endearment with Ellie that had been previously reserved for Sarah. For example, at the beginning of the game when he first tucks Sarah in at night and then later when Sarah is dying, he calls Sarah his "baby girl." Further into the game after Ellie has killed David, Joel comes to her aid and calls Ellie "baby girl." He uses the term once more when rescuing Ellie from the hospital. The decision to make such a connection through language was a small, but important, rhetorical device for Naughty Dog, symbolizing that Joel now regards Ellie as his own child. The care that Joel shows is quite emblematic of the New Father, and this care is communicated through his tenderness and loving words. However, Joel's character doesn't fit the New Man/Father completely. Since Joel consistently takes away Ellie's agency, he partially embodies the Old Man/Father by using force or deception to control Ellie. He also effectively annihilates all presence of a mother by killing Marlene near the end of the game. As well, Joel fails to truly nurture Ellie in ways that help prepare her for life without him. Instead, he unfailingly serves as protector. In many ways, the Joel that appears at the end of the game is a mixture of the Joel at the beginning as New Father and in the middle, as Old Father.

Bloggers' Responses to *TLoU*

The second question asks how the chosen bloggers view the father-daughter dynamic in *TLoU*. For this study, three blogs were examined. The selection criteria included finding blogs with the desired gender and parental characteristics. The blogs also needed to discuss fatherhood in *TLoU*. The addition of a fourth blog from a mother was desired, but one could not be located. In addition, the authors are not specifically identified other than by the gender and parental markers listed by the bloggers. Blogger One (B1) is male and a father. He identifies as a life-long gamer and his entries include game reviews, editorial pieces, and his general experiences with and reactions to games. No occupation is provided. Blogger Two (B2) is male with no children. He works as a software developer and maintains the blog on the side. He solely focuses on video games providing reviews as well as critical commentary. Blogger Three (B3) is female with no children. She currently writes professionally for a website that provides commentary on several types of media, but B3's focus is writing critical commentary of video games.

Out of the three bloggers, B1 relates most closely to the characters as written. As B1 indicates, his connection flows from the fact that he has a young daughter. As a result, the sequence that ends with Sarah's death strongly impacts B1, and he states that he became heavily absorbed in the game due to the father-daughter dynamic. Moreover, B1 specifically identifies with the need for Joel to protect Ellie since, even though she is immune to infection, she is not immune to the other dangers. B1 also points out how Joel and Ellie's relationship developed from an escort/cargo affiliation to a father-daughter relationship where Joel is willing to do anything to help Ellie survive. B1 details how as a father, he would make the same decisions—he would lie to save her life because that is what fathers do even if it meant that the rest of humanity potentially perishes. Furthermore, B1's reading of *TLoU* is tied strongly to the pathos of the storyline. His acknowledgment of his personal status as a father is what connects him to the game. For B1, the need to protect is overwhelming. He even describes watching his own daughter in her crib just to make sure she is still breathing. In regard to Joel as father/protector, B1 provides no comments on the non-diegetic aspects of the game. Instead, his reflection on the developer's decisions relate more to combat mechanics and set design including light, sound, and inability to revisit earlier levels.

In comparison, B2 is a young male without children who connects very differently to the characters. At the beginning of the game, B2 identified with Joel's biological daughter Sarah. He notes that Sarah needs Joel's protection because she is unable to protect herself; however, B2 also notes that he is forced to play as Joel, and therefore, Sarah is stripped of her agency—a decision he laments. Furthermore, B2 calls into question Joel's ability to properly protect Sarah since she is killed only a few minutes into the game. Likewise, B2 does not like being forced into the protector's role for Ellie, and he notices that when danger appears, Ellie merely scurries away while Joel fights. Consequently, Ellie is never truly in danger. Joel's actions seem pointless to B2 since Joel seemingly wants to protect Ellie's innocence in a world where that is impossible but also unnecessary given the apparent lack of threat to Ellie's life. Another issue for B2 is that Joel does not attempt to teach Ellie anything including how to swim even though there is ample time. Having the option to teach Ellie survival skills would give her agency and make her less dependent on Joel, but Naughty Dog's decisions make that impossible. Furthermore, B2 points out that when Ellie is searching for food and medication to help an injured Joel, Ellie basically has the same mechanics as Joel, but is unable to carry as much gear. The player cannot upgrade Ellie's ability or weapons either, which severely limits Ellie. B2's final comments focus on the ending of the game where Joel saves Ellie from the Fireflies, executes Marlene, and lies to Ellie about her ability to save humankind. B2 reflects that without agency, Ellie does not have the choice to save humanity. In fact, B2 labels Joel as a terrible father due to these choices.

Overall, B2 has taken a cerebral approach to the game where he considers both the diegetic and non-diegetic aspects of the game. In comparison to B1, B2 looks outside of the story to critique the father-daughter relationship decisions made by Naughty Dog and reflected in the gameplay. Not only is the blogger making meaning from the story. He is also making meaning by examining the developer's choices and how those choices enhance or inhibit the player's experience. Given B2's job in software development, his profession may contribute to his critique of the developers.

Lastly, B3 begins her entry by identifying as a female and not a father. B3 adds that even though she is not a father, she expected to find some level of emotional connection to the characters in *TLoU* especially as a protector. However, that was not her experience. B3 partially attributes this lack of connection to the inability to play as anyone other than Joel, and even though the relationship between Joel and Ellie takes a while to develop and B2 hoped to develop a connection during that time, she found the experience off-putting. What makes the experience even more difficult is that B3 does not see Joel as a good role model. Part of her issue is connected to the use of violence as the most common solution to all problems. For instance, Ellie is exposed to violence early and often, and she seems to adapt to this mode of living especially after getting permission from Joel to use guns and other weapons. In addition, B3 notes how enemies do not seem to see Ellie during combat. Consequently, the player, as Joel, is not overly inconvenienced by Ellie's presence resulting in a disconnect from the potential father-daughter relationship for B3. B3 identifies other issues that interfere with developing a connection between Joel and Ellie. For example, due to the loss of his daughter, Joel is reluctant to get close to Ellie early in the game. He convinces himself that she is merely cargo.

For B3, Joel is seemingly irritated at needing to deal with a young woman. Conversely, B3 does state that she became attached to Ellie because Ellie is charming. This response is interesting in that Ellie can be insubordinate and foul-mouthed, and she doesn't always do what Joel tells her to do. However, B3 notes, it is as if Ellie needs to be charming to break through Joel's gruff exterior.

In a similar manner to B2, B3 points out Ellie's lack of agency. She notes that all the adults in Ellie's life get to make life-and-death decisions for her, and they lie to allegedly protect Ellie. B3 also connects Joel's decision to lie to his fear of losing another daughter, which, for B3, makes Joel seem selfish. B3 also goes on to explain that despite Ellie's fear of being alone, Ellie might be better off because she could make her own decisions. In the end, B3 states that Joel's decision to lie made her (B3) feel worse, and she questions whether Joel's decision is even realistic. B3 does not believe that real-world parents ever act in the same way as Joel. Given B3's diegetic and non-diegetic commentary, it is possible that her occupation as a writer who critiques video games influenced her critique of Naughty Dog's game-design decisions.

Applying Reader Response to Blog Posts

The third question asks how the three bloggers' responses fit the reader-response framework. As a quick review of reader response theory, the privileged approach asserts that while a reader has some control over the interpretation, the author's intended meaning strongly influences the reader. In contrast, the reader and the author mutually influence one another in a negotiated reading. Lastly, the reader creates unique understandings of the text in a subjective approach (Brooks and Browne 2012). Recall that B1 strongly connects to the relationship between Joel and his biological daughter Sarah as well as the need for Joel to protect Sarah. Additionally, B1 believes that Joel's decisions at the end of the game are appropriate, and even though both Sarah and Ellie are older, B1 sees the need for protection as normal. B1 also does not offer any criticism of Naughty Dog's decisions regarding the way in which the father-daughter relationship is portrayed. While B1 does not directly influence the developer, the developer's decisions certainly reinforce B1's views on a father's role, and while B1 points out the lack of nurturing opportunities for Ellie, it is one small deviation from the rest of his responses that assume protection at all costs. Consequently, B1's response is situated as more of a negotiated reading.

In contrast, B2 identifies more with Sarah and Ellie. If anything, he shows great empathy toward these two female characters and is frustrated by their lack of agency. As a young adult not far removed from his teenage years, B2 relates to both of the young women's struggles. In addition, B2 questions Joel's parental ability since Sarah dies quickly and Joel never invests any time to teach Ellie survival skills. As well, B2 actively questions the diegetic and non-diegetic aspects of *TLoU*. As opposed to B1, B2's reading is more oppositional and subjective. He does not believe that Joel is acting properly and actively critiques Joel's decisions.

In a similar way, B3 criticizes many of the same issues as B2. She has the hardest time connecting emotionally to Joel, and cannot identify with the need to protect Ellie. She, too, resents being forced to play as Joel while also questioning the lack of opportunity to educate Ellie. However, B3 goes even further than B2 when B3 claims that Ellie may have been better off on her own. Ellie needs to emancipate herself. B3 also contrasts with B1 when she states that Joel should not have lied to Ellie. B3 does mention Ellie's charm, and it is possible that B3's identity as a young woman allows her to connect to Ellie on a level that neither B1 nor B2 can. Ellie's insubordination may even be seen as a way of fighting against patriarchy, an experience B3 and Ellie might share. In the end, B3's readings are very much in opposition to Naughty Dog's choices making B3's response strongly unique and oppositional.

Making Meaning—(Re)reading Fatherhood

With the preceding discussion in mind, there are a few thoughts that deserve consideration. For one, while the analysis above reveals how each blogger is situated in terms of reader response, it does not examine how each blogger's reading fits the different fatherhood archetypes. Remarkably, their readings of Joel as father are quite similar; where they differ is as to whether Joel's actions are appropriate. At the beginning of the game, all three bloggers seem to see Joel as a mixture of the Old and New Father as shown through his interactions with Sarah. He serves as provider and protector while simultaneously connecting emotionally. However, his post-pandemic interactions are seen as closer to the Old Father. All three bloggers comment on Joel's role as protector and provider; he is read as emotionally distant while his missed opportunities to teach are seen as regressive. All three bloggers also remark on his growing emotional closeness as the player reaches the end of the game—elements of the New Father.

Even though these similarities exist, there are marked differences and therefore it is necessary to contextualize the bloggers' responses. For example, B1 was directly impacted by the presence of and interaction with his young daughter. As a young male, B2 was better able to identify with the teenagers—Sarah and Ellie—than he could with Joel. B3, as a female gamer, appeared impacted by her experiences with patriarchy. So what does this mean? If anything, we know that while developers control the plot and game mechanics, there is no guarantee that players will all read the game in the same fashion. Instead, it appears that the players and games mutually constitute one another to varying degrees depending on context. Essentially, we have only scratched the surface of these gaming experiences, but progress is being made by identifying which factors impact a player's reading of a game. Using reader response theory provides an additional tool to uncover those factors to gain a deeper understanding of the meaning-making process, especially when culturally situated.

As well, a common assumption in the video game literature is that because the player controls an avatar, there must be some type of identification with that avatar. For example, Giddings and Kennedy (2008) question this assumption and state that the theory does not account for the complexity of a game player's experience. The authors' position connects to culturally situated reader response theory (Brooks and Browne 2012) where the reader's cultural position, including family, peers, and community, is assumed to impact a reader's interpretation. This is especially true in regard to the parental roles and occupational communities that each blogger occupies. By the same token, Elson, Breuer, Ivory, and Quandt's (2014) work on hedonic and eudaimonic gratifications connects three interactive variables that contribute to the gaming experience. These include the gaming narrative, which incorporates the game's story, setting, and plot; the game mechanics, which include the game's rules, restrictions, and feedback that impact interaction; and finally, the playing context or social setting, which involves the gaming device, the location of play, and the presence of other players. I suggest extending the playing context to include the presence (or lack) of family members, as well as the player's personal experiences. Taken together, Giddings and Kennedy's (2008) assertions, as well as Brooks and Browne's (2012) culturally situated reader response and an extended playing context based on Elson, Breuer, Ivory, and Quandt's (2014) study, effectively combine with this examination of bloggers' responses to illustrate the foibles of the identification assumption.

Finally, it would be remiss to not connect the gender studies research to this analysis and the growing body of research focused on fatherhood in gaming. For instance, the research on representation (Dietz 1998; Dill and Thill 2007; Kennedy 2002) extensively examined body type, including hypermasculinity and hyperfemininity, and clothing (or lack thereof). The characters in *TLoU* are more representative of average persons who are fully clothed. Even though *TLoU* could have portrayed its protagonists in hyper-muscular and hyper-sexualized ways, Naughty Dog kept the characters in line with what a person might encounter on any given day. This is a positive step, but not true of all games depicting fatherhood. Voorhees (2016), for example, contrasts Ellie's appearance in *TLoU* with Elizabeth's character in *BioShock Infinite*. While Elizabeth is also a daughter figure, she is portrayed in ways more consistent with the male gaze and exaggerated proportions. Additionally, research interested in females' motivations to play (Carr 2005; de Castell and Jenson 2003; Jenson and de Castell 2008) can benefit from reader-response analyses. Further understanding of how players interpret gameplay can provide deeper and more nuanced insights into the choices that both male and female gamers make. Certainly, games that portray men and fathers who are more nurturing and who do not resort to violence to solve any and all problems have the potential to impact on who chooses to play video games. Lastly, Consalvo (2012) discusses the impact of toxic gamer culture and the challenge said culture poses feminist game studies scholars. *TLoU*, while still rife with violence and depictions of the Old Man/Old Father archetype, moves gamers in a slightly different direction, a nudge if you will. What we do not know is if that movement will have any effect on games culture. However, the possibility exists that it will, and future game studies research more broadly and feminist game studies more specifically should examine whether or not those changes actually take place.

Bibliography

Attwood, Feona. 2005. 'Tits and Ass and Porn and Fighting': Male Heterosexuality in Magazines for Men. *International Journal of Cultural Studies* 8 (1): 83–100.

Bell, Kristina, Nicholas Taylor, and Christopher Kampe. 2015. Of Headshots and Hugs: Challenging Hypermasculinity through *The Walking Dead* Play. *Ada* 7. http://adanewmedia.org/2015/04/issue7-bellkampetaylor/.

Beynon, John. 2002. *Masculinities and Culture*. Buckingham: University Press.

BioShock Infinite. 2013. Video Game. Novato, CA: 2K Games.

Bleich, David. 1976. Pedagogical Directions in Subjective Criticism. *College English* 37 (5): 454–467.

Brice, Mattie. 2013. *The Dadification of Video Games is Real*. Alternate Ending Blog. http://www.mattiebrice.com/the-dadification-of-video-games-isreal/.

Brooks, Wanda, and Susan Browne. 2012. Towards a Culturally Situated Reader Response Theory. *Children's Literature in Education* 43: 74–85.

Carr, Diane. 2005. *Contexts, Pleasures and Preference: Girls Playing Computer Games.* Paper Presented at DiGRA Conference: Changing Views—Worlds at Play, Vancouver, June 16–20. http://www.digra.org/digital-library/publications/contexts-pleasures-and-preferences-girls-playing-computer-games/.

de Castell, Suzanne, and Jennifer Jenson. 2003. Serious Play. *Journal of Curriculum Studies* 35 (6): 649–665.

Chapman, Rowena. 1988. The Great Pretender: Variations on the New Man Theme. In *Male Order: Unwrapping Masculinity*, ed. Rowena Chapman and Jonathon Rutherford, 225–248. London: Lawrence and Wishart Limited.

Chess, Shira, and Adrienne Shaw. 2015. A Conspiracy of Fishes, or, How We Learned to Stop Worrying about #GamerGate and Embrace Hegemonic Masculinity. *Journal of Broadcasting & Electronic Media* 59 (1): 208–220.

Clauson, Jonathan. 2015. Fathers in Video Games: Seeing Ourselves on the Screen. *Christ & Popular Culture Blog.* http://christandpopculture.com/fathers-in-video-games-seeing-ourselves-on-the-screen/.

Connell, Raewyn. 1993. The Big Picture: Masculinities in Recent World History. *Theory and Society* 22 (5): 597–623.

Consalvo, Mia. 2003. The Monsters Next Door: Media Constructions of Boys and Masculinity. *Feminist Media Studies* 3 (1): 27–45.

———. 2012. Confronting Toxic Gamer Culture: A Challenge for Feminist Studies Scholars. *Ada* 1. http://adanewmedia.org/2012/11/issue1-consalvo/.

Dietz, Tracy L. 1998. An Examination of Violence and Gender Roles Portrayals in Video Games: Implications for Gender Socialization and Aggressive Behavior. *Sex Roles* 38 (5/6): 425–442.

Dill, Karen E., and Kathryn P. Thill. 2007. Video Game Characters and the Socialization of Gender Roles: Young People's Perceptions Mirror Sexist Media Depictions. *Sex Roles* 57 (11/12): 851–864.

Dishonored. 2012. *Video Game.* Austin, TX: Arkane Studios.

Edwards, Tim. 2003. Sex, Booze and Fags: Masculinity, Style and Men's Magazines. In *Masculinity and Men's Lifestyle Magazines*, ed. Bethan Benwell, 132–146. Oxford: Blackwell Publishing.

Elson, Malte, Johannes Breuer, James D. Ivory, and Thorsten Quandt. 2014. More than Stories with Buttons: Narrative, Mechanics, and Context as Determinants of Player Experience in Digital Games. *Journal of Communication* 64: 521–542.

Giddings, Seth, and Helen Kennedy. 2008. Little Jesuses and Fuck-Off Robots: On Aesthetics, Cybernetics, and Not Being Very Good at Lego Star Wars. In *The Pleasures of Computer Gaming: Essays on Cultural History Theory and Aesthetics*, ed. Melanie Swalwell and Jason Wilson, 13–32. Jefferson, NC: McFarland.

Griswold, Robert L. 1993. *Fatherhood in America: A History.* New York: BasicBooks.

Holmquest, Broc. 2013. *Ludological Storytelling and Unique Narrative Experiences in Silent Hill Downpour.* Master's Thesis, Bowling Green State University.

Jenson, Jennifer, and Suzanne de Castell. 2008. Theorizing Gender and Digital Gameplay: Oversights, Accidents and Surprises. *Eludamos* 2 (1): 15–25.

Joho, Jess. 2014. The Dadification of Videogames, Round Two. *Kill Screen Blog.* https://killscreen.com/articles/dadification-videogames-round-two/.

Kennedy, Helen W. 2002. Lara Croft: Feminist Icon or Cyberbimbo? *Game Studies* 2 (2). http://www.gamestudies.org/0202/kennedy/.

Kirkland, Ewan. 2009. Masculinity in Video Games: The Gendered Gameplay of *Silent Hill. Camera Obscura* 29 (2): 161–183.

Kücklich, Julian. 2006. Literary Theory and Digital Games. In *Understanding Digital Games*, ed. Jason Rutter and Bryce Jo, 95–111. London: Sage Publications Ltd.

Mackey, Margaret. 2011. *Narrative Pleasures in Young Adult Novels, Films and Video Games.* New York: Palgrave Macmillan.

MacKinnon, Kenneth. 2003. *Representing Men.* London: Arnold Publishing.

Milestone, Katie, and Anneke Meyer. 2012. *Gender and Popular Culture.* Cambridge: Polity Press.

Myers, Maddie. 2013. Bad Dads vs. Hyper Mode: The Father-Daughter Bond in Video Games. *Paste Magazine,* July 30. http://www.pastemagazine.com/articles/2013/07/hyper-mode.html.

Nakamura, Lisa. 2012. Queer Female of Color: The Highest Difficulty Setting There Is? Gaming Rhetoric as Gender Capital. *Ada* 1. http://adanewmedia.org/2012/11/issue1-nakamura/.

Oxford Dictionaries. 2016. *s.v* "Fatherhood". http://www.oxforddictionaries.com/us/definition/american_english/fatherhood. Accessed 11 Jan.

Pleck, Joseph. 1987. American Fathering in Historical Perspective. In *Changing Men: New Directions in Research on Masculinity*, ed. Michael S. Kemmel, 83–97. Newbury Park, CA: Sage.

Pollock, Greg. 2013. Let's Get Real about Fatherhood in Video Games. *Gamasutra Blog.* http://www.gamasutra.com/blogs/GregPollock/20130719/196651/Lets_Get_Real_about_Fatherhood_and_Video_Games.php.

Rabinowitz, Peter J. 1987. *Before Reading: Narrative Conventions and the Politics of Interpretation.* Ithaca, NY: Cornell University Press.

Rosenblatt, Louise. 1982. The Literary Transaction: Evocation and Response. *Theory Into Practice* 21: 268–277.

Royse, Pam, Joon Lee, Baasanjav Undrahbuyan, Mark Hopson, and Mia Consalvo. 2007. Women and Games: Technologies of the Gendered Self. *New Media & Society* 9 (4): 555–576.

Sims, Christo. 2014. Video Game Culture, Contentious Masculinities, and Reproducing Racialized Social Class Divisions in Middle School. *Signs: Journal of Women in Culture & Society* 39 (4): 848–857.

Sipe, Lawrence R. 2008. *Storytime: Young Children's Literary Understanding in the Classroom.* New York: Teacher's College Press.

Taylor, Nicholas, Christopher Kampe, and Kristina Bell. 2015. Me and Lee: Identification and the Play of Attraction in the Walking Dead. *The International Journal of Computer Game Research* 15 (1). http://gamestudies.org/1501/articles/taylor.

The Last of Us. 2013. Video Game. Santa Monica, CA: Naughty Dog.

The Walking Dead. 2012. Video Game. San Rafael, CA: Telltale Games.

The Witcher 3: The Wild Hunt. 2015. Video Game. Warsaw: CD Projekt Red.

Thomas, Kimberly D., and Ronald F. Levant. 2012. Does the Endorsement of Traditional Masculinity Ideology Moderate the Relationship Between Exposure to Violent Video Games and Aggression? *Journal of Men's Studies* 20 (1): 47–56.

Tragos, Peter. 2009. Monster Masculinity: Honey, I'll Be in the Garage Reasserting My Manhood. *Journal of Popular Culture* 42 (3): 541–553.

Tyson, Lois. 2014. *Critical Theory Today: A User-Friendly Guide*. 3rd ed. New York: Routledge.

von Gillern, Sam. 2016. The Gamer Response and Decision Framework. *Simulation & Gaming* 47 (5): 666–683.

Voorhees, Gerald. 2016. Daddy Issues: Constructions of Fatherhood in TLoU and Bioshock Infinite. *Ada* 9. http://adanewmedia.org/2016/05/issue9-voorhees/.

Wahlström, Helena. 2014. *New Fathers? Contemporary American Stories of Masculinity, Domesticity and Kinship*. Newcastle upon Tyne: Cambridge Scholars Publishing.

Witt, David D. n.d. History and Development of the Father Role. http://www3.uakron.edu/witt/father/fanote2.htm. Accessed 15 Jan 2016.

7

He Scores Through a Screen: Mediating Masculinities Through Hockey Video Games

Marc Ouellette and Steven Conway

At first glance, Eric Nystrom's end of practice, impromptu version of Ned Braden's legendary striptease from the movie *Slapshot* seems like a playful moment among friends and fans alike. It is a shared joke, insofar as the popularity of *Slapshot* among fans and players remains unquestioned. The film, starring Paul Newman as Reg Dunlop, the coach of a struggling team that turns to "goon hockey" to revive itself, recently received a celebration of the fortieth anniversary of its release during the National Hockey League's signature All-Star weekend, and it remains widely recognized as one of the very best sports films of the last half-century (McDonald 2017). However, as Ouellette (2008) argues, the original striptease comes as a protest against the brawling style, and in this regard, Nystrom's gesture becomes even more significant, and not just because it was also an effort to raise funds for a charitable cause (Cruickshank 2008).

The movie version features the reversal or parody of the epic warrior's preparation for battle.[1] Braden removes all of his armor as part of his refusal to fight: his protest against the excess of hypermasculine violence. For Nystrom's part, he is performing a parody *of* a parody within his own biting satire; his performance constitutes a *contra*-masculine gesture so gratuitous it has the opposite effect: Nystrom's masculinity is untouchable. It will never be questioned: He is

M. Ouellette (✉)
Old Dominion University, Norfolk, VA, USA

S. Conway
Swinburn University of Technology, Melbourne, VIC, Australia

© The Author(s) 2018
N. Taylor, G. Voorhees (eds.), *Masculinities in Play*, Palgrave Games in Context,
https://doi.org/10.1007/978-3-319-90581-5_7

a tough hockey player and a willing fighter. He is also the son of Bob Nystrom, a Stanley Cup winning hero and a legendarily hardy hockey player. At the time, the younger Nystrom was a member of the National Hockey League's Calgary Flames, an organization known for its historic brawls with the rival Edmonton Oilers—the so-called Battle of Alberta—particularly during the Wayne Gretzky era, when the Oilers were more known for finesse and scoring than for physicality. Indeed, the final scene of *Slapshot* occurs after Dunlop eschews the brawling style for the championship game. As a younger, college-educated player, Braden had protested the fighting throughout the season, providing one of the central conflicts of the movie. However, once informed of the presence of dozens of scouts, Dunlop and the Chiefs return to their brawling ways. The spectacle of a gigantic brawl prompts and forms the back-drop for Braden's performance, highlighting the multiple and contradictory trajectories of masculinity within the game, the sport, and the film.

Yet these are not the only contradictions, for Nystrom's performance high-lights the ways in which one media shapes and conditions the experience of producing and/or performing within another. This is most obvious given the contrasts between and among his role in the game, the charitable cause that occasioned his performance, and the inspiration for the film's original. Moreover, the playfulness is shared via social media; indeed, it seems produced with this level of surveillance in mind: a panoptical performance that operates both inter-textually (assuming audience recording; knowledge of *Slapshot*) and intratextu-ally, without acknowledging the contradictions within hockey's well-documented hypermasculine environment (Allain 2012; Robidoux 2001; Silverwood 2015).

Ironically, hockey has been the sport most resistant to the impact of "new media" and the data-driven surveillance they bring to the game. From the glowing Fox puck to the growing list of statistics being collected to the advanced statistical tools like the (controversial) Corsi score, we would argue that video games are changing the way sports, like hockey, soccer, and so on, are played, consumed, and experienced.[2] They do so not only through the generation of statistics but—more importantly—through the threat posed to hegemonic masculinity by exposing its constructedness as performance, undermining any rhetorical claim to a basis in nature. Quite simply, then, *gender is performed in and through one's body.*

Therefore, we should acknowledge that how one performs masculinity is historically bound up with rituals and techniques targeted towards a male body. Noted Canadian sport sociologist Kristi Allain, whose work focuses on gender in winter sports, finds that the literature and the language about hockey shows that "the bodies of boys and men are not to express beauty and grace, nor are they to be examined" (2012, 364). Scrutiny calls into the question the immanence and the inevitability of masculine performance. As renowned French philosopher of sport Jean-Marie Brohm (1989) ruminates, the type of masculinity expressed through sport is also conducive to late capitalism because sport develops

> *a standardised image of the body*, regulating the way the adolescent relates to his or her own body and seeking to establish the ideology of the body as a sort of automated machine. As a "character school," sport creates authoritarian, aggressive, narcissistic and obedient character types, preparing young people for integration into society and training them to operate as alienated machines on the capitalist market. (1989, 180, italics in original)

In a postindustrial, knowledge economy operating under the aegis of the database, what could be more appropriate to "establishing the ideology of the body as a sort of automated machine" than the essential automated machine of our time, the computer? When the latent relationship between sport and technology becomes manifest, and the athlete becomes cyborg, what happens to our notion of masculinity? How is it challenged, negotiated, and (re)presented? Using Steven Conway's (2010, 2012) threefold typology of hyper-, contra-, and hypo-ludicity, we unpack the paradox of a masculinity discursively situated as both natural and technological—a negotiated understanding of not masculinity but *masculinities* that resists reduction.

Ludus Body

The need to dictate compliant subjectivities for social integration is a central concern of Michel Foucault's. For Foucault there is no such thing as masculinity, simply *masculinities*, that is, a technique/technology for generating a persona conducive to social stability and reproduction. Not surprisingly, then, Gerald Voorhees offers:

> [o]nly in sport is the sustained, practical mastery of one's body essential to not only play but play well in a manner that enables winning. Energy must be conserved, muscles expended and relaxed to preserve continued performance, and maximum effect achieved through the exertion of the least requisite force. Despite the appearance of physical excess, the body is restrained, its performance an exemplar of instrumental rationality. (Voorhees 2015, 78)[3]

As Brohm noted above (1989), modern sport is immanently oppressive, demanding acquiescence to a specific enactment of the body: proportion, motility, voice, language, dress, and so on. In enactment, the "player" subjectivity forces one's entire identity to be projected through the narrow prism of "sprinter," "wrestler," "footballer," and so on: the fluidity of identity, so obvious in the paidic mode of play, is made static through the instrumentalization of the ludic (Caillois 2001). Meanwhile autotelic, open, improvised play, or *paideia*, with its qualities of imagination, exploration, and whim have been historically demonized or infantilized as a waste of time: unserious, unproductive for the child (or implicitly, girls). Such play destabilizes the meaning of the phenomenological world; for example, the world of ice hockey, a discursive formation so tightly regulated that any paidic moment, such as Nystrom's striptease, begs the immediate question from the audience: why is he doing that? Luckily for Nystrom, his performance was clearly signified as operating within the bounds of ice hockey culture, as a loving tribute to a well-known film on the sport; therefore, any disciplinary action would have been viewed very dimly by the hockey community.

Ludic Technique

In fact, the dance Nystrom does has become so familiar through the ritual of watching *Slapshot*, which has an iconic status among hockey players, but also because of the ritual of (re)enacting the performance by hockey players (Boyle 2014). Watching the video on social media platforms like *YouTube* and *Twitter* also becomes part of the ritual. As Conway writes (2012), one of the key aspects of video games is their imbrication with ritual and the effects, in work, in effort, of perfecting operations in and through the ritualized play and performance.

The three fold typology Conway develops (2010, 2012)—hyper-ludicity, contra-ludicity, and hypo-ludicity—affords a means of studying both digital games and masculinity, for the ludic processes map onto the development and the construction of masculinity, as Ouellette and Thompson (2017) argue in studying the tenuous merger of masculinity and technology afforded by digital games in the post-9/11 period. According to Conway (2010, 2012), hyper-ludicity is where some actant or actants, within the diverse network that come together as "game," provide for the user supreme agency over the gamestate. For example, broadband can be hyper-ludic if others are on slower, dial-up modems: high-resolution and refresh rate monitors if playing a first-person shooter; traditional "power-ups" such as Mario's mushrooms or Pac-Man's power pellet; advanced knowledges and bodily skills may also enable hyper-ludicity, as evidenced by a Chess Grandmaster, or Zlatan Ibrahimovic's control of the ball playing soccer.

Contra-ludicity occurs when an actant (or actants) within the game network refuse, push back against, and overall impede the player. Lag in a real-time multiplayer game is contra-ludic and includes bugs and glitches (which might also be hyper-ludic in the right scenario), "power-downs" in-game such as diseases, faulty items and hostile spells, enemy characters and AI, inadequate knowledges and bodily skills.

Finally, hypo-ludicity is the absence of play for the user: somewhere within the network of play, an actant is outright refusing the player's engagement. Computer crashes are hypo-ludic as are electricity outages, heavy rain during tennis matches or grands prix races, and a rigged game of cards. Simply put, hypo-ludicity often occurs when the rubber band of hyper- or contra-ludicity stretches too far and snaps. As a player pays money to automatically pass a difficult level within a mobile game, this hyper-ludicity becomes hypo; similarly, hacks and cheats used in a multiplayer situation can prove so resistant (contra-ludic) to other users' engagement that they transcend contra into hypo-ludic features.

Here, the enhancement of play coincides precisely with the enhancement of masculinity. However, it is the grind of contra-ludicity and hypo-ludicity that contribute the most to the project—of this paper, of the digital games, and of masculinity—through the "gamework" (Ruggill et al. 2004) that goes into producing, performing, and proving masculinity. While the work of the game can be acknowledged and appreciated the work of masculinity cannot.

Simply put, if hypermasculinity is the achievement for competition, then hypo-ludicity and contra-ludicity are the test itself. These are the contests that must be passed on the way to proving what might be understood as *masculine-hood*, which is still in Western culture synonymous with *manhood*. Here, we are reminded of Eve Sedgwick's (1996) axiom that masculinity does not always pertain solely to men. Thus, our question becomes one of determining how the experience of the digital informs, influences, and infuses with the experience of the sport. This becomes particularly important given the perceived antagonism between technology and masculinity. We recognize the distinction between the real and the digital as an artificial binary, one which actually serves to mask the mythic imbrication of masculinity *qua* sport, and *vice versa* by reifying its projection as immanent and therefore apart from experience.

This is significant because, like Nystrom's striptease, ludicity speaks to the very contradictions upon which the performance of masculinity rests. It is at once feminizing to be on display and to enact the striptease, as well as emasculating to perform conspicuously outside the limits of rational, goal-oriented play. Yet this overt display of hypo-ludic disarmament is hypermasculine *as provocation*, as a confrontational gesture of precisely the kind hockey and other sports associate with masculinity, and yet attempt to resist because it exists as pure contradiction: The hypo-masculine striptease is hypermasculine.

Morphic Masculinities

Despite the nearly three decades and scholarship on gender as play and performance, Game Studies remains fixed in its focus on sex role theories and approaches. As Bergstrom et al. offer, "What remains in most of this work is a predominant, indeed, an almost intuitive reflex to crudely attribute difference as demarcated by male/female sex binaries" (2011, 32). These approaches, then, limit the type and scope of performance that can be studied, as well as the analysis itself. They cannot encompass the possibility for play to entail anything but fixed gender roles. Indeed such critiques reinscribe gender roles even as they seek to dismantle by limiting the available subject positions. If the positions are fixed, then alternative constructions and identities are rhetorically excluded as anomalies, as the detritus of monolithic formations. Simply put, then, "It takes no intellectual effort (or political will) to simply describe stereotypical patterns and choices, and then to explain them by reference to stereotypes" (Jenson and de Castell 2010, 32). In other words, as Ouellette (2011) has argued elsewhere, there exists a plurality of gender formations across a spectrum, as opposed to a binary pairing, and video games provide a platform for playing and performing them.[4]

Indeed, this is the key contribution of Australian sociologist R. W. Connell's (1995) landmark study of "masculinities"—in the plural—in which the Australian sociologist adapts the Gramscian conception of hegemony to explain the ways in which masculinities exist in through negotiations. Since the traditional binary opposition model of gender tends to obscure power relations within genders, Connell employs the concept of "hegemonic masculinity" rather than the loose term "patriarchy." The key distinction arises because hegemonic masculinity:

> embodies a "currently accepted" strategy. When conditions for the defense of patriarchy change, the bases for the dominance of a particular masculinity are eroded. New groups may challenge old solutions and construct a new hegemony. The dominance of *any* group of men may be challenged by women. Hegemony, then, is a historically mobile relation. (p. 77)

As Ouellette (2008, 2011) argues, the effect of hegemonic masculinity as a "currently accepted strategy" can be seen in the hybrid form of the sports film. As occurs in the earlier cited instance of Nystrom's performance of the final game in *Slapshot*, the forms are not only related, they merge with and/or suture onto each other. Every one of them is coded and ritualized in its relationship to masculinity. Thus, if the elements of a game-derived technique and technology affirms or even bolsters masculinity, then it is embraced. More significantly, Ouellette's work combines the Susan Jeffords' (1989, 1994) classic studies of masculinity in 1980s action films with Varda Burstyn's award-winning study (1999) of masculinity and sport. Burstyn notes that historically sport provides a surrogate for the proof of manhood entailed by war and at present offers an embodied counter to the "soft" masculinities that result from increasing technologization of the work place. Here, she cites Jeffords recognition that popular cultural productions of the post-Vietnam era, technology is overwhelming presented as being antithetical to masculinity. In short, the American (over) reliance on technology rather than on masculinity led to defeat. Intriguingly, neither Burstyn nor Jeffords cites sports films and both overlook video games entirely. Yet the omnipresence of technology, hypermasculinity, and play make video games an important locus for the study of cultural productions that threaten or diminish the coherence of the masculine myths. Most notably, anything that opens masculinity to surveillance and scrutiny, particularly on the basis of statistical analysis and measurements, is dismissed as being the product of non-players, that is, soft masculinities. In this way, the contradiction centers on the emphasis upon performance over result. That is to say, sport is all about achieving a better score than one's opponent, often at all costs; paradoxically, the defense against technologization is founded upon the belief there is something innately masculine that cannot be codified, quantified, scrutinized, and measured.[5]

Remediation as R-emasculation in Hockey

In this regard, the *NHL* series of video games of the 1990s began to add and track a wide range of statistics beyond the typical official stats of goals, assists, points, and penalty minutes. Indeed, many of the stats were of little concern to fans of live action hockey and some were invented. Here, the mid-90s introduction of "one-timer," a type of shot, as a tracked statistic and measured ability, stands out for its inclusion and fetishization within the digital games. Employing a one-timer affords video game players a power up on their shot. No such advantage exists on real ice, where the principle advantage of the one-timer occurs if and only if the goalie cannot react quickly enough to the rapidly changing direction from which the puck is coming, as opposed to the rapidity with which the puck is flying. Moreover, the power of the shot can be tracked via a glowing puck. The harder the shot, the redder or glowing the trail becomes.

What becomes interesting is the adoption of this technology in broadcasts of live-action hockey in the 1990s. The league expanded rapidly into the United States, and unfamiliar fans found it difficult to track the puck. Fox added a glowing corona to the puck, similar to the one that appears around the puck-carrier in a video game (Barry 2016). As much as there might be a hyper-ludic effect, there is also a potential for contra-ludic effects: the one-timer might look great, offer the power up, but it might not be the best available play and it might not be the most heroic as understood by the sport-media complex. In other words, the hardest kind of shot, the one that would give the most glow, might not be the best option, in either case. Also, the one-timer means setting up a teammate—supporting another player's hyper-ludicity—as well as being the recipient—that is, receiving help and admitting to effeminate interdependence; not a self but a self-in-relation. In fact, this highlights one of the central contradictions of video games, for the self-in-relation traditionally has been considered a predominantly, if not strictly, feminine mode of identification. While the technology seemingly affirms masculinity via the glowing puck, it sets up a situation of dependence, as well. The puck provides proof but it also means measuring masculinity.

Concordantly, players of the team-based digital sport games rely and/or depend on the ever-changing non-player characters (NPCs) to support and assist the player.[6] Thus, the learning curve of the sport might not occur but the learning curve of the digital game is taken into account by the ludic formulation. In fact, the in-game action reflects a system in which the whole team, even its stars, exist to support and nurture the player. This is key because it highlights how the ludic processes map onto the production of masculinity, both in the game and in live-action sports. What becomes clear is that the elements of digital games produce, alter, and resist typical understanding of live-action sport, even as they reproduce the original and, more importantly, even as these elements become part of live-action sports, as well.

For example, Marc Bergevin, the General Manager of the Montréal Canadiens, was disparaged by fans and media for his comment, "My reality, it might not be the same as the PlayStation that I play at night" (as cited in Gordon 2015). Bergevin followed that with a joke about the ease of swapping players on his console as compared to the actual requirements of making a trade. Yet fans and media reacted with incredulity. Montréal sportscaster, Brian Wilde (2016), for one, taunted Bergevin on Twitter after other teams made a trade, tweeting, "Well, it appears Bergevin was wrong. The NHL does make PlayStation trades." His post was re-tweeted over 150 times, including several by other journalists. Underlying Bergevin's comments and Wilde's taunts is the tension between the proven, bodily masculinity of the hockey player and the soft, technologically subservient masculinity of the player. In particular, it lays bare the threat to masculinity posed by the increased statistical study afforded by video games and the concurrent, and as we will show, concomitant rise of advanced statistical measurements. In the mind of fans and journalists, at least, the line between their knowledge (and expectations) and that of management no longer exists, in large part because of the statistical measures provided in and through video games.

Thus, nowhere is the conflation of the digital emulation's elements (and outcomes) with the physical sport's aspects more apparent than in the contradictory reception and deployment of game-derived features and statistics. In this regard, the role of the sport star and the user-as-star becomes particularly intriguing. In keeping with the masculine myth, celebrity in sport is codified within the digital game as hyper-ludicity: the more famous, the more ludicity, *ipso facto* the more masculine. This runs counter to the myth of hard work, endurance, and commitment to training so often espoused as essential to sporting accomplishment, highlighted by Conway (2014):

> We are therefore confronted by a paradoxical state of affairs within the digital interpretation of sport: without hyperludicity, the celebrity avatar would not be famous, and without fame, the celebrity avatar would not be hyperludic. The extraordinary ability and charisma of the sport celebrity as perpetuated by the cultural industries are thus translated into a model comprehensible within the information economy, a form of legal-rational authority defined and encoded through finite rules, categories, and the solidity of numbers. (pp. 146–147)

Appropriate to the emphatic visibility of the star, the "net-cam" has been embraced for revealing heroic saves by goalies and magical goals by players, but the "helmet-cam" on officials has been dismissed as too revelatory or intrusive, despite its ice-level, first-person point of view. The contrast becomes more salient given responses like that of Kurtis Larson, in *The Toronto Sun* (2013). In an interactive online article, Larson recounts instances when "ice girls," hockey's equivalent of cheerleaders, "went above and beyond the call of entertainment duty" and revealed a bit too much in front of one of the net-cams. While the NHL removed the video, *The Toronto Sun* has not, to the delight of dozens of commenters.

Where it is alright to further objectify an always already objectified "ice girl," anything that might lead to an interrogation of masculinity is too threatening to the culture. Like net-cam, "ref-cam" can be considered a product of the development of video games and the contingent effort by broadcasters to mimic the infinite possible camera angles available in digital games[7]: From sports games to action-adventure blockbusters such as *Horizon Zero Dawn* (Guerilla Games 2017), the remediation (Bolter and Grusin 2000) of the camera, as apparatus for the innately masculine practice of voyeurism, is more than ever apparent within the medium.

Yet, the *Globe and Mail*'s Eric Duhatschek (2014) bemoans the elimination of ref-cam after just "one month." In claiming the technology was too intrusive, the league was acknowledging it demystifies the players by showing their fouls and failures—that is, the things the referee sees—quite conclusively. Even so, the Fox Puck was dismissed as a silly gimmick, yet its basic premise is no different than the halo/corona or color change used to designate the puck-carrier in the digital game (Hartley 2010). Moreover, the velocity of any shot becomes a celebrated topic and proof of manhood, as metonymic of virility. These are key features of highlight packages and "analysis," as well as the video games. Even so, the technology was dismissed as silly, gimmicky, and inauthentic, the creation of marketing executives, geeks, and those who did not understand the game.

Similarly, the in-game version of the measures corresponds with a perception and sometimes a practice of increasing a player's power. The key failure of hyper-ludicity is that it builds masculinity as it builds progress through the game, most notably by adding to the prowess and mastery, as opposed to power, of the player/avatar combination. Thus, the (previously mentioned) work of the game is the production of masculinity in and through its algorithm and its operations. Hyper-ludicity produces and even blends with masculinity, particularly through the aspects that relate to performance and performativity.

Producing Masculinity

However, it should be noted that the presumed aggressive or dominant versions of hegemonic masculinity are not the only versions of masculinity that correspond with masculine forms. Yet, it is precisely at the intersection of algorithm and performance that the cracks and ruptures are revealed. The very instant masculinity must be rehearsed, practiced, or drilled; it cannot be anything but a production. The relationship, or imbrication, with an algorithm reveals that masculinity operates according to rules; henceforth, masculinity can be measured and assessed. It can also be simulated and reproduced, giving access to those who might otherwise not be able to participate in the sport.

Few elements of the games embody the contradictory depictions of masculinity like the fight mechanic. Controversially, hockey is the one major sport that allows (and even tacitly condones) fighting, with NHL vice-president

Colin Campbell calling safety advocates, including the head of the trainers' association "Greenpeace pukes" and "tree huggers" (as cited in AP 2016).[8] Yet, in any version of hockey, either in live action or in a digital game, fighting constitutes a hypermasculine display that is at once hypo- or contra-ludic. Fights occur because of and through the very real performances of hegemonic masculinity and offer a reminder of sport as a surrogate for combat. In short, masculinity becomes its own worst enemy.

The earliest game to feature fighting was Adventure Artworx's *International Hockey* for the Commodore 64, released in 1985 (preceded by the company's 1984 *Slapshot Hockey*, which did not feature fighting). Even in this primitive, cartoonish form, the outcome remains the same: the game stops, the player loses agency to change the game, and there is a penalty assessed. While *Pro Sport Hockey* (TOSE 1993) and *NHL94* (EA Sports 1993) offer "real" players and teams, any player, including a star, could receive a major penalty. In the older game, the instigator of the fight had to face a penalty shot, that is, a direct attempt to score. A similar mechanic appears in *Face-Off* (Mindspan 1989). In the contemporary versions, the player's team loses one in-game asset for five minutes of game play (or more). In short, the action takes place entirely outside the scope of the content. The game stops. The fight exists only for its own sake and it is arguable whether it has any impact on the game at all; as with the camera and the gameworld, the spectacle is its own reward.

In its *NHL* series, EA Sports attempts to make the fighting mechanic into a mini-game. Starting with its *NHL14* revision, EA Sports adapted the mechanic of its *Fight Night* boxing series for this purpose. Amazingly, EA's own designer hails the new mechanic as less intrusive than the previous one, which was shipped starting with *NHL10* (Hartley 2013). This is only the latest such "mashup." One of the first simulation style hockey games, *Actua Ice Hockey* (Gremlin Interactive, 1998) used the soccer engine from *Actua Soccer* (1995) and elements of *Virtua Fighter* (1993) since all were produced by the same studio. In the physical sport, fighting is a pointless intrusion that has little to do with the outcome but has everything to do with masculinity. The video game version only confirms the necessity of protecting masculinity.

Moreover, the punishment includes losing the fight and losing a player for at least five minutes; there can only ever be a contra-ludic, sometimes hypo-ludic outcome. The point becomes more significant given that the game engine upon which the *NHL* simulation is built is borrowed from the successful *FIFA* series (ibid.). As Rory Smith (2014) recounts in the *New York Times*, soccer players and managers have embraced the development of video games because they reveal tendencies and patterns based on measurable, translatable data and algorithms. Duncan Alexander, head of a leading British data provider, draws a direct link between the rise of video games, starting with *Football Manager*, and the rise of statistics in the sport: "The chronology between the popularity of the game and the use of numbers in soccer [...] is broadly similar" (as cited in Smith 2014); Alexander's firm provides data to professional soccer teams. Despite the obvious intersections, including the *FIFA* physics engine and the player data required to run it, hockey clings to mythic "codes" of masculinity, in the video game and in the sport. The contradictions become even more pronounced given the need to add an otherwise extraneous element, the fighting mechanism, to a purely statistically driven game algorithm: The avatars' fists serve as capricious shield to protect the masculine myth.

Transludic Man

It is not surprising, then, that the fighting mechanic has been hailed by reviewers (and some players) as a kind of reward, that is, spectacle, as noted earlier. On ESPN's *Grantland* site, hockey columnist Sean McIndoe (2014b) notes the role of the fighting mechanic and its contradictory heritage: "Look, you don't have to like the continued existence of fighting in real hockey. But fighting in hockey video games is freaking fun, especially when it's done well. Nobody has ever done it as well as *NHLPA '93*." More interesting is the fact that ESPN created *Grantland* as a medium for covering the intersections of sports and pop culture. In his column the previous week, the "NHL Dictionary," McIndoe (2014a) mocks hockey fighting, hockey statistics, and hockey video games fans. In this last regard, he cites the "one-timer" as a statistic invented for and by video games, along with the concomitant belief that this is the only way to score in the (actual) NHL. Similarly, the NHL only began counting "hits" after the work stoppage of 2005–2006. *NHL94* (EA Sports 1993) and its successors have counted hits, while the *NHL Hitz* (Midway, 2003) series is built around the violence. If sport is a surrogate of war, through the fighting mechanism and its questionable utility, video games then become a kind of meta-surrogate, offering a commentary on the construction of masculinity not only in the sport but in the wider culture as well.

Like fights, hits exist primarily within the transludic space, which is defined as the space among and between the players and the game, whether players are competing against one another or an AI opponent (Ouellette and Ouellette 2013, 2015). In both cases, the act exists as a part of but also apart from the game. Even so, the importance placed on fight mechanics in game reviews, in game engines and in *Let's Play* videos are mirrored in popular fan sites dropyourgloves.com and hockeyfights.com, among others. On these sites, fights from live-action games are scored and charted as might occur for a boxing match, as well as in a video game. In fact, some players have uploaded nothing but in-game fights from their video games as their contribution to the intertextual web of masculine endeavors. Not only do these resemble a brawling game like *Streetfighter* or *Mortal Kombat* more than they do a sports game, they are encumbered by the added weight of the fight mechanic. What becomes clear, then, is that the production of masculinity in and through play remains at the forefront of the game's ostensible scoring system. While a statistic like Corsi or Fenwick might signal domination, a fight and a game have an obvious winner and obvious loser, irrespective of the process. Thus, the ludic masculinity favors ends over means.

The contradictions become more pronounced given the ways that Conway's third entry in his typology, hypo-ludicity, contributes to the production of masculinity insofar as and because it represents a diminishment or a loss of agency. This is no mere emasculation, though that could be entailed in the process. It is not surprising, then, that Conway writes, "as the game removes the very essence of control and agency so necessary to the experience of not only winning and losing, but playing a game. [...] hypo-ludicity offers nothing but absence: of empowerment, of resistance, of agency" (2012, 38). Although Conway offers Bethesda Softwork's *Elder* Scrolls series as an exemplar because of its requirement that players search interminably for resources, he could also have included any drill and practice regime in any sports game. This is an important reminder that masculinity is routinized as part of a regime.

The Ouroboros

Nevertheless, this is not the extent of the functions of hypo-ludicity within a given game. Quite the contrary, hypo-ludicity can actually have positive effects, even through the mindlessness of drill and practice routines. This is their very contingency and the statistical tracking, at least since *NHL 94* (EA Sports 1993), bears this out. Thus, hypo and contra-ludicity are as much about means as they are about ends. This stands in stark contrast to the presumption that masculinity inherently or naturally produces and demands a winner-takes-all or win-at-all-costs approach. Nowhere is this more pointed and controversial than in the ongoing debate surrounding advanced statistics in hockey. These advanced statistics are necessarily similar to the algorithms used to produce the video games, vehicles for the celebration of masculinity.

This is not an assumption or a projection. Since *NHL 94*, the games have charted a wide variety of each player's skills: puck handling, skating, shot, hitting, fighting, "one-timers," and so on.

Thus, it should be surprising that Corsi and similar measures of player prowess have been shunned and worse by hockey commentators, journalists, and others. In calling statistical analysis a fad, Jack Todd of the *Montréal Gazette* (2014) claims hockey is built on "emotion and chaos," which cannot be quantified. The *Toronto Sun*'s Steve Simmons (2014) echoes this belief that the game cannot be "naturally or easily analyzed with math." Yet, the statistics and their relation to hockey as masculinity become quite clear: the games extract, condense, crystallize, and package the very same routines and criteria used to otherwise celebrate masculinity. In short, the only kind of unpacking of masculinity is precisely the hypo-ludicity performed by Nystrom, as cited earlier. He is never under threat, even as he protests the contrived spectacle. The strip does not suggest vulnerability; rather, it states implicitly that his masculinity is beyond question. It just is.

Thus it becomes clear that the building of masculinity and the empowerment of the character become one and the same. The ludic function reinforces the cultural imperative and vice versa. Obviously, this begs the question of correlation vs. causation, as well as which came first. Ultimately, if we recognize the shift in the portrayal of manhood, it does not really matter which was first because one conditions the other as an (overtly phallic) ouroboros. Regardless, the rituals and codes of masculinity are not present or are shifted so that games have become one of the central places and venues for men to learn to be men, especially when the bodily sense of masculinity no longer matters. Thus, games become a ritual of traditional masculinity, in which the player, coached by a hegemonic masculine figure reclaims manhood. Moreover, this process is built right into the kernel of the algorithm. Whereas the world of soccer openly embraces the imbrication of advanced statistics, video game and sport, the world of hockey clings to a regressive past. Indeed, in remediating *Fight Night* as an integral part of the game, it denies its very premises. Here, it is well worth noting that the popular film *Money Ball* (2011), based on the success of the Oakland A's baseball team through the adoption of advanced statistics, features a fit Brad Pitt and portly Jonah Hill as the player turned General Manager and the statistical wizard, respectively. The contrast in their appearances is not an accident. Even as it affirms the figure of the nerd, popular culture makes it clear which formation of masculinity is preferred: Pitt gets top billing and Hill's character works for Pitt's. The important question, then, is whether the determinism of technology will continue to be viewed as incompatible with certain kinds of masculinities, privileging as it does the cyborgian self-in-relation, rather than the supremely hypermasculine, natural self.

Notes

1. Satire includes parody, not the other way around; hence, the specificity.
2. The Corsi rating is a relatively simple of measure of the shot attempt differential that occurs when a given player is on the ice. The intent of those developing the statistic was to provide a means of measuring of puck possession and therefore dominance in a given game. However, it fails to account for the benefit or debit of teammates or the level of competition faced, among other criticisms.
3. The Foucauldian definition of technology is very much rooted in the Heideggerian tradition, where technology (*techné*) is an epistemic tool—a standardised model for knowledge production, distribution, and reception.
4. Indeed, it was the present authors' previous works, particularly in the areas of gender, technology and video games that drew them to this topic and to contribute to a growing body of work that does examine gender as fluid rather than fixed. The volume to which this chapter contributes should be included in that process.
5. Here it is worth noting one of the biggest trades in recent memory, that of Shea Weber going from Nashville to Montréal in return for P. K. Subban, The trade was controversial not only because of Subban's popularity in Montréal, it also resulted in the firing of the Canadiens' statistical analyst, who disagreed with the trade on the basis of the numbers (Engels 2016).
6. Even early baseball simulations, on machines as primitive as a Commodore C64, included the option of having the computer play as both sides. Hockey games did not include this feature until recently. Early hockey games were simple adaptations of *Pong* styled games, and more closely resembled digital versions of air hockey.
7. For example, in a photo essay celebrating *New York Times* photographer Barton Silverman's pioneering techniques for capturing sporting events, Silverman reveals that his first attempts required wires frozen under the ice and large wooden boxes in the net (MacDonald 2012).
8. Emails among NHL executives on the topic of player safety, including fighting, were subpoenaed as part of a lawsuit by former players. The former players allege that the league has disregarded player safety in favour of profits. The emails reveal executives not only referring to injured players as "soft," but also saying that injured players should have been penalized for putting themselves in positions where they could be hurt—by illegal hits (AP 2016).

Bibliography

Allain, Kristi A. 2012. 'Real fast and tough': The Construction of Canadian Hockey Masculinity. In *Rethinking Society in the 21st Century: Critical Readings in Sociology*, ed. MichelleWebber and Kate Bezanson, 359–372. Toronto: Canadian Scholars' Press.

Associated Press. 2016. Declassified NHL Memos, Emails Detail Concussion Debate. *SportsNet.ca*, March 29. http://www.sportsnet.ca/hockey/nhl/declassified-nhl-memos-emails-detail-concussion-debate/.

Barry, Sal. 2016. 20 Years Later, a Look at the FoxTrax Puck's Complex Legacy. *The Hockey News*, January 23. http://www.thehockeynews.com/news/article/20-years-later-a-look-back-at-the-foxtrax-pucks-complex-legacy. Accessed 22 Nov 2016.

Bergstrom, Kelly, Victoria McArthur, Jennifer Jenson, and Tamara Peyton. 2011. *All in a Day's Work*. Proceedings of the 2011 ACM SIGGRAPH Symposium on Video Games, 31–35. New York: ACM Press.

Bolter, Jay D., and Richard A. Grusin. 2000. *Remediation: Understanding New Media*. Cambridge, MA: MIT Press.

Boyle, Eric. 2014. Requiem for a 'Tough Guy': Representing Hockey Labor, Violence and Masculinity in *Goon*. *Sociology of Sport Journal* 31 (3): 327–348.

Brohm, Jean-Marie. 1989. *Sport: A Prison of Measured Time*. London: Pluto Press.

Burstyn, Varda. 1999. *Rites of Men: Manhood, Politics, and the Culture of Sport*. Toronto: University of Toronto Press.

Caillois, Roger. 2001. *Man, Play and Games*. Trans. Meyer Barash. Champaign: University of Illinois Press.

Connell, R.W. 1995. *Masculinities: Knowledge, Power and Social Change*. Berkeley: California University Press.

Conway, Steven C. 2010. Hyper-ludicity, Contra-ludicity, and the Digital Game. *Eludamos: Journal for Computer Game Culture* 4 (2): 135–147.

———. 2012. We Used to Win, We Used to Lose, We Used to Play': Simulacra, Hypo-ludicity and the Lost Art of Losing. *Westminster Papers* 9 (1): 28–46.

———. 2014. Avastars: The Encoding of Fame within Sport Digital Games. In *Playing to Win: Sports, Video Games, and the Culture of Play*, ed. Alan Brookey and Thomas P. Oates, 133–151. Bloomington, IN: Indiana University Press.

Cruickshank, Scott. 2008. Nystrom Striptease Scores for Charity. *Calgary Herald*, March 1. http://www.faceoff.com/hockey/teams/calgary-flames/story.html. Accessed 22 Nov 2016.

Duhatschek, Eric. 2014. After One Month, What Happened to the Ref Cam? *Globe & Mail*, November 5. http://www.theglobeandmail.com/sports/hockey/duhatschek-first-month-of-nhl-season-sees-early-surprises-disappointments/article21469322/. Accessed 22 Nov 2016.

Engels, Eric. 2016. Former Canadiens Analyst Matt Pfeffer Clarifies on Subban Trade. *SportsNet.ca*, July 14. http://www.sportsnet.ca/hockey/nhl/former-canadiens-analyst-matt-pfeffer-clarifies-subban-trade/.

Gordon, Sean. 2015. Lack of Fan Respect for Habs Coach Therrien 'Disappoints' GM Bergevin. *Globe and Mail*, May 15. http://www.theglobeandmail.com/sports/hockey/canadiens-cut-ties-with-veterans-gonchar-weaver-malhotra/article24454430/. Accessed 23 May 2016.

Hartley, Shaun. 2010. FoxTrax: It Is Time for the Glow Puck to Return to the NHL. *Bleacher Report*, September 9. http://bleacherreport.com/articles/460539-foxtrax-it-is-time-for-the-glow-puck-to-return-to-the-nhl. Accessed 22 Nov 2016.

Hartley, Matt. 2013. EA Sports Channels Brian Burke, Aims to Try a Little Truculence with *NHL 14*. *The Financial Post*, August 28. http://business.financialpost.com/fp-tech-desk/post-arcade/ea-sports-channels-brian-burke-aims-to-try-a-little-truculence-with-nhl-14?__lsa=b477-00f5. Accessed 23 May 2016.

Jeffords, Susan. 1989. *The Remasculinization of America: Gender and the Vietnam War*. Bloomington, IA: Indiana University Press.

———. 1994. *Hard Bodies: Hollywood Masculinity in the Reagan Era*. Brunswick, NJ: Rutgers University Press.

Jenson, Jen, and Suzanne de Castell. 2010. Gender, Simulation, and Gaming: Research Review and Redirections. *Simulation & Gaming* 41 (1): 51–71.

Larson, Kurtis. 2013. Chicago Blackhawks Ice Girl Forgets About Goal Cam. *The Toronto Sun*, December 18. http://blogs.canoe.com/slam/hockey/chicago-blackhawks-ice-girl-forgets-about-goal-cam/. Accessed 14 Feb 2017.

MacDonald, Kerri. 2012. Camera in the Net? Might Just Work. *New York Times*, April 9. http://lens.blogs.nytimes.com/2012/04/09/camera-in-the-net-might-just-work/?_r=0. Accessed 14 Feb 2017.

McDonald, Joe. 2017. 'Slap Shot' 40th Anniversary Reunion Weekend Really Captured the Spirit of the Thing. *ESPN.com*, February 26. http://www.espn.com/nhl/story/_/id/18770934/nhl-slap-shot-40th-anniversary-reunion-weekend-really-captured-spirit-thing. Accessed 18 June 2017.

McIndoe, Sean. 2014a. Grantland Dictionary: NHL Edition. *Grantland*, January 14. http://grantland.com/features/sean-mcindoe-nhl-grantland-dictionary/. Accessed 14 Feb 2017.

———. 2014b. 'NHLPA' 93' vs. 'NHL' 94': The Ultimate Showdown. *Grantland*, January 21. http://grantland.com/the-triangle/nhlpa-93-vs-nhl-94-the-ultimate-showdown/. Accessed 14 Feb 2017.

Ouellette, Marc A. 2008. "Everybody Else Ain't Your Father": Reproducing Masculinity in Cinematic Sports, 1975–2000. *Reconstruction: Studies in Contemporary Culture* 7 (3). http://reconstruction.eserver.org/073/contents/073.shtml.

———. 2011. 'Next Time We Go Bowling': Play and the Homosocial in the *Grand Theft Auto IV* Series. In *Learning the Virtual Life: Public Pedagogy in a Digital World*, ed. Peter Pericles Trifonas, 161–177. New York: Routledge.

Ouellette, Michelle E. and Marc A. Ouellette 2013. 'Married, with Children and an Xbox': Compromise in Video Game Play. In *Everyday Play*, ed. Samuel Tobin. http://mediacommons.futureofthebook.org/tne/pieces/married-children-and-xbox-compromise-video-game-play. Accessed 22 Nov 2016.

————. 2015. "Make Lemonade": The Pleasantly Unpleasant Aesthetics of Playing *Portal*. In *"The cake is a lie": Polyperspektivische Betrachtungen des Computerspiels am Beispiel von Portal*, ed. Britta Neitzel, Tomas Hensel, and Rolf F. Nohr, 151–173. Münster and Berlin: Lit-Verlag.

Ouellette, Marc A., and Jason Thompson. 2017. *The Post-9/11 Video Game: A Critical Examination*. Jefferson, NC: Macfarland.

Robidoux, Michael A. 2001. *Men at Play: A Working Understanding of Professional Hockey*. Montreal: McGill-Queen's University Press.

Ruggill, Judd E., Kenneth S. McAllister, and David Menchaca. 2004. The Gamework. *Communication and Critical/Cultural Studies* 1 (4): 297–312.

Sedgwick, Eve Kosofsky. 1996. Gosh, Boy George, You Must Be Awfully Secure in Your Masculinity. In *Constructing Masculinity*, ed. Maurice Berger, Brian Wallis, and Simon Watson, 11–20. New York: Routledge.

Silverwood, Victoria. 2015. *"Five for Fighting": The Culture and Practice of Legitimised Violence in Professional Ice Hockey*. Doctoral Dissertation, Cardiff University.

Simmons, Steve. 2014. Why Hockey's Trendy Advanced Stats are a Numbers Game. *The Toronto Sun*, May 20. http://www.torontosun.com/2014/05/20/why-hockeys-trendy-advanced-stats-are-a-numbers-game. Accessed 14 Feb 2017.

Smith, Rory. 2014. How Video Games Are Changing the Way Soccer Is Played. *New York Times*, October 13. https://www.nytimes.com/2016/10/14/sports/soccer/the-scouting-tools-of-the-pros-a-controller-and-a-video.html. Accessed 22 Nov 2016.

Todd, Jack. 2014. Year of the Number with Hockey Analytics. *Montréal Gazette*, September 28. http://montrealgazette.com/sports/jack-todd-year-of-the-number-with-hockey-analytics. Accessed 14 Feb 2017.

Voorhees, Gerald. 2015. Neoliberal Masculinity: The Government of Play and Masculinity in E-Sports. In *Playing to Win: Sports, Video Games, and the Culture of Play*, ed. Robert Alan Brookey and Thomas P. Oates, 63–91. Bloomington, IA: Indiana University Press.

Wilde, Brian. [BWildeCTV]. 2016. Well, It Appears Bergevin Was Wrong. The NHL Does Make PlayStation Trades. #Hall #Oilers. *Twitter*, June 29. https://twitter.com/BWildeCTV/status/748241030416318465. Accessed 1 Jul 2017.

Part II

Now You're Playing with Power Tools: Gendering Assemblages

8

Militarism and Masculinity in *Dungeons & Dragons*

Aaron Trammell

The fifth edition of *Dungeons & Dragons Players Handbook* (Mearls and Crawford 2014) has done extraordinary work in diversifying a character set which had at one point typified the white supremacist and misogynist representations of Sword and Sorcery fiction.[1] When at one point fans like P. M. Crabaugh, a fan essayist for *Dragon Magazine*,[2] had offered instructions for including people of color in the predominantly "caucasian" settings of these fictive worlds, a cursory review of the new *Players Handbook* shows that this advice has been taken to heart. The inside cover features a dark-skinned Moorish warrior valiantly raising a sabre over the fallen and toppling bodies of a group of goblins (Mearls and Crawford 2014, 1). A well-armored "oriental"[3] female samurai stands holding a sword in the book's chapter on "Personality and Background" (140). A brown-skinned dwarven cleric stands with hands open conjuring a magical blade in the included spellbook (247). Of the 86 illustrations in the manual depicting characters, 63 depict characters posed with weaponry of some sort (76 if you consider magical evocations and ballistics). For all of the great strides that *Dungeons & Dragons* has made in promoting a more inclusive player base, this sense of inclusivity problematically reaffirms the patriarchal, militaristic, and masculine structures of our society. This chapter considers the construction of masculinity in *Dungeons & Dragons* and explains its ever-present connections to military weaponry, strategy, culture, and technology.

A. Trammell (✉)
University of California, Irvine, CA, USA

© The Author(s) 2018
N. Taylor, G. Voorhees (eds.), *Masculinities in Play*, Palgrave Games in Context,
https://doi.org/10.1007/978-3-319-90581-5_8

129

Methodologically, I take a historical approach that is grounded in Foucauldian genealogy. I argue that the cultures of masculinity in *Dungeons & Dragons* can be discursively traced through published manuals and articles about the game.

I draw on manuals and fanzines from the 1970s located in the Ray Browne Popular Culture Archive as well as several volumes of *The Dragon*, which were published on CD-ROM as "The Dragon Magazine Archive" by TSR Hobbies in 1999. Here, I compare the representations of masculinity found in these historic texts to the ways that masculinity is represented today in the fifth edition of *Dungeons & Dragons*. In staging this comparison, I consider how depictions of masculinity have progressed over the 40-year life span of *Dungeons & Dragons* and also how they have stayed the same.

If we are to advocate for a feminist aesthetic of game design,[4] it is important to understand how masculinity is represented, ritualized, and shared longitudinally. Despite its roots in a homogeneous and sexist gaming community, *Dungeons & Dragons* has changed significantly in the past 40 years. The game no longer assumes a male player and has taken several steps toward implementing an inclusive gender vocabulary. Still, other representational spaces of masculinity remain: the game continues to feature heavy militaristic and patriarchal overtones that are now inclusive of both men and women. Does gender reform in the language and representation of role-playing games adequately address the insidiousness of patriarchal institutions like the military? And, as game design aesthetics have moved toward a more inclusive understanding of gender, what understated and perhaps counter-hegemonic practices of masculinity have been lost to our culture?

Although questions of gender in gaming were, once upon a time, located squarely within the representational practices of the software industry—see Justine Cassell and Henry Jenkins' (2000) collection *From Barbie to Mortal Kombat: Gender and Computer Games*—questions of gender in games today have diversified. The new diversity of approaches toward understanding gender in games encompasses many new voices in the queer games movement—where queer and trans players, authors, and designers have questioned the relationship between games, gender, and sexuality[5]—and approaches, like those contained in this volume, which seek to understand masculinity as an invisible and under-theorized social norm.

By better understanding masculinity, feminist scholars, players, and designers can hope to better participate in an earnest and candid conversation about identity in games. Games scholar Benjamin J. Triana (2015, 33), when writing about masculinity in the Western genre *Red Dead Redemption*, explains, "The artificial environment of a video game provides the opportunity for reproducing a Western environment and procedurally exploring claims about appropriate masculine values and beliefs about the world." I would push this claim one step further, and suggest that the artificial environments of games reproduce the environments, biases, and norms of Western Civilization, and in so doing reveal much about what masculinity scholar R. W. Connell (2005) would refer to as the invisible and hegemonic characteristics of masculine identity (xviii).

Although the invisible pressures of hegemonic masculinity certainly affect us all, it is important to consider how the negotiation of these pressures often results in the emergence of alternate in-between identities. Sociologist Lori Kendall (1999), for instance, discusses how the "nerd" identity is a mash of masculine and feminine characteristics, "The nerd stereotype includes aspects of both hypermasculinity (intellect, rejection of sartorial display, lack of 'feminine' social and relational skills) and feminization (lack of sports ability, small body size, lack of sexual relationships with women)" (265). Kendall argues that the negotiated nerd and geek masculinities occupy a subordinate position to hypermasculinity on a continuum of gender performance. This chapter shows how similar forms of subordinate masculinity are reinforced through game manuals and paraphernalia, but holds back from embracing the same sort of granular analysis that Kendall evokes. To show whether or not one performs hyper- or subordinate masculinity is secondary to this chapter's main goal. This goal is to reveal the descent of masculinity across media and consumer, showing how similar constructions of masculinity emerge within *Dungeons & Dragons* sourcebooks and within the discussions of *Dungeons & Dragons* players.

I will sketch a blueprint for understanding the way that masculinity has been constructed within the *Dungeons & Dragons* player community in this chapter. First I will show how masculinity has been established as a sort of glue that was able to join lonely men looking for friends across America. Then I will note its recurrence as a style of writing that assumes a masculine subject via a militaristic and patriarchal set of game rules. Finally, I offer some player accounts of masculinity from within the structure of *Dungeons & Dragons*, specifically *Dragon Magazine*.

Lonely Men Seeking Other Lonely Men

To understand the militaristic and masculine mechanics of *Dungeons & Dragons*, it is important to first consider the community that the game is embedded within. Before there was *Dungeons & Dragons*, the same hobby communities played *Diplomacy*. *Diplomacy* was a strategic board game that was released commercially by Avalon Hill in 1959. The game takes place in Europe during World War I. In it, each player controls the military of a European nation and schemes, plots and strategizes with the other players to dominate the map. Although *Diplomacy* couldn't be considered a role-playing game like *Dungeons & Dragons*, it did contain role-playing elements. Notably, as players assumed the roles of nations, they would take on the roles of leaders and diplomats, play-acting their reaction to combat and conflict.

Because the core game mechanics of *Diplomacy* were perfectly tuned to the social dynamics of negotiation, *Diplomacy* games were best played in with complete groups of seven players. When the game was played with less, players reported strategic and experiential wrinkles that found the game to be slightly unbalanced and less fun. Additionally, the social skills required by *Diplomacy*—negotiation, trust, and trickery—improved after repeated play; the game rewarded devoted players more than it rewarded casual play. For these reasons, it was difficult for many to find a group to enjoy *Diplomacy* with. *Diplomacy* played best with seven, and this left players around America with less than seven friends with an exciting yet infrequently played game. To make matters worse, those who could find a group of several players were seldom rewarded with the challenging and rewarding gameplay offered by that in a full and experienced group. In this way, lonely men across the country sought other lonely men to play *Diplomacy* with.

In Sherry Turkle's (1984) study of hackers at MIT in the 1980s, she found that loneliness often worked to create strong community bonds. Counterintuitively, loneliness serves as an anchor for counterculture: "It is a culture of people who have grown up thinking of themselves as different, apart, and who have a commitment to what one hacker described as 'an ethic of total toleration for anything that in the real world would be considered strange'" (196). A thriving several hundred person underground play-by-post community of board game enthusiasts would certainly appear odd to most. But for many lonely men across America seeking to play *Diplomacy*, nothing could be more exciting!

The solution to the community's geographic isolation lay in the pages of *The Avalon Hill General* which published a column entitled "Opponents Wanted" in order to help lonely players across America find friends to play *Diplomacy* with. Although the first "Opponents Wanted" column dated back to May 1964, and only contained one entry for Afrika Korps (another Avalon Hill game) the column boomed in the months that followed. Best described in a letter by International Federation of Wargamers president Len Lakofka (1971):

In the United States the hobby of wargaming has always been a fluid entity. Prior to the emergence of Avalon Hill Games, the hobby of wargaming was limited, almost exclusively, to small groups of miniature figures collectors who, on occasion, would create rules so that they could recreate battles for their collections. When the Avalon Hill Company pioneered the adult wargame, in board game style, many more persons were introduced to the competitive aspect of wargaming. Still, a person would by an AH game, play it with a friend or two, but then, most often, find a void in which no new competition could be found.

The General was the first step in creating a broadly based permanent market of "hard core" wargamers and a means via which persons, interested in the hobby, could contact one another. Of course I refer to the 'opponents wanted' column of this magazine. (2)

After making these points, Lakofka explains that the fanzines which were inspired by the "Opponents Wanted" column went on to inspire player groups across the country to set up play-by-mail *Diplomacy* games within fanzines that they would self-publish. This "hard core" contingent of *Diplomacy* players would be instrumental in developing *Dungeons & Dragons*.

Gary Gygax and Dave Arneson are widely credited with the development and invention of *Dungeons & Dragons*. The two were familiar with one another from the play-by-mail *Diplomacy* scene, and even began distributing rules for the early variant of *Dungeons & Dragons*, a wargame called *Chainmail*, via fanzine to other interested players who subscribed to their fanzine, *The Domesday Book*.

Although the game would mature and develop over time, it's important to note that Gygax used the publishing model of *The Avalon Hill General* to support *Dungeons & Dragons* in its initial runs. Where fanzines such as *Alarums and Excursions*, *The Dungeoneer*, *The Haven Herald*, and *The Wild Hunt* would take on the role of the supplemental fanzines that had at one point been directly associated with play-by-mail *Diplomacy*—supporting non-canonical modifications, supplements, and fictions—*Dragon Magazine* would take the role of *The Avalon Hill General*. *Dragon Magazine* became the in-house publication of TSR Hobbies establishing a quasi-official dialogue around the company's role-playing products.

Reflecting upon the networks of fans that constitute the role-playing hobby, it's hard not to notice the impact of isolation and loneliness on the development of gaming. The "hard core" gaming market noted by Len Lakofka is notable for both their purported zeal and their reported isolation. Alongside the affective dynamics, which surround loneliness, lie many of the insights that Sara Ahmed (2010) points to in her essay "Happy Objects." For Ahmed, a happy object is notable less for what it represents, and more for what feelings we expect it to invoke (33). Role-playing games (and *Dungeons & Dragons*, in specific) are happy objects insofar as players expect them to evoke feelings of camaraderie and fun. The nature of this construction as an expectation and not necessarily an evocation is key, based on whether or not the expectation is met players might react to playing the game in any number of ways.

I refer to role-playing games as a happy object here, because the expectation of community was a clear catalyst for the games' embryonic networks. This expectation cuts both ways, as the community that players expected to engage with reflects many of the values that the community itself had built into its games. Specifically, the militaristic tropes of combat worked to produce a specific sort of player—one that valued the rational, quantitative, and oppositional mechanisms that were constitutive of the game's rules.

These brief historical notes point to the ways that role-playing games like *Dungeons & Dragons* relied on an infrastructure of players to curate and maintain its rules. Just as the fan communities that played *Diplomacy* took on an active role in modifying the game's rules, so too did the player base of *Dungeons & Dragons*. The corporate interests who curated these fan bases, Avalon Hill (*Diplomacy*) and TSR Hobbies (*Dungeons & Dragons*), were attentive to the ideas, ideals, and modifications produced by fans, and often allowed engaged players to publish in their official magazines, *The Avalon Hill General* and *Dragon Magazine*. The participatory dialogue between publishers and fans is key to understanding the longitudinal dynamics of these products, given the circulation of ideas invoked by the form. As this chapter turns to the representation of masculinity in game mechanics, it is important to note that these ideas were actively cycling both through the official products published by TSR Hobbies and the fan communities that would later consume and modify them.

Learning to Dude

As Mia Consalvo (2007) notes in *Cheating*, hobby publications were not only sources of news about games, but also a way to groom inexperienced players into the techniques and skills necessary to play various games (31–33). Articles in the "Classified Information" section of *Nintendo Power* magazine were a way to cultivate a fan base of players that understood how to advance in games that would have been otherwise too difficult to navigate for beginning players. If we consider how strategies of cheating had been cultivated through industry publications, we must also consider how industry and hobby publications had encouraged players to take on other attitudes when playing games.

This section considers how *Dragon Magazine* cultivated an ethic of masculinity within its constituents that was intended to both thwart loneliness and preserve the militaristic and patriarchal values that lay at the core of *Dungeons & Dragons* gameplay. By examining these early moments where masculinity is incorporated into the rules and practices surrounding gameplay, we can ascertain a sense of what elements of masculinity have continued within cultures of gameplay in the present.

Early editions of *Dungeons & Dragons* took on a tone that assumes that the players participating were men. For evidence, one need search no further than Volume 1 of the original ruleset—*Men & Magic*. Aside from the obvious—the casual invocation of "men" in the title—the illustrations contained within the volume also spoke to a deliberately groomed sense of masculinity. Almost all of the heroic characters contained within were muscle-bound men (Fig. 8.1), except for one small exception: an illustration of a voluptuous witch and a nude Amazon (Fig. 8.2) (Gygax and Arneson 1974a). The assumption here is that the game would be played in casual groups with locker-room interests. The character archetype which would later come to be known as "Fighters" was described in this edition as "Fighting-men," yet another minor yet important mode of cultivating and grooming a player audience (6).

Other manuals in the series maintain this somewhat sexist and implicitly masculine tenor. The second manual *Monsters & Treasure* contains a reference table for the different monsters one might encounter in the game. It explicitly

16

Fig. 8.1 A barbarian from the original D&D rulebook

Range: 24".

BEAUTIFUL
WITCH

AMAZON

27

Fig. 8.2 A witch and an amazon from the original D&D rulebook

lists "men" as a type of monster that might be encountered during the game's adventures. Interestingly, the often female-gendered "mermen" make an appearance on the list with no mention of their female counterparts, mermaids (Gygax and Areneson 1974b, 7). Women are included on the list; they are generally denoted through rules that allow for the control of the assumedly male player characters. Pixies and Nixies can "charm" player characters and lure them to a watery death. Dryads are referred to as "beautiful tree spirits" and have similar powers (15–16). Medusa are listed without gender as "it", but depicted in the manual's imagery as female (9, 28). Finally, female werewolves or "lycanthropes" are thrust into a presumably feminine role fighting at three times their normal power to protect their young. Similarly, female centaurs are infantilized and grouped with centaur children—preferring not to fight at all (14).

The final rulebook in the original series of manuals was *Underworld & Wilderness Adventures*, which contained rules for how characters were encouraged to interact with their environment. The manual continues to list "men" as a distinct and womanless category distinct from others. Combat and referee tips are included here as well. Given that *Dungeons & Dragons* had been developed as a merger of some of the role-playing elements native to *Diplomacy* and the hard statistical combat elements borrowed from other wargames like *Napoleonic Wars* and *The Kriegspeil*, a dice-based statistical combat system was core to the gameplay. In addition to this system, *Dungeons & Dragons* inherited a system of authority through which players would be forced to accept the world-making decisions made by the referees (Gygax and Arneson 1974c, 12–14). This authoritative and somewhat patriarchal structure saturates all gameplay—it is derivative of military structures of authority that require soldiers to report up the chain of command to superior officers.

These various elements are key to understanding how masculinity is constituted in early role-playing materials. Players are assumed to be male, interacting in a world where men are the primary social actors. Militaristic abilities are an important part of the natural order of this world, as players are expected to defeat other mystical creatures through martial combat. When women enter the martial sphere, they are made monstrous (lycanthropes) or forced to seduce men through a set of abilities keyed in to their beauty. Finally, players are made to adhere to the militaristic dynamics of command as they report to the referee and await a description of how they are interacting with the environment.

The early rules of *Dungeons & Dragons* reinforce group dynamics that allow for an organized and ordered expression of masculinity. Players are given the agency to act through violent and sexual fantasies with rules that focus on combat and construct women as seductresses looking to control men. Because women are absent from the above description it seems apt to describe it only as an ordered space of agency, where expression is possible only insofar as group dynamics and authority figures can condone and allow it.

The Infamous Harlot Table

Perhaps the most famously sexist example of the gendered dynamics of *Dungeons & Dragons* is the "Harlot" table which was published a half decade later in 1979 within Gygax's *Advanced Dungeons & Dragons* manual *Dungeon Master's Guide* (see Fig 8.3). This table expands on the random encounters already established in the basic rules of *Dungeons & Dragons*. Specifically, it details rules for randomly generating the socioeconomic backgrounds and motivations for a variety of "harlots" that players might encounter in the game. The table's clearly misogynist language has been widely criticized by a variety of web sources,[6] and is often cited as an example of gendered rules in *Dungeons &*

Goodwife encounters are with a single woman, often indistinguishable from any other type of female (such as a magic-user, harlot, etc.). Any offensive treatment or seeming threat will be likely to cause the woman to scream for help, accusing the offending party of any number of crimes, i.e. assault, rape, theft, or murder. 20% of goodwives know interesting gossip.

Harlot encounters can be with brazen strumpets or haughty courtesans, thus making it difficult for the party to distinguish each encounter for what it is. (In fact, the encounter could be with a dancer only prostituting herself as it pleases her, an elderly madam, or even a pimp.) In addition to the offering of the usual fare, the harlot is 30% likely to know valuable information, 15% likely to make something up in order to gain a reward, and 20% likely to be, or work with, a thief. You may find it useful to use the sub-table below to see which sort of harlot encounter takes place:

01-10	Slovenly trull	76-85	Expensive doxy
11-25	Brazen strumpet	86-90	Haughty courtesan
26-35	Cheap trollop	91-92	Aged madam
36-50	Typical streetwalker	93-94	Wealthy procuress
51-65	Saucy tart	95-98	Sly pimp
66-75	Wanton wench	99-00	Rich panderer

An expensive doxy will resemble a gentlewoman, a haughty courtesan a noblewoman, the other harlots might be mistaken for goodwives, and so forth.

Fig. 8.3 The infamous "harlot table," taken from the first edition of *AD&D Dungeon Master's Guide*

Dragons. This chapter considers how the harlot table helps to reveal the depth to which a patriarchal order has been embedded within the rules of *Dungeons & Dragons* and therefore how the games rules foster a sense of masculinity amongst the players.

The "Harlot" table is embedded within a master list of random encounters entitled the "CITY/TOWN ENCOUNTERS MATRIX," which explain the various types of encounters that players might have in a city environment. Within this master list are several other clearly gendered townsfolk that players are liable to encounter when exploring an urban space. A patriarchal and heteronormative social order is inscribed within these descriptions. Women occupy one of three stereotypical and archetypical roles in the list, they are "harlots," "goodwi[ves]," or "night hags". Meanwhile the other folk of the city are either assumedly or explicitly men and therefore responsible for a majority of the commerce, intrigue, and crime taking place in the city on a day-to-day basis.

Rules for including "harlots" in the city adventures of characters are interesting as all included "harlots" are given an adjective descriptor which implies a relationship to a presumably masculine player character. Harlots are "slovenly," "brazen," "cheap," "typical," "saucy," "wanton," "expensive," "aged," and worse. In addition to these problematic descriptors, the harlot table offers explicit rules for adding additional depth to "harlots":

> Harlot encounters can be with brazen strumpets or haughty courtesans, thus making it difficult for the party to distinguish each encounter for what it is. (In fact, the encounter could be with a dancer only prostituting herself as it pleases her, an elderly madam, or even a pimp.) In addition to the offering of the usual fare, the harlot is 30% likely to know valuable information, 15% likely to make something up in order to gain a reward, and 20% likely to be, or work with, a thief. (Gygax et al. 1979, 192)

Not only are harlots given descriptions, which situate their value to a presumably male player, but there is also a slight chance that they can possess additional value as an information source. Set this positive value against the alternate possibility that the "harlot" encountered might be a liar or thief and degree to which women are treated like juvenile sex objects in the rules of *Dungeons & Dragons* is made clear.

The "Harlot" table concludes by explaining that, "An expensive doxy will resemble a gentlewoman, a haughty courtesan a noblewoman, the other harlots might be mistaken for goodwives, and so forth" (192). Harlots find utility in the patriarchal social order by only by self-objectification and sexuality; otherwise women must accommodate the positionality of noblewoman or goodwife.

Rules for goodwife encounters are straightforward; goodwives are prude and fragile. The rules explain that, "Any offensive treatment or seeming threat will likely cause the woman to scream for help, accusing the offending party of any number of crimes, i.e. assault, rape, theft, or murder" (192). Additionally, goodwives are written to be "indistinguishable" from other females, interchangeable and practically objects. "Noblewomen" are found being doted upon by their servants, "[they] will have a sedan chair, carriers and linkboys (at night)" (192). Also like the "goodwife," noblewomen are indistinguishable from other women of a similar social strata; "noblewomen can likewise be mistaken for a courtesan or procuress" (192). "Goodwives" and "noblewomen," the two examples of women who cleanly fit into the patriarchal order, are indistinguishable and interchangeable with other women in the game, relegating them to the role of background flavor.

"Night hags" are to be used rarely in the game, only in suitable narrative moments and locales (192). Despite being typecast as a monster encounter as opposed to the social encounter one might have with a "goodwife" or "harlot," "night hags" exemplify the only remaining role for women in patriarchy—if women cannot be objectified, they become obstacles for men to overcome.

The social order implied by the list positions men in positions of social and economic value throughout. Take the laborer for example, "Laborer encounters are with a group of 3–12 non-descript persons loitering on their way home to or from work. These fellows will be rough customers in a brawl. There is a 10% chance for each to be a levy in the city watch, with commensurate friends and knowledge" (192). Men are "fellows" who work and brawl with one another, while women can either acquire independence by marketing their sexuality as "harlots," or maintain the patriarchal structure by acting as a "goodwife."[7]

Many other men can be encountered in the city. The list includes a "Press Gang" of typically macho and "burly sailors or soldiers," ruffians with clubs, "guardsmen," "watchmen," "gentlemen," and "tradesmen," among others (191–192). Typical to the descriptions of men operating around the city are rules noting the respect they command from others, their likelihood to engage in combat, and material wealth.

The rules governing city encounters in *Advanced Dungeons & Dragons* offer a snapshot of how the game's designers construed urban life and how it replicates and typifies a patriarchal structure. Not only do the examples within this section show how limited female agency was in a typical *Dungeons & Dragons* campaign, but they also show how masculine agency is constructed along the lines of material wealth and martial power. The men that players are likely to run into command respect because of the ways that they fit into a city's thriving (or failing) economy as skilled tradesmen, merchants, or military.

The social order produced by *Dungeons & Dragons* city encounter rules is a microcosm of the social order produced by the game's authoritarian and patriarchal structure. These early city settings cultivated a sense of masculine empowerment amongst the players experiencing them. They represent a world where men have access to powerful economic positions, modest (yet socially integral) positions as craftsmen, and, of course, positions in the always relied-upon military. The tables for random city encounters are paired with an illustration that accurately depicts this social order (Fig. 8.4). In this illustration a rampaging magician-bandit blasts a member of the city guard while heroes and brawny ruffians pour from a tavern. A lifeless body burns in the fore-

Fig. 8.4 An illustration following the "harlot table," taken from the first edition of *AD&D Dungeon Master's Guide*

ground. In the background a covered goodwife shrieks and flees while a common tradesman watches with stoic interest from his window (193). When examining this illustration, I cannot help but see it as a reflection of the play spaces typically engineered by players and referee of a typical *Dungeons & Dragons* game. Players have significant freedom to enact their masculine fantasies in a bounded world that allows them to traipse, romp, and cavort through a world where the most important social actors are men.

On Beards, Dwarves, and Women

In *Dragon Magazine* #28, published August 1979, an article entitled "The Dungeons Master's Guide—Developers' Notes & an Interview with the Author" offered developers notes on the newly released *Dungeon Master's Guide* from several members of the design team. In addition to the notes left by author and designer Gary Gygax, other notables like Jeff Leason, Len Lakofka, Lawrence Schick, Jean Wells, Allen Hammack, Mike Carr, and James T. Ward were given some space to explain their thoughts on the design process. Notably, Jean Wells, the first and only woman to be employed by TSR Hobbies at that time, left an enigmatic remark that reflected many of the debates occurring behind closed doors. Apart from complaining about what, in her opinion, were overly frivolous representations of elves in the *Dungeon Masters Guide*, Wells ended her notes with a strong point: "Finally, let it stand that I say, 'Dwarven women DO NOT have beards, Gary!" (Gygax et al. 1979, 4).

Some of the other designers offered their thoughts on the topic, too. The other twelve designers, all men, were in consensus—they claimed that dwarven women DO have beards and that the new rules reflected this point. One designer Allen Hammack wrote quite smugly, "With the lopsided score of TSR 12, Jean 1, the mini-controversy of whether dwarven women have beards has been laid to rest. They do" (4). Gygax also was sure to weigh in on the controversy, as in the same column the editors of *Dragon Magazine* inquired what his thoughts on the topic were. His reply assumed a typically patriarchal tone as he assured readers that his account of dwarven women was more reliable than any other:

> It's fairly common knowledge. I don't believe I know anyone who *ever* met a female dwarf who *didn't* have a beard, so I don't know what more there is to be said about the matter. I'm not quite sure what the hoopla is—perhaps somebody who is uninformed or who has never dealt with dwarves *en masse* would assume that because *homo sapiens* females generally don't tend to have beards, dwarven females are likewise. But they all, of course, have beards. They're not so bald as the males, though. (46)

Not only does Gygax insult Wells' intelligence in this note—he refers to her as "uninformed"—he also assumes a tone reminiscent of locker-room horseplay and gatekeeping. He grants authority to those who agree with his account, and belittles the intelligence and logic of those who would hold a different opinion. In this quick design note, Gygax reinforces many of the group dynamics of masculinity—specifically, maintaining a hierarchical and patriarchal pattern of knowledge.

The debate did not soon let up. Four months later, in December 1979, in her column for *Dragon Magazine* Wells recounts how players had stopped her at conventions to weigh in on the debate with her. She wrote:

> [At Gen Con[8] m]any people stopped me in the hall to either agree with me wholeheartedly, or disagree with me and then tell me that I was crazy. Everyone knows that dwarven women have beards, they said. It did not stop there. Oh, no! We have even been getting mail on the issue. It is not too bad, but I don't like being accused of making an issue out of the subject. (Wells 1979, 14)

Reading between the lines, it's clear that Wells was receiving both internal pressure from TSR Hobbies about the fans that she had catalyzed against Gygax on the topic, as well as external pressure from fans hassling her and mimicking Gygax's language—calling her crazy, stupid, and worse. Wells shuts down future conversation on the topic by telling people writing with their thoughts on the topic not to bother and to "save your breath" (14). She closes by explaining, "Dwarven women may indeed have beards, Gary, but not in my world" (14). Wells writes as if she was being bullied, using curt language and cutting off further conversation.

Because Wells was being hassled by fans as well as critiqued by the management of TSR Hobbies, it's important to take seriously the ways that this historical vignette highlights the forms of patriarchal gatekeeping coalescing around *Dungeons & Dragons*. The question of whether or not female dwarves have beards is ridiculous and fictional, and it highlights the degree to which spurious argumentation plays into masculine group dynamics. Not only did figures within the design team of TSR Hobbies take arbitrary sides on the topic, and dismiss Wells' perspective as foolish, but Gygax's public statement catalyzed some fans to mimic his stance and publically approach and belittle Wells. The bearded female dwarf stands as an example of how knowledge is disseminated in patriarchal structures, and shows how game rules—however insignificant they may seem—are often taken to heart and replicated by players in surprising, literal, and occasionally spiteful ways.

The rules, game, and brand of *Dungeons & Dragons* are happy objects. They catalyze a community of excited fans around them and establish a set of normative protocols for how they should be challenged and interacted with. And, because of the positive affects they produce in most players, when Jean Wells challenged them, the community passionately turned against her. Within this processes, some ideas (like bearded dwarven women) are normalized, and used as a form of social gatekeeping—thus maintaining the order of hegemonic masculinity.

Passing in a Masculine Culture

Aside from being a fiction, the bearded female dwarf stands as a symbolic representation of the pervasiveness of masculinity within the early cultures of *Dungeons & Dragons* players. If women were to play *Dungeons & Dragons*, they had to accept much of the masculine baggage that came along with the game. Patriarchal authority and knowledge structures had to be accepted and taken for granted, homosocial representations of masculinity were everywhere in the game's rulebooks, and martial prowess was the definitive mode of conflict resolution and self-worth. All players of *Dungeons & Dragons* have to don the dwarven beard to some degree and accept these masculine tropes as self-evident in the game's world and rules.

There is a sense that the hierarchical and cooperative structures of the *Dungeons & Dragons* system are undoubtedly complicit in priming workers entering the technological sector for the forms of management that they would encounter throughout their careers. Although some like Doug Thomas and John Seely Brown (2009) have argued that the tools of cooperation developed by players of MMORPGs (and thus, by association, *Dungeons & Dragons*) are highly sought by managers in the technological sector, I remain critical of this trend. Drawing on the feminist scholarship of Sally Hacker (1989), I feel that it is important to recognize the degree to which the bureaucratic structures of role-playing games are fetishized in the masculine technological sector. White-collar workers learn how to work within patriarchy from role-playing games. They become aware of the ways that unspoken social rules are connected to systems of representation that prioritize a patriarchal social order.

If all players have to accept the customs of masculinity that come along with the game, it's important to question the degree to which players still have agency: can these tropes of masculinity be subverted? To some extent, it's clear that designers and players still have a great deal of agency in this area. As noted in the introduction, much of the representational tunnel vision of *Dungeons & Dragons*' early design has been abandoned in favor of an ethic of diversity. No longer do women exist only to tantalize teenage consumers as sex objects in the pages of the games manuals, now women are represented as heroic equals to men. In this sense, there has been a great deal of progress regarding the way women are represented in *Dungeons & Dragons*. Although the problematic trappings of the "Harlot" table have been all but abandoned, the games designers have opted to pull women into the space of masculinity as opposed to illustrate or design for a broader array of masculine tropes. Jakko Stenros and Tanja Sihvonen (2015) have done tremendous work in depicting representations of queer characters in the history of role-playing games; it could be a strong starting point for game designers seeking alternate visions of masculinity in role-playing game design.

Despite these valiant efforts toward patching the game's representational design, I still find myself troubled by the prevalence of militarism in *Dungeons & Dragons*. Combat is still relied on as a central mechanic for conflict resolution, and play is still organized through a hierarchical chain-of-command. These militaristic tropes saturate the games representational strata as well, as pointed out earlier, with "badass" depictions of women and people of color maneuvering though combat zones in a number of masculine and macho poses. As fan communities and designers continue to ponder and discuss the politics of inclusivity in games, new questions can emerge from questioning masculinity as opposed to simply maleness. As representation in games comes to be inclusive of all, we must inquire what the politics of the worlds are: Are we including players of diverse backgrounds? How does appearance become a problematic and dominant approach for understanding who is included or excluded in gaming culture? When masculinity is reduced to appearance, as the example of bearded dwarves proves above, we lose track of its most toxic aspects, including the silencing of feminine and minority voices and the circulation and affirmation of baseless knowledge.

Notes

1. Robert E. Howard, author of the Conan series, has been critiqued for incorporating his racist beliefs into his character and world design. Please see Gary Romeo's (2002) "Southern Discomfort," for a thorough yet forgiving overview of how Howard's racist beliefs affected his writing.
2. *Dragon Magazine* was TSR Hobbies and Wizards of the Coast's flagship magazine for all things role-playing. Intended to cultivate an audience of role-playing fanatics, *Dragon Magazine* was first published in 1975 as *The Strategic Review*. It took on various titles during its history, including *Dragon* and *The Dragon*. The magazine's final issue was published in September 2013.
3. I have argued elsewhere that despite the manual's excellent work in developing an inclusive and multi-ethnic world, it still falls prey to what Edward Said would refer to as "orientalism." It reduces the complexity of various "exotic" Asian, African, and South American cultures to a single stereotypical imaginary (Trammell 2016).
4. There are a number of approaches that might help flesh out this category. For the purposes of this essay, a feminist aesthetic of design is any that seeks to cultivate an appreciation for difference in a game's representational and mechanical

content. This is perhaps best reflected in the work of Gillian Smith (2016), who writes, "A feminist and proceduralist approach to game analysis lets us examine more than just the ways that diversity is *shown* to the player by designers, artists, and writers, it also helps us see how players can *perform* and *play* with identity." Others like Naomi Clark and Merritt Kopas (2014) have argued that the turn toward queer game design is itself a turn toward approaching and appreciating non-normative identity.

5. Bonnie Ruberg (2016) maintains an excellent collection of essays and books central to queer game studies.

6. The "harlot" table has been the object of much consternation in the past few years, appearing in websites like *Boing Boing* (Donovan 2014) and *Vice* (Johnson 2008).

7. I have intentionally left out a few descriptions of positions on the list that accommodate both men and women such as "beggar" and "thief" as I felt that they were both more or less interchangeable as poor and invisible in the city's landscape.

8. Gen Con is a hobby convention devoted to role-playing and role-playing enthusiasts. It was developed by Gary Gygax to help support *Dungeons & Dragons*. Gen Con is an annual event that persists today.

Bibliography

Ahmed, Sara. 2010. Happy Objects. In *The Affect Theory Reader*, ed. Melissa Gregg and Gregory J. Seigworth, 29–51. Ashville, NC: Duke University Press.

Cassell, Justine, and Henry Jenkins. 2000. *From Barbie to Mortal Kombat: Gender and Computer Games*. Cambridge, MA: The MIT Press.

Clark, Naomi, and Merritt Kopas. 2014. Queering Human-Game Relations: Exploring Queer Mechanics and Play. *First Person Scholar*. http://www.firstpersonscholar.com/queering-human-game-relations/.

Connell, R.W. 2005. *Masculinities*. 2nd ed. Berkley, CA: University of California Press.

Consalvo, Mia. 2007. *Cheating: Gaining Advantage in Video Games*. Cambridge, MA: The MIT Press.

Donovan, Tim. 2014. #NotAllRolePlayers: A History of Rapey Dungeon Masters. *Vice*. http://www.vice.com/read/notallroleplayers-a-history-of-rapey-dungeon-masters.

Gygax, Gary, and Dave Arneson. 1974a. Men & Magic. In *Dungeons & Dragons: Rules for Fantastic Medieval Wargames Campaigns Playable with Paper and Pencil and Miniature Figures*, 1st ed. Lake Geneva, WI: Tactical Studies Rules.

———. 1974b. Monsters & Treasure. In *Dungeons & Dragons: Rules for Fantastic Medieval Wargames Campaigns Playable with Paper and Pencil and Miniature Figures*, 1st ed. Lake Geneva, WI: Tactical Studies Rules.

————. 1974c. Underworld & Wilderness Adventures. In *Dungeons & Dragons: Rules for Fantastic Medieval Wargames Campaigns Playable with Paper and Pencil and Miniature Figures*, 1st ed. Lake Geneva, WI: Tactical Studies Rules.

Gygax, Gary, et al. 1979. The Dungeons Master's Guide—Developers' Notes & an Interview with the Author. *The Dragon* 28, Lake Geneva, WI: TSR Hobbies.

Hacker, Sally. 1989. *Pleasure, Power, and Technology: Some Tales of Gender, Engineering, and the Cooperative Workplace*. Boston, MA: Unwin Hyman.

Johnson, Joel. 2008. Great Moments in Gygax: Random Harlot Table. *Boing Boing*. http://gadgets.boingboing.net/2008/03/05/great-moments-in-gyg.html.

Kendall, Lori. 1999. Nerd Nation: Images of Nerds in US Popular Culture. *International Journal of Cultural Studies* 2 (2): 260–283.

Lakofka, Len. 1971. Avalon Hill Philosophy—Part 26. *The Avalon Hill General* 7 (6). Baltimore, MD: The Avalon Hill Company.

Mearls, Mike, and Jeremy Crawford. 2014. *Dungeons & Dragons Player's Handbook*. 5th ed. Renton, WA: Wizards of the Coast.

Romeo, Gary. 2002. Southern Discomfort. *Sand Roughs* 4. http://www.robert-e-howard.org/sandroughs4.html#_edn6.

Ruberg, Bonnie. 2016. Queer Game Studies 101: An Introduction to the Field. *Our Glass Lake*. http://ourglasslake.com/queer-game-studies-101/.

Smith, Gillian. 2016. A Proceduralist View on Diversity in Games. *Journal of Games Criticism* 3 (1), ed. Aaron Trammell and Zack Lischer-Katz. http://gamescriticism.org/articles/smith-3-a.

Stenros, Jakko, and Tanja Sihvonen. 2015. Out of the Dungeons: Representations of Queer Sexuality in RPG Source Books. *Analog Game Studies* 2 (5). http://analog-gamestudies.org/2015/07/out-of-the-dungeons-representations-of-queer-sexual-ity-in-rpg-source-books/.

Thomas, Douglas, and John Seely Brown. 2009. Why Virtual Worlds Can Matter. *International Journal of Learning and Media* 1 (1): 37–49.

Trammell, Aaron. 2016. How Dungeons & Dragons Appropriated the Orient. *Analog Game Studies* 3 (1). http://analoggamestudies.org/2016/01/how-dun-geons-dragons-appropriated-the-orient/.

Triana, Benjamin J. 2015. Red Dead Masculinity: Constructing a Conceptual Framework for Analyzing the Narrative and Message Found in Video Games. *Journal of Games Criticism* 2 (2). http://gamescriticism.org/articles/triana-2-2/.

Turkle, Sherry. 1984. *The Second Self: Computers and the Human Spirit*. Cambridge, MA: MIT Press.

Wells, Jean. 1979. Sage Advice. *Dragon Magazine* 32. Lake Geneva, WI: TSR Hobbies.

9

At the Intersection of Difficulty and Masculinity: Crafting the Play Ethic

Nicholas A. Hanford

An Intersection of Performances

The Skulls battles in *Metal Gear Solid V: The Phantom Pain* (MGSV; Konami Productions 2015) are a well-known pain in the ass. These supersoldiers who surround Snake take incredible amounts of damage and show up periodically throughout the game. They move fast and have heightened senses, pushing the skills learned through previous missions to an extreme. In many cases I was unable to move past them or kill them. Between their quickness and damage resistance, the Skulls repeatedly closed the distance, killed Snake, and left me in frustration. Dying three times in a row in these fights meant being prompted to lower the difficulty. The tradeoff for submitting to the system is to look upon Snake wearing a chicken hat while running through the desert of Afghanistan as well as a cap being placed on my score for the mission.

Donning the chicken hat in MGSV makes me nervous that I am doing some disservice to the game at hand. The same hesitation is present when I select "Cakewalk" prior to starting *Binary Domain* (Yakuza Team 2012). I am reminded quickly that my preferences for smooth playthroughs without a constant chorus of failure and punishment are not accepted as completely legitimate. My performance does not pass the tests of dedication these systems require for entry into the gamer world.

N. A. Hanford (✉)
Rensselaer Polytechnic Institute, Troy, NY, USA

© The Author(s) 2018
N. Taylor, G. Voorhees (eds.), *Masculinities in Play*, Palgrave Games in Context,
https://doi.org/10.1007/978-3-319-90581-5_9

Video games are a medium built upon challenge and difficulty. Whether that difficulty emanates from the artificially intelligent actors within the game world or from a human player, players are expected to overcome. Through hard work and the gathering of skill within a system, the player must face their challenges, learn from their mistakes, and change their actions to continue within the game. Like this general performance of video game play, the performance of gender is based upon what Butler (1999) calls the "stylized repetition of acts" that are either accepted or demeaned.

When it comes to men playing video games, two performances intersect to create meaning and shape identities. For both of these performances challenge and effort are key forces in the shaping normative notions of both masculinity and play. As Adrienne Shaw (2013) has noted, the "gamer" identity is strongly wrapped up in the amount of work and investment one puts into gaming. The effort that gamers put into their play becomes a badge of commitment and their abilities merit their use of the term. This cycle of legitimacy and work has a multitude of effects, from the shaming of women at gaming conventions to the common critique of Anita Sarkeesian not playing enough games to critique them (Rouner 2014).

The performativity of gamers and the accompanying boundary policing works concurrently at these interpersonal levels as well as at a textual level. In this chapter I will investigate the interrelations between effort and challenge in the context of the "gamer" identity by discussing the strategies games employ to celebrate or demean certain players or kinds of play while legitimizing others. By expanding on the work of Jesper Juul (2009a) in his discussion of punishments within game systems, I propose a broad category of *gender offense punishments* that demonstrates the various ways video games have crafted an image of the gamer that is contingent on the effort of players.

This study further contextualizes how we understand the "hardcore" male gamer as the audience of video games. A great deal of work has been done to show how the figure of the gamer is instantiated throughout gaming discourses, but there is a lack of work that describes how video games themselves influence the position and enforce particular viewpoints on the role of play in people's lives. After discussing previous research that explains the work of difficulty in games and situating this gamer audience, I will describe three genres of gender offense punishment: menu embarrassment, character attacks, and restriction of textual completion. Additionally, I will show how these textual strategies converge to create a *play ethic* for gamers. This ethic grounds the legitimacy and boundary policing in the texts gamers encounter and the experiences they draw upon.

This analysis allows for a more extensive view on how the gamer audience is created and sustained. Elucidating how representations of difficulty and work within video games inform concepts of gamer legitimacy provides a different angle on the masculinities games create. This study informs our knowledge of gaming culture, while also exposing an arena where play can be used to subvert meanings of games. Additionally, this work can afford clarity for designers to craft different representations of difficulty and challenge in the future.

Constructing the Gamer

Erecting the norms of gaming has been a long process and generally revolves around the establishment of the white, heterosexual male as the sole legitimate audience for games. From the work of Cassell and Jenkins (2000) to Sarkeesian (2013), the textual strategies for ensuring the masculine gendering of games have been analyzed and explained in great detail. These studies have emphasized the lack of equal representation within game worlds, demonstrating how games themselves contribute to a sexist gaming subculture.

The gamer identity has formed through a variety of means. Analyzing how the popular magazine *Nintendo Power* displayed the gaming populace in the 1990s, Cote (2015) showed a significant skewing toward a male audience. During the studied timeframe (1994–1999) male contributions to the magazine in the form of letters, articles, artwork, or as subjects of photographs were the clear majority of content. This is only one demonstration of a pervasive trend throughout the history of games.

Even though the journalistic representation of games is largely steady, both Diane Carr (2005) and Helen Thornham (2008) demonstrate that the appeal of games to men and women is complicated by game genres and player preferences. By looking at young women's preferences, Diane Carr (2005) concluded that access to certain genres was a simple way to break down the proposed gender differences in playing preference. In a study of gaming's place in multiple households over the course of several years, Thornham (2008) demonstrates the internalization of the marketed gender roles in various households, impacting the norms of how games are played as a social activity. These studies show that while the marketing of games clearly gender what games men and women should play and that the preferences might be internalized, they are not the final say on performing gameplay.

The ideal gamer is not solely male, but also identifies as a "hardcore" player (Kerr 2006). Even as audiences have expanded over time, this hardcore gamer is one that plays a routine subset of games. As Vanderhoef (2013) summarizes, "The video game industry treats the term casual as a beneficial target consumer, a potential profit, but this enthusiasm is tempered by the subtle devaluation and more blatant feminization of this same market." These processes of separating the casual and hardcore markets by the industry have worked their way into the gaming subculture, furthering the stratification of gamers by gamers. The formal, gamic qualities (Juul 2009b) and informal, social rules (Consalvo 2009) have crafted a distinct hierarchy of how games are viewed.

The separation of players along the casual/hardcore border has been an important force in the legitimacy of individuals and this stratification takes place in a medium where legitimacy is seen as being earned through effort. The more a gamer plays through a game, the more social capital and gamic credibility they receive in support of their identity. James Paul Gee (2007) celebrates the space that video games afford people in that they offer a safe space for failure. Here the credibility gamers earn is tied to skill or the time invested within the game.

However, praising the presumed meritocracy of games does not take into account the issues arising from this viewpoint. Discussing the role of leveling systems in crafting this meritocratic façade, Paul (2013) writes, "Under a presumption of proper balance, leveling systems work as an alibi for video games and the inequality that can be wrought in their meritocratic spaces by making abstract effort result in concrete, visible results." This challenges the validity Gee (2007) lends games as a space for learning and the actual place of work within gaming. As Paul further points out, more generally, the discourses of meritocracy have long maintained paths to salvation that are built upon the necessity of inequality. Although gamers earn their credibility through various social methods, the work that they do within games is always directed as challenges are made evident.

Guiding Gamers Through Difficulty

The study of difficulty within video games has largely focused on the experience of gameplay and the basis of engagement with the medium. Video games, according to Espen Aarseth (1999), are an ergodic medium, composed of texts that require effort to move through them. This resistance is where many locate the pleasure of gameplay. As Costikyan (2002) notes, difficulty in games acts as a means of keeping the audience engaged. Further, Naomi Clark (2014) writes, "Overcoming difficulty is deeply appealing to us as human beings for good reason: it can give us confidence in our own ability to learn and even master difficult aspects of our lives" (118). Through the coding of difficulty and creation of challenge, games create spaces where work is a necessity to alter behavior and overcome challenge.

Game studies enforces understandings of difficulty and challenge that are tied to the learning of the game system and game world. The ideal player is constructed through the rules and situations presented to them by the game world with a core loop of failure, punishment, and the alteration of player action providing players an avenue for progression in the game. As Juul (2013) writes, "Though we may dislike failure as such, failure is an integral element of the overall experience of playing a game, a motivator, something that helps us reconsider our strategies and see the strategic depth in a game, a clear proof that we have improved when we finally overcome it" (9). Thus, it is through failure that the play of the game is determined and valued, while the player is constructed through this process.

Further, game worlds provide players with a variety of means for how they should engage in order to progress. Kristine Jørgensen (2013), in expanding our understanding of interfaces by looking at various gameworlds, writes, "Gameworlds use processes and behaviors with which we are familiar in other contexts as representative of game-system processes. This approach contextualizes the game mechanics and provides a framework for how to understand them" (144). By using the gameworld as an interface, players are directed along with their behavior for the purposes of overcoming resistance, their performances melding with the needs of the system.

The building of resistance within a gameworld is how difficulty is crafted and communicated to the player. Games will often employ a variety of strategies, like hints and tutorials, in order to guide the player through. These strategies, described by Carl Therrien (2011) as slowly developing as games left the arcades and entered the home, aid the player in giving implicit and explicit directions to the player. Although this may be the norm for games, Christopher A. Paul (2011) has described the inaccessibility of *EVE: Online*, which obscures the basic rules and actions players must know in order to succeed by presenting them with a deluge of information upon beginning. Only through hard work and the investment of time can these kinds of systems be understood.

The difficulty and challenges of games have also often been used to discuss the relationships between games and social relationships. Roger Caillois (2001), in discussing the social work of merit and chance, links the rise of games of skill, *agôn*, with the emphasis on equalitarianism in Western societies. Where Caillois (2001) reads games as the social means many cultures used to eliminate the divine will of chance and emphasize meritocratic ideals, some recent authors have looked to games as allegories for forces of privilege and oppression in the real world. John Scalzi (2012) discusses the easy difficulty in video games as a means to explain the privilege of straight, white men by picking apart generic video game mechanics of skill points, abilities, and leveling up. Building off of this, Samantha Allen (2013) writes on how to explain the complex interrelations that are a part of understanding intersectional oppression through *Halo*'s Skulls mechanic. She writes, "Each sort of marginalized social identity comes with its own set of 'skulls' that can interlock and produce a complicated and unpredictable effects." Establishing and furthering the links between difficulty and social relationships are necessary as games become more dominant parts of our media ecology.

Situating the Gamer

The focus of this chapter is not on masculinity *per se*, but it is important that we situate where the gamer masculinity I am building on interacts with theories of masculinities in general. Masculinities shift and are translated along geographic and temporal lines (Reeser 2010). While the gamer masculinity is something that emerges from contemporary Western spaces, its intersections with other masculinities flow through the valuation of work and effort.

The place of hard work and effort in the performance of gender has long been a central theme for the creation of hegemonic masculinity (Connell 1990). Men's worth has been tied to the work that they perform and the power that it possibly affords them. Successes that derive from men's work are often attributed to strong work ethics or the overcoming of adversity (Harris 1995). Even as this work and its effects have been largely used to establish male power and dominance over women, the success of some men also creates hierarchies of how different work is valued (Tolson 2004). These cultural undercurrents had kept masculinity in a certain stability, at least into the last decade of the twentieth century.

However, the place of work in the Western world changed as industrial jobs became replaced with more precarious service-based work. As Susan Faludi (2000) writes, "The shipyard represented a particular vintage of American masculinity, monumental in its pooled effort, indefatigable in its industry, and built on a sense of useful productivity, or work tied to service" (p. 55). The tying of masculinity to a strong work ethic, one that generally derived from industrial imaginings of labor, sustains the drive for work to be a central part of masculine identities. This sentiment is echoed by Catano (2001), who emphasizes the connection of work with self-reliance in the portrayal of steel workers. With the fracturing of masculinity that coincided with the emergence of a globalized, postindustrial economy, the crisis of masculinity is snugly tied to the decrease in stable opportunities for work.

Even though the existence and extent of contemporary crises of masculinity have been questioned (Hanke 1998), we must still note that the shifts in the last several decades have been important. Michael Kimmell (2008) situates the crisis of masculinity in the liminal space between boyhood and adulthood, emphasizing the importance of media on crafting new hegemonic masculinities. In this world old ideas of effort and work are somewhat shirked and spread off into different areas of a man's life. Kimmell explains away video games as time-wasters that hold men back, but the satisfaction of effort within these realms cannot be denied.

Gender Offense Punishments

Within the study of games, difficulty and effort have been positioned as objects of game design. In describing how game difficulty functions as a result of various punishments, Juul (2009a) outlines four kinds: energy, life, setback, and game termination punishments. These mechanisms work by punishing the player through the loss of their time, what he notes as being "the most fundamental currency of games" (p. 238). These punishments require the player to recomplete parts of the game and alter their behavior in order to continue playing.

The strategies outlined below are not direct expressions of challenges or difficulty within game worlds; instead, they are ways that this difficulty is represented to the player. Whereas the punishments Juul (2009a) outlines are manifested in the rules and mechanics of the game, gender offense punishments generally operate at a representational level, giving name and image to the challenge mechanics being communicated to the player. Whereas Juul's punishments emerge solely from the relationship between the player and the software, the punishments I outline draw upon masculine ideals of work and effort to create meaning.

While this chapter presents a theoretical extension of Juul's taxonomy of punishments in games to demonstrate the link between gender performance and difficulty, it is largely a work of interpretation and identification of consistent, but unrelated, examples. The theorization relies on various textual analyses, all read with the theoretical lenses of Juul's punishments as well as Butler's (1999) "stylized repetition of actions" while searching out the areas of games where masculinity, meritocracy, and challenge or difficulty cross paths.

It must be stated up front that the readings of these texts are inflected by my own perspective as a straight, white man who is a part of the intended audience for many of the games listed. Because this is an act of interpretative theory-building, the textual analyses are limited in their applicability to the different audiences who play games. Additionally, this study does not seek out possible means of challenging or subverting the design decisions and their effects. I hope that this can act as a jumping off point for further research of how the effects of difficulty, challenge, and skill interact and converge in the experience of video game play.

Menu Embarrassment

The difficulty menu is a powerful tool for the display of meritocracy and an expedient method for establishing the meaning of various levels of resistance a game offers. Menus establish a clear pecking order to gamers, providing them with a hierarchy of presumed or necessary skill. Many games use some variety of easy-normal-hard designations for difficulty levels, but it is also a common convention for games to use different words or phrases to convey these levels of difficulty. I will discuss a few examples to highlight the various masculinities that these signifiers relay.

One of the most famous examples of this kind of gender offense punishment can be seen in *Wolfenstein 3D* (id Software 1992), *Wolfenstein* (Raven Software 2009), and *Wolfenstein: The New Order* (MachineGames 2014). The four settings given to the player in these games at the outset are, from lowest to highest difficulty, "Can I play, Daddy?," "Don't hurt me," "Bring 'em on!," and "I am Death Incarnate!" These four difficulties are paired with a particular avatar image of B. J. Blazkowicz. The lowest difficulty settings, "Can I play, Daddy," portrays Blazkowicz wearing a baby's bonnet while sucking on a pacifier. This sort of infantilization of the player in difficulty selection screens is a common affair, with games like *Viewtiful Joe* (Capcom Production Studio 4 2004) and *Doom* (id Software 1993), both using infantile or childish descriptions as signifiers for their lower difficulty settings. By stratifying difficulty in these ways, and the necessary effort and skill for being successful, games stratify masculinities according to age, emphasizing the connection between skill and manhood.

Difficulty setting labels often mirror the subject matter of the game itself. For example, many military shooters use a scale that is comparable to that which is used by *Call of Duty* (Infinity Ward 2003): Greenhorn, Regular, Hardened, and Veteran. These classifications often question the skill or proficiency of the player at hand. Although these difficulty ranges may be accurate to the subject matter, they normalize and legitimize higher difficulties by connecting them to socioeconomic positions within a profession. Rhetorically, the difficulty settings employed by these games offer a simple way to establish the boundary for legitimate play and the level of social capital gained through the playing of a game. Playing *Halo 4* (343 Industries 2012) on its "Legendary" setting easily dispenses a player's bona fides in the game, legitimating their use of the gamer identity.

On the other side of the spectrum, many games describe higher difficulty settings through words and phrases that create senses of power or raw manliness. Additionally, *PO'ed* (Any Channel 1996), a first-person shooter for the first PlayStation, alluded to Bruce Feirstein's (1982) *Real Men Don't Eat Quiche* with its highest difficulty setting being called "I don't Eat Quiche."

This kind of gender offense punishment occurs prior to gameplay in many cases, as a player is just beginning the game or franchise. Demeaning and mocking those who play on lower difficulties establishes the barrier for legitimate play. Players are directed to a particular style of engagement and openly mocked if desiring an easier or faster game type. These designations often call into question a players' willingness to commit to the game or their developmental abilities and progress. Additionally, a lack of skill within the game or a desire to learn the game from easier difficulty settings is portrayed as undesirable for the gamer being projected by these texts. Where the seeming objectivity of the game system dispenses life or setback punishments equally, these punishments are meted out to create a distinct hierarchy of play.

Character Attacks

Gender offense punishments also occur during the course of the playing of a video game. These often take the form of transforming player-characters themselves or giving the character items that directly impact the play of the game and the player's score or rating of particular levels or missions.

Punishing the player by transforming the character often occurs after the player has selected to play the game on a lower difficulty setting. For example, when the indie game *I Wanna Be the Guy* (O'Reilly 2007) is played on "Medium"—its lowest difficulty setting—the player character is given a bow in their hair, while save points, which are labeled "WUSS," also appear. Going along these lines, after failing a level multiple times of *'Splosion Man* (Twisted Pixel Games 2009), the player will have the option of skipping the level completely. Named "Way of the Coward", this option forces the player-character to wear a tutu for the entirety of the next level if this option is chosen.

In addition to games altering characters or the game world, demeaning items are often given to a player who fails several times in a row. As discussed above, after failing three times during a single mission, players of *Metal Gear Solid V: The Phantom Pain* (Kojima Productions 2015) are given the option of wearing a chicken mask that allows them to go unseen by a few enemies. However, the player is ultimately penalized for this through their mission score, which is directly tied to how much in-game currency is made for completion of a mission. In this way character attacks resemble the punishments outlined by Juul (2009a) more closely. They do not directly attack a player's time, but devalue the time and effort put forth.

Restricting Textual Completion

Lastly, many video games have employed the strategy of restricting certain levels or endings from players who choose to play games on lower difficulty settings. These sorts of punishments range from having different plotlines available to different difficulty levels to completely cutting off progression within the game when on lower difficulties. This practice enforces the view that gamers must earn the content that they have paid for.

One extreme example of this kind is in *Twisted Metal 2* (Sony Interactive Studios America 1996). When playing the campaign on the lowest setting, the game will show a large stop sign and display the following:

NO LOSERS ALLOWED BEYOND THIS POINT
YOU MUST SWITCH TO MEDIUM OR HARD TO CONTINUE.

This prevents the player from continuing on easy for the remaining three levels of play. Like this game, *Contra 4* (WayForward Technologies 2007) stops the player before the regular ending with a screen that reads, "You'll never see the ending on Easy!" These endings are surprising and harsh in order to correct the sinful practices of the player.

These sorts of strategies deny completion of the game, serving not only as gender offense punishments but also as Juul's (2009a) game termination punishments. Through these restrictions, the time invested by players becomes completely devalued. If searching for textual resolution, the player must atone for their choice of difficulty setting by starting the game over at a new difficulty and playing it in its entirety. Where legitimate gamer masculinity was challenged by lack of effort, the priest in the machine offers reconciliation with a Hail Mary and a few more hours of gameplay.

Crafting the Play Ethic

The examples of gender offense punishments that I discussed above are only a small sampling of how effort and difficulty are portrayed in games. They are the textual sites where difficulty becomes gendered, which act as intersections between the performance of gamer masculinity outside the game and that of the player within it. The learning that occurs within a gameworld, as well as the learning of gender roles, transpires through performance and response. This learning occurs over time, through the experience of multiple texts and their convergence with various social forces. In his discussion of how MMORPG guilds are built and played, Jeremy Aroles (2015) writes, "belonging to a virtual community is not given but consists in a performance that relies on a multitude of factors. Therefore, the notion of belonging is best expressed in terms of becoming rather than being" (p. 13). The player experiencing these is always becoming a part of the system while also becoming part of the gamer masculinity.

Performing at this intersection is how a particular *play ethic* is created by video games. This is the play ethic that spawns the idea that certain levels of investment are required to be considered a gamer. Like the boundaries that are created between masculinities when work ethic and merit are contested, the play ethic erects the borders between gamer and non-gamer. Through the textual strategies outlined, these borders are mirrored back to the gamer who accepts and performs them.

Because of their strong representation within the medium, the space of the video game has long been seen as one of freedom for men. Cassell and Jenkins (2000) discuss this intersection, writing:

> Boys can use games to escape into a fantasy world which allows them to prepare themselves for the requirements of adult masculinity. ... The cultural prescriptions for masculinity are harsh and exacting. Few boys can feel secure about achieving a sufficient degree of masculinity. The pressure is relentless—and these games provide a fun, painless opportunity for boost their sense of masculinity and let off some steam. (86–87)

I agree that the ease of identification with characters may provide men with a greater feeling of escapism in games; we must realize that deviations from the norms of gamer investment are met with different pressures. Their play is infantilized and emasculated as their space of leisure is questioned on the grounds of labor.

When we understand gender offense punishments as being tied to the labor of play, we can see that video games are an important space for the retaking of the masculine subject. Where hard work was often entailed through a man's profession, a postindustrial society creates a world that does not involve the same images of masculinity. Writing on these trends specifically in the United States, Susan Faludi (2000) demonstrates how this shift has infected the work of Hollywood, discussing Sylvester Stallone's desire to do his own stunts as a reinforcement of real work. The increasing reliance on immaterial labor has left hegemonic masculinity searching for new spaces where labor and effort would be apparent.

Video games offer a space where the increased mixture of leisure and work provides fertile ground for the rededication of Western masculinity to the subject of hard work and mastery. As the video game became more and more of a private function, moving from the arcade to the living room, the rubric for their legitimacy of gamers had to be resituated. No longer could the pecking order of masculinity be determined by watching over the shoulder of someone at a cabinet. Instead video games themselves ensured that skill and personal investment would continue to be emphasized as determinants of gamer credibility. This is not a new phenomenon, as Lori Kendall (2000) demonstrates by looking at masculinity in Multi-User Domains (MUDs). Kendall finds pliability with the word "nerd," but stresses that "[e]ven when used pejoratively to support structures of hegemonic masculinity, it can confer grudging respect for technical expertise" (p. 262). The hierarchies of legitimacy that emerge from gamer and nerd spaces use gender offense punishments to craft a play ethic, maintaining hegemonic boundaries to gamer credibility.

Conclusion: Valuing Different Masteries

In *Tomb Raider* (Crystal Dynamics 2014) I was a graceful soldier; my Lara Croft danced between enemies and was unwavering in the face of danger. She was out for vengeance and could not be stopped. While the avatar might often mutter her unwillingness to kill and desire to leave the island, the character I was molding was ruthless. She didn't have to learn the ways of the island because it was within her the entire time. This Lara Croft did not have to produce and grow to perform her place in the world. My avatar occasionally skulked across the island, but I had no reason to fear traversing this world. Instead of worrying about positioning or sneaking enemies, I could focus on the environment around me or create new metrics of success on the vicious island.

Mastery in the study and design of games is often seen as the result of investment and practice in a gameworld. It is the stuff of speedrunners and high score pursuers. It has spawned aphorisms like "a game should be easy to learn but difficult to master" and models like the flow channel (Clark 2014). Mastery is the absolute knowledge of a system and the muscle memory to defeat it at its best. These notions put the difficulty of the game and the effort of the player front and center in the study of games and the valuation of their kinds of engagement.

However, we must resist only studying mastery. Focusing on the configurative notion of difficulty that prevents boredom and promises progression restricts the possibilities of gameplay and game studies. Playing on easy affords players and researchers new avenues for studying and playing. However, it is only through further disruption of the gamer identity and its ties to the play ethic of games that these avenues can be valued and their own masteries understood.

Low difficulty modes could offer researchers a place to expand on the boundaries that video games offer for performance. Like Kücklich's (2007) suggestion of using cheat codes to investigate how different modes of play alter the game text, lower difficulties allow us to expand the limits of play within a game world and to focus on the performances and creativity of players. Further, by understanding play at lower difficulties as resisting normative gamer masculinity, we are able to understand this play as being valuable for creating alternate play styles and player outlooks.

This study shows that the performance of the masculine gamer is seen not only within who plays or for how long but in the intricacies of the games players engage with. As Eskelinen and Tronstad (2003) have noted, games act as systems that configure and direct the performances of players. While the authors restrict their conceptualization to the performance within the game space, it is necessary to expand these configurative practices outward from games themselves into the construction of particular masculinities. Expanding legitimacy to different performances of gameplay is one way to slowly alter the gamer identity.

Ultimately it will not solely be the work of game developers to cease using tired stereotypes in describing difficulty settings or mocking a player who cannot finish a level without mechanical aid. Instead, there needs to be an additional thrust within the gaming subculture that accepts and encourages the playing of games on lower difficulties. Respecting these play styles allow us to further our understanding of how different individuals can use games and how meaning is created in different ludic situations where overcoming challenge might take a backseat.

Even in places where mastery is not the end product of gameplay, further study of those playing on low difficulty modes allows for new understandings of how games fit into people's lives. Putting *Metal Gear Solid 3: Snake Eater* (Kojima Productions 2011) on its "Very Easy" mode guaranteed that my inability to master the forced perspective of the game would not regularly cause backtracking. Because of this, the game did not become a burden or chore to get used to and melded with my life. For a player who has little leisure time, lower difficulty levels allow for games to not be huge time investments, closing the gap in usage between typical "casual" and "hardcore" games. Furthering the humanistic study of games requires understanding the wide range of engagements that video games afford individuals. Whether games are played at their highest or lowest difficulty level provides different angles on their possibilities for creating meaning by the designer and the player alike.

Bibliography

343 Industries. 2012. *Halo 4*. Xbox 360. Microsoft Studios.

Aarseth, Espen. 1999. *Cybertext: Perspectives on Ergodic Literature*. Baltimore: The Johns Hopkins University Press.

Allen, Samantha. 2013. The Other Difficulty Mode: What Halo Can Tell Us About Identity & Oppression. *First Person Scholar*. http://www.firstpersonscholar.com/the-other-difficulty-mode/. Accessed 30 Oct 2016.

Any Channel. 1996. *PO'ed*. PlayStation. Accolade.

Aroles, Jeremy. 2015. Performance and Becoming: Rethinking Nativeness in Virtual Communities. *Games and Culture*. https://doi.org/10.1177/1555412015616714.

Butler, Judith. 1999. *Gender Trouble: Feminism and the Subversion of Identity*. New York: Routledge.

Caillois, Roger. 2001. *Man, Play and Games*. Urbana, IL: University of Illinois Press.

Capcom Production Studio 4. 2004. *Viewtiful Joe*. PlayStation 2. Capcom.

Carr, Diane. 2005. Contexts, Gaming Pleasures, and Gendered Preferences. *Simulation & Gaming* 36 (4): 464–482.

Cassell, Justine, and Henry Jenkins. 2000. *From Barbie to Mortal Kombat: Gender and Computer Games*. Cambridge: MIT Press.

Catano, James V. 2001. *Ragged Dicks: Masculinity, Steel, and the Rhetoric of the Self-Made Man*. Carbondale: Southern Illinois University Press.

Clark, Naomi. 2014. Resistance. In *A Game Design Vocabulary*, ed. Anna Anthropy and Naomi Clark, 117–154. Upper Saddle River, NJ: Addison-Wesley.

Connell, Raewyn. 1990. A Whole New World: Remaking Masculinity in the Context of the Environmental Movement. *Gender and Society* 4 (4): 452–478.

Consalvo, Mia. 2009. *Hardcore Casual: Game Culture Return(s) to Ravenhearst*. Paper Presented at the Annual Meeting of the Foundations of Digital Games, Orlando, FL.

Costikyan, Greg. 2002. I Have No Words & I Must Design: Toward a Critical Vocabulary for Games. In *Proceedings of Computer Games and Digital Cultures Conference*, ed. Frans Mäyrä, 9–33. Tampere, Finland: Tampere University Press.

Cote, Amanda C. 2015. Writing 'Gamers': The Gendered Construction of Gamer Identity in *Nintendo Power* (1994–1999). *Games and Culture*. https://doi.org/10.1177/1555412015624742.

Crystal Dynamics. 2014. *Tomb Raider*. PlayStation 4. Square Enix.

Eskelinen, Markku, and Ragnhild Tronstad. 2003. Video Games and Configurative Performances. In *The Video Game Theory Reader*, ed. Bernard Perron and Mark J.P. Wolf, 195–220. New York: Routledge.

Faludi, Susan. 2000. *Stiffed: The Betrayal of the American Man*. New York: Perennial.

Ferstein, Bruce. 1982. *Real Men Don't Eat Quiche*. New York: Pocket Books.

Gee, James Paul. 2007. *Good Video Games + Good Learning: Collected Essays on Video Games, Learning and Literacy*. New York: Peter Lang.

Hanke, Robert. 1998. Theorizing Masculinity With/In the Media. *Communication Theory* 8 (2): 183–201.

Harris, Ian M. 1995. *Messages Men Hear: Constructing Masculinities*. Bristol, PA: Taylor & Francis.

id Software. 1992. *Wolfenstein 3D*. PC. Apogee Software.

———. 1993. *Doom*. PC. GT Interactive.

Infinity Ward. 2003. *Call of Duty*. PC. Activision.

Jørgensen, Kristine. 2013. *Gameworld Interfaces*. Cambridge: MIT Press.

Juul, Jesper. 2009a. Fear of Failing? The Many Meanings of Difficulty in Video Games. In *The Video Game Theory Reader 2*, ed. Bernard Perron and Mark J.P. Wolf, 237–252. New York: Routledge.

———. 2009b. *A Casual Revolution: Reinventing Video Games and Their Players*. Cambridge: MIT Press.

———. 2013. *The Art of Failure: An Essay on the Pain of Playing Video Games*. Cambridge: MIT Press.

Kendall, Lori. 2000. 'Oh No! I'm a Nerd!': Hegemonic Masculinity on an Online Forum. *Gender and Society* 14 (2): 256–274.

Kerr, Aphra. 2006. *The Business and Culture of Digital Games: Gamework/Gameplay*. London: Sage Publications Ltd.

Kimmell, Michael. 2008. *Guyland: The Perilous World Where Boys Become Men*. New York: HarperCollins.

Kojima Productions. 2011. *Metal Gear Solid HD Collection*. Xbox 360. Konami.

———. 2015. *Metal Gear Solid V: The Phantom Pain*. PlayStation 4. Konami.

Kücklich, Julian. 2007. Homo Deludens: Cheating as a Methodological Tool in Digital Games Research. *Convergence* 13 (4): 355–367.

MachineGames. 2014. *Wolfenstein: The New Order*. PlayStation 4. Bethesda Softworks.

O'Reilly, Michael. 2007. *I Wanna Be the Guy*. PC.

Paul, Christopher A. 2011. *Don't Play Me: EVE Online, New Players and Rhetoric*. Paper Presented at the Annual Meeting of the Foundations of Digital Gaming, Bordeaux.

———. 2013. *Resisting Meritocracy and Reappropriating Games: Rhetorically Rethinking Game Design*. Paper presented at the annual meeting of the Association of Internet Researchers, Denver, CO.

Raven Software. 2009. *Wolfenstein*. Xbox 360. Activision.

Reeser, Todd W. 2010. *Masculinities in Theory: An Introduction*. Malden, MA: Wiley-Blackwell.

Rouner, Jef. 2014. 8 'Criticisms' of Anita Sarkeesian that Are Utter Bullshit. *Houston Press*. http://www.houstonpress.com/arts/8-criticisms-of-anita-sarkeesian-that-are-utter-bullshit-6382966. Accessed 26 Feb 2016.

Sarkeesian, Anita. 2013. Damsel in Distress (Part 1) Tropes vs Women. *Feminist Frequency*. http://feministfrequency.com/2013/03/07/damsel-in-distress-part-1/. Accessed 27 Feb 2016.

Scalzi, John. 2012. Straight White Male: The Lowest Difficulty Level There Is. *Kotaku*. http://kotaku.com/5910857/straight-white-male-the-lowest-difficulty-setting-there-is. Accessed 30 Oct 2016.

Shaw, Adrienne. 2013. On Not Becoming Gamers: Moving Beyond the Constructed Audience. *Ada: A Journal of Gender, New Media, and Technology* 2. https://doi.org/10.7264/N33N21B3.

Sony Interactive Studios America. 1996. *Twisted Metal 2*. PlayStation. Sony Computer Entertainment.

Therrien, Carl. 2011. *'To Get Help, Please Press X' The Rise of the Assistance Paradigm in Game Design*. Paper Presented at the Annual Meeting of the Digital Games Research Association, Utrecht.

Thornham, Helen. 2008. 'It's a Boy Thing' Gaming, Gender, and Geeks. *Feminist Media Studies* 8 (2): 127–142.

Tolson, Andrew. 2004. The Limits of Masculinity. In *Feminism and Masculinity*, ed. Peter F. Murphy, 69–79. New York: Oxford University Press.

Twisted Pixel Games. 2009. *'Splosion man*. Xbox 360. Microsoft Game Studios.

Vanderhoef, John. 2013. Casual Threats: The Feminization of Casual Video Games. *Ada: A Journal of Gender, New Media, and Technology* 2. https://doi.org/10.7264/N3V40S4D.

WayForward Technologies. 2007. *Contra 4*. Nintendo 3DS. Konami.

Yakuza Team. 2012. *Binary Domain*. Xbox 360. Sega.

10

Orchestrating Difference: Representing Gender in Video Game Music

Michael Austin

You may have seen them in retail stores or online: cotton swabs packaged and sold as multi-tools for men, ballpoint pens "for her," "brogurt," or "lady hammers" and other pink power tools. Unnecessarily gendered products have gotten a lot of online buzz lately as people raise awareness of inherently sexist marketing practices that reinforce gender hierarchies through packaging and advertising. And as more products become needlessly gendered, some retailers are fighting back. Big-box store Target has recently pledged to stop dividing its toy section by gender, arguing that hyper-feminized toys may overemphasize the roles conventionally associated with a specific gender (Hains 2015), an argument corroborated by many psychologists, such as Weisgram et al. (2014). Yet, products continue to be gendered in an effort to appeal to consumers. And this often applies to video games, most notably in the mid-1990s through the "pink games" movement (Cassell and Jenkins 1998) but continuing today with "casual" games designed around the (imagined) desires and constraints of the white, middle-class, cis-gendered female user (Chess 2017).

The representation of gender within video games has also been strikingly dichotomous, markedly slanting toward hetero-normative masculinity, that is, toward a performance of masculinity that is heterosexual/gynophilic and conforms to traditional, complementary gender roles and hegemonic power structures that favor men and expressions of overt male dominance. The performance of hegemonic masculinity sets itself up as being superior to all other

M. Austin (✉)
Howard University, Washington, DC, USA

N. Taylor, G. Voorhees (eds.), *Masculinities in Play*, Palgrave Games in Context,
https://doi.org/10.1007/978-3-319-90581-5_10

forms of masculinity and "require[s] all other men to position themselves in relation to it, and it ideological legitimate[s] the global subordination of women to men" (Connell and Messerschmidt 2005, 832). In games, this trend is most visible in the gender of the avatar that players can choose to represent themselves and the perception of the stereotypical ways in which these avatars react to the player's input. Historically, video games have not been especially diverse in terms of the gender representation of their constituent characters (Beasley and Standley 2002; Dietz 1998; Dill et al. 2005), and according to the "virtual census" of represented identity in games published in 2005, things have not gotten much better (Williams et al. 2009).

While most academic attention on representation of gender in video games focuses primarily on the misrepresentation of women, the representations of male video game characters are also often troublesome. Men are regularly depicted in video games as conventionally tall, dark, and handsome; they frequently cover their overly muscular bodies with torn clothes, giant guns, and bandoliers of bullets, and they stand in dominating, aggressive stances (Provenzo 1991, 100). According to games critic David Houghton (2010), they fit "the primal hunter/gatherer type [with] arm-cripplingly ripped biceps, necks too muscley to turn, emotion dials stuck on 'aggressive grimace' and a 50% lack of chest coverings" (2).[1] Furthermore, numerous video games involve performances of "militarized masculinity," or gameplay that is constructed around violence and combat in order to appeal to young male audiences (Kline et al. 2005, 247). The point of many games is to fulfill one's "manly duty" by saving the damsel in distress or avenging the death of a weaker (often female) friend or loved one. Video games can also afford young male players the opportunity to perform more extreme forms of masculinity than they would be able to in their everyday life (Jansz 2005, 231–232). Conversely, rather than evoking the virility, duties, and female trophies associated with idyllic manhood, some video games can be seen as opportunities for adult males to "return to their adolescence to play without the responsibility of adulthood" (Burrill 2008, 15), or to act as "everyday Peter Pans," embracing a form of playful masculinity that embraces consumerism, fantasy, and childhood (Voorhees 2014, 78–79).

While the representation of gender has been approached primarily as a visual phenomenon, might these politics of representation extend into aural domains? Music is a key component of video games, and it conveys information to players about a game's plot, setting, and mood. It often guides players in gameplay, warning them of impending dangers or rewarding them for jobs well done. Music often serves as a game's signature, rendering it immediately recognizable with just a few notes—for example, have you ever heard the first few seconds of Koji Kondo's calypso "Ground Theme," heard in level 1-1 of *Super Mario Bros.* (Nintendo 1985), without immediately thinking of the game or its mustachioed protagonist? In this chapter, I investigate the music in video games, examining the ways in which a game's score can contribute to—or undermine—the gendering of a game. I will begin by describing ways in which music more generally has been analyzed for its gendered meanings and ways it has been used historically as a gendering force. I will then go on to discuss music in popular titles in the fantasy game genre and will examine the extent to which it interposes a (sometimes seemingly unintentional) gendered aesthetic, especially through the use of orchestration (or instrumentation).

Music and Gender

Although there is much disagreement about exactly *how* music communicates meaning, music is generally understood to be a vessel that carries social and cultural mores and values. And some of these values are regularly bound up with notions and expectations regarding gender. Music has been described as "a dynamic mode of gender and sexual signification" (Taylor 2012, 603), "an essentially gendered discourse" that is meaningful only within a context of gender, race, and ethnicity (which unfortunately is often essentialized) (Treitler 2011), and is "always already fraught with gender-related anxieties" (McClary 1991, 17). In this section, I argue that orchestration and other musical elements are especially laden with gendered meanings that fuel these anxieties, and they play into and perpetuate stereotypes about gender that persist to this day.

Orchestration, or the instruments used in a musical work, helps to provide a game with the cinematic quality players have come to expect in recent years, and is an essential musical tool for video game composers. As video game music has blossomed from the 8-bit bleeps and bloops of early cabinet and console games to the fully orchestrated scores of contemporary titles, the cultural associations attached to various musical instruments are also attached video games by way of their score. Kevin Dawe (2005) points out that musical instruments "are richly symbolic of our potential to externalize physically and social our needs, aspirations, allegiances and creative energies" (59). Musical instruments also carry with them issues of gender and the power dynamics associated with gender differences, including male exclusivity and gendered division of labor, namely, the notion that certain instruments should only be played by men. Musical instruments are used to demarcate gendered space;

for example, there was a long-held belief that women should not be allowed to perform in church or other public spaces. Further, musical instruments can often be used to represent male control over technology, demonstrated when women are denied access to particular instruments or are perceived as incapable of acquiring the manual dexterity to play an instrument proficiently (Doubleday 2008).

The gendered ideology connected to various instruments has a long history, sometimes traceable back to the beginning of recorded music history. The ancient Greeks associated stringed instruments and their music with Apollo, civility, and manhood, while wind instruments were associated with Dionysian excess, sex, emotion, chaos, and women. The use of horns as hunting *accouterment*, and the use of the trumpet and percussion for military purposes, cultivated reputations for these instruments as male artifacts, especially since males traditionally performed these activities and women were banned from serving in military careers. Women were also prohibited from taking part in the exclusively male guild system of Renaissance Europe, so they had no opportunity to "learn the special *clarino* technique—and partake in the high privileges and salaries of the royal trumpeteers" (Steblin 1995, 131). Women were also discouraged from joining brass bands until the 1930s (Herbert 1991, 65–66). And above all else, women were expected to preserve their feminine allure by only playing "appropriate" instruments. Gustave Kerker (1904), a prominent Broadway musical director, wrote:

> Nature never intended the fair sex to become cornetists, trombonists, and players of wind instruments. In the first place they are not strong enough to play them as well as men; they lack the lip and lung power to hold notes, which deficiency makes them always play out of tune … Another point against them is that women cannot possibly play brass instruments and look pretty, and why should they spoil their good looks?. (217–218)

As with the trumpet, women were also discouraged from playing other large instruments, mostly because straddling a cello or carrying a sousaphone was considered unladylike or too physically demanding. Instead, women were directed toward the "clavier," lute, zither, and harp because they all have "soft, delicate plucked stringed sounds and serve moreover primarily as accompaniment instruments. Thus they reinforced the prevailing notions of the female sex as 'weak' and 'secondary' … The strong soloistic instruments, such as the violin, oboe, or trumpet were reserved for males only" (Steblin 1995, 139).

This prejudicial attitude continues today. In February 2017, London's Royal Albert Hall commissioned a survey in preparation for a concert performance by female trumpeter Alison Balsom, one of the top concert trumpet players in the world. Their study found that only 2% of the 2000 adults surveyed considered the trumpet a "woman's instrument," while 3% would associate the violin with men (Burin 2017). Similarly, according to a 2001 study from the University of Washington, children as young as five years old have already been acculturated to believe that saxophones and drums are appropriate for boys and that flutes and oboes were girls' instruments (Pickering and Repacholi 2001).

The ability to mass-produce pianos for the home led to a sharp rise in the popularity of piano music in the nineteenth century, particularly among women. Combined with the rise of the Victorian "cult of domesticity" and the fact that men alone (with rare exception) held positions as professional musicians, piano playing became a hallmark of cultured home life, and women were taught in finishing schools how to manage the home and to leisurely pursue cultural activities such as painting, singing, and playing the piano, especially since amateur music-making in the home was stigmatized as a predominantly female activity. Richard Leppert (1993) recounts that the piano "was the ubiquitous and unrivaled instrument of the bourgeois home" and that it "located itself almost exclusively among amateurs as a female instrument" (134). Further, he states that the piano "reflected and produced associations, both sonoric and visual, between pleasure, sexual desire, hatred, murder, and women" (150).

The harp is similarly situated and feminized; according to Curt Sachs (1940), the harp was "particularly assigned to the feminine province of musical expression, where its ornamental shape was an added attraction. It has been a lady's instrument since the days of Marie Antoinette, both at home and in the orchestra, and composers have stressed its aptitude for tenderness and mystery" (401). Despite the fact that harps are large and heavy, they still retained their feminine associations, and the "unladylike" necessity to straddle the harp in order to play it is overlooked.

If musical instruments can be gendered, can the music played on these instruments also convey gendered ideology? In her groundbreaking book, *Feminine Endings*, Susan McClary (1991) questions the ways in which gender is represented within music itself, the way gendered language is used to discuss music, and how gendered discourse influences the analysis and reception of music and musicians. McClary first discusses the "musical constructions of gender and sexuality," citing the *stile rappresentativo* (or "representative style") of the seventeenth century, particularly in the operatic work of Claudio Monteverdi, in which music represents the interplay of sexuality/pleasure and fulfillment of these desires. She writes that "music is ... very often concerned with the arousing and channeling of desire, with mapping patterns through the medium of sound that resemble those of sexuality" (8). Second, she problematizes the "gendered aspects of traditional music theory," especially the use of terms such as "masculine" and "feminine" to describe strong/weak and dominant/subservient musical themes and cadences. She makes the disclaimer that she is "not undertaking a Freudian search for unintentional phalluses," but argues that she instead is "relying on the common semiotic codes of European classical music: the gestures that stereotypically signify 'masculine' or 'feminine,' placidity or violence, the military or the domestic realm, and also the standard narrative schemata that underlie most nineteenth-century instrumental movements" (68). Her third question centers around "gender and sexuality in musical narrative" (12). Here, she describes the proclivity of some analysts to ascribe masculine or feminine qualities to narrative tropes to such a point that main themes are male protagonists and subordinate themes are the tractable female obstacles that are overcome as the themes return to the home key at the close of the piece. As a result of the inevitable masculine victory in this "struggle," there can be no such thing as a "feminine ending." Her fourth method takes issue with "music as a gendered discourse"; for instance, McClary argues that music is seen as a more feminine activity by those who define music "as the most ideal (that is, the least physical) of the arts; by insisting emphatically on its 'rational' dimensions; by laying claim to such presumably masculine virtues as objectivity, universality, and transcendence; by prohibiting actual female participation altogether" (17). Last, McClary discusses the "discursive strategies of women musicians," and calls women composers, performers, and scholars to question traditional forms of patriarchy within the musical professions.

McClary's arguments about the gendering of musical discourse find evidence in the writings of several other musicologists and theorists. Charles Ford (1991) argues that the dominant modulation (or temporarily shifting the tonality within a piece of music to a closely related key) is masculine because it is "associated with greater energy because it requires a sharpening of the fourth scale-step, a striving upwards to affirm the fifth as a new tonal center in its own right" (52). He also argues that metric dynamism is also masculine, whereas "decorative stasis" connotes femininity, writing:

> Mozart's feminine music, with its fluid a-periodicity, and decorative prolongation of single pitches and arpeggios, reflects this lack of persona in that it is more akin to that which he wrote for ensembles, rather than that for individual males. Feminine music is a distinct sub-style, formed to express an historical, male representation of feminine sensibilities, as static, decorative and anonymous moments of the natural tonality, which are wholly exhausted, or insistent, in their function as the incarnation of male desire. (138)

According to Ford, masculine music is teleological and makes progress toward a goal; feminine music sits in its place and plays a subservient accompanying role to the masculine main themes as an embellishment to the melody.

Discussions about the expression of emotion through music are also gendered. Catherine Clement (1999) argues that men in operas who express pain or show other signs of emotional weakness are somehow subjected to the same fate as tragic heroines, thus gendering them feminine to their contemporary critics. According to Richard Leppert (1993), "connections between music, woman, and sexuality, inevitably masked by the conditions of Victorian domesticity, were acted out explicitly on the contemporaneous operatic stage and were likewise hinted at in music journalism, where references to passionate emotion abound" (186). Frederick Chopin's music was criticized for being effeminate because of its emotional quality; according to James Huneker (1900), "the poetic side of men of genius is feminine, and in Chopin the feminine note was over emphasized—at times it was almost hysterical—particularly in these nocturnes" (142). Similarly, Fred Maus (1993) lamented the fact that music theorists often eschewed expressions of emotion in their rhetoric and analyses for fear of coming across as feminine.

Music for Dudes

Appealing both to emotions and gendered ideals, companies can often capitalize on the ways in which young men consume music by playing up gendered stereotypes within music used in advertising, and in the case of video games, within the product itself. Masculine music plays an important role in the marketing of male-targeted content. This is especially evident in music written for televised sports. Ken McLeod (2011) discusses the masculine nature of television sports themes, and the way they are coded as aggressive and heroic, writing:

> ABC's Wide World of Sports ... was introduced by a brassy musical fanfare, composed by Charles Fox, over a montage of sports clips and with a dramatic accompanying voice of by [host Jim] McKay ... Fox's theme was a stirring orchestral arrangement that, in addition to the unison brass chord opening fanfare, featured aggressive military snare drum beats and harsh downbeat dissonances that sonically painted and highlighted the classic phrase 'the agony of defeat' ... The overwhelming aesthetic embodied by the music is one of masculine tension and struggle culminating in heroic martial victory. (217–218)

McLeod goes on to argue that the masculine image projected in a television soundtrack is especially important for American football, since it reinforces and reflects the sport's strong cultural preoccupation with masculinity. To capitalize on this obsession, composers and programmers "have seemingly sought to reproduce the aurally tough, combative and macho image of the game … such an image is actively in keeping with the league's marketing image" (218).

Just as particular types of music can be used to appeal to a certain gender and play to gendered ideals, preference for a particular musical genre can vary by gender, and the use of a particular genre in media—such as video games—can help to reach a particular gender at market, or more importantly, play a role in gendering the media, relying on and reinforcing stereotypes. According to some (positivist) studies, males prefer louder music (Staum and Brotons 2000) with an exaggerated beat (McCown et al. 1997), while females prefer softer, dance-type music, which emphasizes emotions and romance, such as pop or R&B (Christenson and Peterson 1988; Maidlow and Bruce 1999). In her book, *A Composer's Guide to Game Music*, Winifred Phillips (2014) discusses at length the relationship between a video game's genre and the music genre conventionally associated with it. For instance, percussion, drums, rock music, and "the epic drama of the 'Elite' orchestra" are associated with shooters, life simulations require musical variety "with an emphasis on a friendly, positive energy," and stealth games employ "moody orchestral and synth combinations" (85–95). Since various music genres appeal to males and females unequally, with hard rock, rap, classic rock, and metal music more often associated with males (especially in fighting and sports games) and pop, dance, and adult contemporary more closely associated with females (as in puzzle games and other more casual genres), various game experiences could be gendered by the genre of music used within them.

Gendered Music in Fantasy Games

As alluded to above, there is a close connection between video game genre and music genre, and precedent set by older games and industry conventions can lead players to expect a particular genre of music within a particular game genre. For example, fantasy games often employ music in the style of sacred and secular Medieval or Renaissance music to invoke the aesthetics of feudal Europe. Examples of this convention can be heard in the Gregorian chant in the opening sequence of music for games in the *Halo* series (Microsoft 2001–2017), the lute and krumhorn used in the score for *Final Fantasy: Crystal Chronicles* (The Game Designers Studio 2004), and the prominence of chant in the first game of the *Assassin's Creed* series (Ubisoft 2007–2016). The instruments used in this particular style of music also evoke customary associations with gender. As with other "feminine" instruments mentioned earlier, Sanna Iitti (2006) writes that certain timbres, "such as those of the harp, lyre and guitar typically produce, tend to relate to things that have always been associated with femininity: weakness, lyricism, fragility, gentleness" (36). When the music in a fantasy game is not explicitly neo-Medieval or neo-Renaissance in style, a game's composer usually resorts to standard orchestral music, relying on a conventionally cinematic score to support the game's narrative and help to immerse the player within the gameworld.

In the remaining pages of this chapter, I will examine several fantasy games as case studies to demonstrate the various ways in which the music used in these games works to gender the game and its constituent elements. This is most often accomplished through the instrumentation used within a game's score, but it can also be achieved through a game character's singing style, or even simply through the genre or style of music used to represent a particular character.

Final Fantasy IV (1994)

In *Final Fantasy VI* (Square Co., Ltd. 1994), the differences in music used to represent male and female characters are quite striking, and the music plays to gendered musical stereotypes in both the genres/styles and orchestration that are used by composer Nobuo Uematsu. Locke Cole is one of the primary male protagonists in *Final Fantasy VI*. This playable character is a treasure hunter, and he fulfills several masculine stereotypes within the game, especial as protector of women and avenger of wrongdoings. His leitmotif, or reoccurring theme, is particularly epic, and includes fanfares and flourishes played by a robust MIDI orchestra, accompanied by militaristic snare drums. This music is heard during Locke's heroic mission to protect Terra Branford (who is simply known as "Girl" in the game's dialog sequences). The leitmotifs and themes that represent other men also exhibit this heroic quality. Prince Edgar Figaro and his brother Prince Sabin, who share a leitmotif, are represented by a royal brass fanfare with timpani and cymbal crashes. Their theme can be heard anytime the player enters Figaro Castle. Likewise for Setzer Gabbiani, a male gambler who owns the "Blackjack," an airship; he too is represented by a heroic orchestral fanfare, replete with a soaring trumpet melody and accompanied by running descending eighth notes, timpani, and snare drum. This music can be heard as the background music for the airship cabins.

Terra Branford (also known as Tina in the Japanese version of the game) is a playable female character in *Final Fantasy VI*. Her storyline is central to the game, as evidenced in her appearance in the game's logo and much of its other artwork. Thus, her leitmotif can be heard during the game's opening credits, ending theme, in the overworld map in the World of Balance, and in several of the game's other cues, such as "Searching for Friends," "Metamorphosis," and "Save Them!" In almost every instance, "Terra's Theme," usually a ballad of sorts, is played on "feminine" instruments such as flutes/ocarinas, oboe, strings, and so on. However, due to her role as one of the primary protagonists of the game, her theme is recontextualized in more masculine situations, such as when she is battling espers (or magical beast) at the sealed gate, when it can be heard being played by loud brass instruments in dissonant chords.

Celes Chere is also a playable female character in *Final Fantasy VI*. She is a Magitek knight and Locke Cole's love interest. Despite being one of the Empire's top generals, her theme is gendered as overtly feminine, and appears in moments of extreme femininity or personal tragedy.[2] We first hear "Celes Theme" when she sings the "Aria di Mezzo Carattere" ("Aria of Half Character") while impersonating Maria, an opera singer, during the in-game production of the opera *Draco and Maria* (also known as *The Dream Oath*).[3] Much like the other iterations of this theme, the aria is scored for arpeggiated harp accompaniment, with a thicker orchestral texture to enter at the second stanza. Later in the game when Celes awakes from a coma on Solitary Island, she tries to repay Cid, her grandfather, for taking such good care of her with food. If she catches a poor-quality fish to feed him, Cid dies of food poisoning, and Celes attempts suicide. As she walks to the edge of the cliff from which she is to throw herself, "Celes Theme" can be heard, with long sustained string chords, harp arpeggios, and the melody played in a high register by a celeste. In 1994, a live version of "Aria di Mezzo Carattere" was released on the album "Final Fantasy VI: Grand Finale" (Uematsu 1994), sung by Italian soprano Svetla Krasteva. Even in this version, the theme is an especially feminized aria about a woman longing for her hero, performed by Krasteva in the *bel canto* style with string and arpeggiated harpsichord accompaniment.

Dragon Age: Origins (2009)

In the score for *Dragon Age: Origins* (BioWare 2009), composed by Inon Zur, the distinction between "male music" and "female music" is clearly marked. Zur often uses drums and low brass to accentuate the game's dark and epic aesthetic. The game's main theme begins with a timpani roll and horn solo over sustained strings, immediately establishing the epic tone of the game through music. The horn continues as a countermelody beneath a short vocal fragment (sung by female vocalist Aubrey Ashburn in a language invented for the game), but the horn continues as an aggressive wall of brass sound and war drums soon overtakes the voice in a display of heroic, masculine power.

During gameplay, when the player joins the Grey Wardens in a ceremonial drinking of darkspawn blood, the cinematic music heard at this point of the game undulates below the action, rising to accentuate plot points and moments of suspense. While two other candidates for the order fail to prove themselves worthy (and die as a result of their unworthiness), the player drinks from the chalice and successfully proves his worth. As he does, militaristic snare drums, orchestral strings, and choir—signifying bravery, heroism, and male competence—grow louder and louder, fading out as the player experiences the hallucinogenic effects of his drink. The "Grey Wardens Song," heard on the official soundtrack, is especially militaristic, highlighting the status of these characters as warriors and guardians, and further emphasizes the player's duty to perform "masculine" duties as a newly conscripted Grey Warden. The orchestration of this piece includes uilleann pipes (or smaller Irish bagpipes more suitable for playing indoors than their larger Scottish counterpart), hammer dulcimer, orchestra with dominant brass (especially trombones), marching band percussion, and a choir part scored to the extreme ends of the singers' vocal range (i.e. the male choristers sing very low, and the female chorus members sing very high). When the choir is first heard, it is a very low, raspy male chorus singing in the game's invented language. The entire choir soon enters, interjecting with the Grey Wardens' creed, "In peace, vigilance; in war, victory; in death, sacrifice." Likewise, the musical cues representing other men in the game, such as "The Dwarven Nobles" and "King Endrin," also feature orchestral music with heavy low brass, prominent horn section, and militaristic drumming.

Other music within *Dragon Age: Origins* is coded feminine, especially music intended to represent women or accompany their actions. For example, "Morrigan's Love Song" is gendered feminine, sung in a mezzo-soprano register by Morrigan, over arpeggiated guitar chords, celtic flutes, and airy synth pads. The song is also styled as a classical crossover/operatic pop song, reminiscent of the oeuvre of Irish ensemble Celtic Woman, Welsh singer Charlotte Church, or American lyric baritone Josh Groban, and processed with lots of reverb. The first-time players hear the award-winning "I Am the One," written by Inon Zur and Aubrey Ashburn, and performed by Ashburn herself; it is played over the final credits of the game. This version of the song, like

"Morrigan's Love Song," is a Celtic/classical cross-over song, sung in a woman's register, with lush string and arpeggiated guitar accompaniment, and ample reverb. In *Dragon Age: Inquisition* (BioWare 2014) (the sequel to *Dragon Age: Origins*), the song is performed in a tavern by the minstrel Maryden Halewell (a non-playable character) in Haven Tavern.[4] Here, too, the song is performed with florid, arpeggiated guitar accompaniment, and the audio is processed with much more reverb than the tavern would naturally produce in the real physical world. In fact, all tavern songs performed by Maryden Halewell are stylized as feminine.

The Elder Scrolls V: Skyrim (2011)

The epic music that Jeremy Soule composed for *The Elder Scrolls V: Skyrim* (Bethesda Game Studios 2011) spans a wide range of orchestral timbres, genres, and dynamics. Some portions of this music are overtly masculine. For example, the game's main theme, "Dragonborn," was recorded using a choir of more than 30 men and boys shouting and singing in "Draconic," a pseudo-Scandinavian language invented for the game. It is especially bombastic, and is thus further gendered masculine in its use of full orchestra that largely features brass instruments. Conversely, much of the overworld music is romantic, almost Wagnerian, in nature, and is heard when the player explores the world of Skyrim. The music is adaptive, and changes depending upon where the player is in the game world. As the player leaves a city, pastoral music, played on soft orchestral strings and harps, accompanies them on their journey. With its undulating string pads, muted choirs, subtle harmonic progressions, and evocative melodies, the overworld music is rather neutral in its depiction of gender, and instead, it more accurately represents the atmosphere, landscape, and topography of the areas of the gameworld in which it is heard. As a player gets nearer to danger, the music changes drastically, and war drums and brass instruments alert the player to prepare for combat. Here the music becomes much more assertive, brash, and thus, more masculine, when the hero is called upon to fulfill his duty and fight.

Furthermore, bards can be found throughout Skyrim, usually performing in taverns on their lyre-lutes, flutes, and drums, and singing epic ballads (in the traditional sense). Since all bards seem to play all instruments equally, there is nothing particularly gendering about the instruments on which they perform in the game (even though the lyre-lute would historically be gendered feminine in the real world). Within the game, there are also quests that involve collecting these bardic instruments. After the player becomes a full member of the Bards College, they will be sent on various quests by the college's faculty. Pantea Ateia, the Imperial Master Vocalist at the Bards College, will ask the player to complete an in-game quest to retrieve her stolen flute. Likewise, Inge Six Fingers, the lyre-lute instructor at Bards College, will send the player on a quest to retrieve Finn's Lute for her. Giraud Gemane, Breton Dean of History at the Bards College, will ask the player to retrieve Rjorn's Drum and return it to him in exchange for increased battle skill and armor. As you can see, the gender of the faculty member that requests a particular instrument conforms to expectations regarding the gendering of instruments for performance purposes; that is, a man requests the traditionally "male" instrument (Giraud Gemane requests the drum), and the women (Pantea Ateia and Inge Six Fingers) request traditionally "female" instruments (flute and lyre-lute, respectively).

Why Aural Representation Matters

Just as visual representations of gender in video games are important signifiers of cultural attitudes about gender and encode acceptable forms of gender performance, the aural representation of gender in video games is equally significant. When composers of video game music rely on gendered tropes, stereotypes, and clichés in their scores—either of their own volition, unconsciously, or acquiescing to pressure from executives from a game's creative department or market research team—they, at best, create hackneyed music that derives much of its meaning from—and contributes to—centuries of sexism, misogyny, patriarchy, and hegemonic heteronormativity. This can often undermine even the best intentions of representing and interpreting female characters in gender non-conforming ways. Consider *Tomb Raider* (Core Design et al. 1996) and its title character, English archaeologist Lara Croft. Croft's physical appearance has been the subject of much academic scrutiny due to the fact that she was rendered with an unnaturally small waist and disproportionally large breasts, making her an object for the male gaze to sexualize and fetishize. Sheri Graner Ray (2004) describes her as "a hypersexualized female caricature that is, essentially, 'eye candy' for male players" (33). But despite her exaggerated female features, some critical reception of Croft situates her in a masculine or gender queer role. She has been described as an action heroine, femme fatal, and even a vehicle for potentially transgendering experiences (Kennedy 2002). But perhaps most importantly, Lara Croft served as an aspirational figure—one of the first playable female protagonists in an action-adventure game—that young female players of

Tomb Raider could admire for performing and negotiating her femininity (for better or worse) in a powerful way.

Aurally, this was not the case. Unlike some of the fantasy games described above that use individual leitmotifs to represent each character, there is no "Lara's Theme" in *Tomb Raider*; however, the cinematic music used throughout the game, although purposefully suspenseful and mysterious, is also stereotypically "feminine," especially in instrumentation/orchestration. The opening theme music for the game is first heard on the game's menu screen and begins with a simple, unaccompanied oboe solo, high in the instrument's range. This melody rarely strays from its small, 3-note *tessitura*, even when it is later played by a solo violin, and sung by artificial male and female voices. This melody is accompanied at first by sustained string pads that are soon replaced by harp arpeggios. The cue, "Longing for Home" is orchestrated using vibraphone arpeggios over sustained string notes. The melody of this cue is played first by oboe and flute, and later by strings. "A Friend Since Gone" is similarly orchestrated, with oboe and clarinet playing the main melody over mostly sustained strings and guitar arpeggios. Even the action music in *Tomb Raider* is gendered feminine, rarely using brass as a melodic timbre, and relying heavily on lyrical, melodic music rather than heroic fanfares or epic orchestral cues. The cue called "Let's Run" is very string-heavy, utilizing quick pizzicato (or plucked) and short bowed string figures. It is accentuated with occasional short, syncopated brass interjections. When writing the music that is heard when Lara battles the T-Rex in the Lost Valley, composer Nathan McCree eschews brass altogether, opting to use only frantic string and marimba motives, and cymbals (to accentuate important beats). So, although the visual representation of Lara Croft is open to interpretations that highlight her strength and bravery, the music in the game characterizes her as demure and fragile.

Conversely, affirmative representations of gender via music in video games can also have a positive influence on game players, helping to buck arbitrary, negative, or harmful gender stereotypes. They can also provide players with a safe place for player to explore (and subvert) performances of gender norms and expectations. For example, in a research study on male all-state flutists in Texas, one student interviewed for the study cited the fact that Link from *The Legend of Zelda: Ocarina of Time* (Nintendo EAD 1998) played the ocarina as the reason he decided to play a traditionally female instrument (Taylor 2009). I also often wonder if the driving, militaristic percussion and fanfare melody in the score of *Metroid* (Nintendo R&D1 et al. 1986) helped lead many of us to believe that Samus Aran was male rather than female, surreptitiously demonstrating that heroic music can represent female characters just as well as it denotes male protagonists.

Not only does this chapter represent a first step in discussing whether or not video game music is gendered; it also lays some necessary groundwork for other investigations into *how* music can be used to represent the gender identity of characters within a game, to gender game mechanics and the actions of a player, and to gender entire video games and franchises more generally. Although I only discuss a few of the ways orchestration contributes to, undermines, or complicates the visual representations of gender within a video game in this chapter, I strongly believe that other elements of music, such as genre, themes/leitmotifs, texture and ensemble size, volume/amplitude, harmony, form/structure, could shape or subvert our understanding of gender in video games in similar ways. And because of the myriad ways gender and music can be intertwined, video game composers have a unique responsibility—and opportunity—to critically evaluate their use of gendered tropes and techniques whenever possible and to reimagine the ways they use music to represent gender within a game. As I mentioned earlier, Susan McClary (1991) argued that Western classical music relies on common semiotic codes to signify masculinity and femininity. She warns "these codes change over time" since "the meaning of femininity was not the same in the eighteenth century as in the late nineteenth, and musical characterizations differ accordingly" (8). She is not bothered by the fact that classical music evokes a certain eroticism, or that it articulates male sexuality. She is, however, concerned that "the erotic continues so often to be framed as a manifestation of feminine evil while masculine high culture is regarded as transcendent"; she draws troubling implications to this when she notes that "the pervasive cultural anxiety over women as obstacles to transcendence justifies over and over again narratives of the victimized male and the necessary purging or containment of the female" (68). Furthermore, she laments that these codes "are informed by the prevalent attitudes of their time," but persist for long periods of time because they are "strikingly resilient" (8). So, although we as listeners may not be consciously aware that particular instruments are used to represent masculinity in a video game's score—and perhaps even the music's composer is unaware of these associations—the cultural baggage that comes with these connections lives on, long after their original usage, and we carry that baggage into all of our listening experiences, including our video game playing. Careful attention and continued scrutiny of the musical representation of gender within video games can go a long way toward changing unnecessarily gendered perceptions and achieving parity in the status of women within this media, and can help to foster healthier representations of masculinity, even if these are heard rather than seen.

Notes

1. It is important to note that although the bodies of male video games can be as uncovered as their female counterparts, there nakedness is seen as a demonstration of virility and a performance of hegemonic masculinity, not an expression of sexuality.
2. Perhaps Celes' most famous in-game quote: "I'm a general, not some opera floozy!"
3. Due to the limitations of the Sony SPC700 component of the Nintendo S-SNES audio processing unit of the SNES, Celes does not actually sing, but the synthesized "ooh" sounds are translated though supertitles controlled by the player.
4. Maryden Halewell is voiced by Russian-American pianist and classical crossover artist Elizaveta Khripounova.

Bibliography

Beasley, Berrin, and Tracy C. Standley. 2002. Shirts vs. Skins: Clothing as an Indicator of Gender Role Stereotyping in Video Games. *Mass Communication & Society* 5 (3): 279–293.

Burin, Rick. 2017. In the News: Alison Balsom Trumpets Gender Equality Ahead of Hall Show. *Royal Albert Hall News Service*, February 3. http://www.royalalberthall.com/about-the-hall/news/2017/february/in-the-news-alison-balsom-trumpets-gender-equality-ahead-of-royal-albert-hall-show/.

Burrill, Derek A. 2008. *Die Tryin': Videogames, Masculinity, Culture*. New York: Peter Lang.

Cassell, Justine, and Henry Jenkins. 1998. Chess for Girls? Feminism and Computer Games. In *From Barbie to Mortal Kombat: Gender and Computer Games*, ed. Justine Cassell and Henry Jenkins, 2–45. Cambridge, MA: The MIT Press.

Chess, Shira. 2017. *Ready Player Two: Women Gamers and Designed Identity*. Minneapolis: University of Minnesota Press.

Christenson, Peter, and Jon Brian Peterson. 1988. Genre and Gender in the Structure of Music Preferences. *Communication Research* 15 (3): 282–301.

Clement, Catherine. 1999. *Opera, or, The Undoing of Women*. Minneapolis: University of Minnesota Press.

Connell, R.W., and James W. Messerschmidt. 2005. Hegemonic Masculinity: Rethinking the Concept. *Gender & Society* 19 (6): 829–859.

Dawe, Kevin. 2005. Symbolic and Social Transformation in the Lute Cultures of Crete: Music, Technology, and the Body in a Mediterranean Society. *Yearbook for Traditional Music* 37: 58–68.

Dietz, Tracy L. 1998. An Examination of Violence and Gender Role Portrayals in Video Games: Implications for Gender Socialization and Aggressive Behavior. *Sex Roles* 38: 425–441.

Dill, Karen E., Douglas A. Gentile, William A. Richter, and Jody C. Dill. 2005. Violence, Sex, Race and Age in Popular Videogames. In *Featuring Females: Feminist Analysis of the Media*, ed. Ellen Cole and Jessica Henderson Daniel, 115–130. Washington, DC: American Psychological Association.

Doubleday, Veronica. 2008. 'Sounds of Power': An Overview of Musical Instruments and Gender. *Ethnomusicology Forum* 17 (1): 3–39.

Ford, Charles. 1991. *Cosi?: Sexual Politics in Mozart's Operas*. Manchester: Manchester University Press.

Graner Ray, Sherri. 2004. *Gender Inclusive Game Design: Expanding the Market*. Hingham, MA: Charles River Media.

Hains, Rebecca. 2015. Target Will Stop Labeling Toys for Boys or for Girls. Good. *Washington Post*, August 13. https://www.washingtonpost.com/posteverything/wp/2015/08/13/target-will-stop-selling-toys-for-boys-or-for-girls-good.

Herbert, Trevor, ed. 1991. *Bands: The Brass Band Movement in the 19th and 20th Centuries*. Philadelphia: Open University Press.

Houghton, David. 2010. Are Video Games Really Sexist? *GamesRadar.com*, January 19. http://www.gamesradar.com/are-video-games-really-sexist.

Huneker, James. 1900. *Chopin: The Man and His Music*. New York: Charles Scribner's Sons.

Iitti, Sanna. 2006. *The Feminine in German Song*. New York: Peter Lang.

Jansz, Jeroen. 2005. The Emotional Appeal of Violent Video Games for Adolescent Males. *Communication Theory* 15 (3): 219–241.

Kennedy, Helen W. 2002. Laura Croft: Feminist Icon or Cyberbimbo? On the Limits of Textual Analysis. *Game Studies: The International Journal of Computer Game Research* 2(2), December. http://www.gamestudies.org/0202/kennedy.

Kerker, Gustave. 1904. Opinions of Some New York Leaders on Women as Orchestral Players. *Musical Standard* 21 (535): 217–218, April 2. Reprinted in Women in Music: An Anthology of Source Readings from the Middle Ages to the Present, ed. Carol Neuls-Bates, 202–203 (Boston: Northeastern University Press, 1996).

Kline, Stephen, Nick Dyer-Witheford, and Greig de Peuter. 2005. *Digital Play: The Interaction of Technology, Culture, and Marketing*. London: McGill-Queen University Press.

Leppert, Richard. 1993. *The Sight of Sound: Music, Representation, and the History of the Body*. Berkeley, CA: University of California Press.

Maidlow, Sarah, and Rosemary Bruce. 1999. The Role of Psychology Research in Understanding the Sex/Gender Paradox in Music—Plus Ca Change.... *Psychology of Music* 27 (2): 147–158.

Maus, Fred Everett. 1993. Masculine Discourse in Music Theory. *Perspectives of New Music* 31 (2): 264–293.

McClary, Susan. 1991. *Feminine Endings: Music, Gender, and Sexuality*. Minneapolis: University of Minnesota Press.

McCown, William, Ross Keiser, Shea Mulhearn, and David Williamson. 1997. The Role of Personality and Gender in Preferences for Exaggerated Bass in Music. *Personality and Individual Differences* 23 (4): 543–547.

McLeod, Ken. 2011. *We are the Champions: The Politics of Sports and Popular Music*. Farnham: Ashgate Publishing.

Phillips, Winifred. 2014. *A Composer's Guide to Game Music*. Cambridge, MA: The MIT Press.

Pickering, Samantha, and Betty Repacholi. 2001. Modifying Children's Gender-Typed Musical Instrument Preferences: The Effects of Gender and Age. *Sex Roles* 45 (9): 623–643.

Provenzo, Eugene F., Jr. 1991. *Video Kids: Making Sense of Nintendo*. Cambridge, MA: Harvard University Press.

Sachs, Curt. 1940. *The History of Musical Instruments*. London: J. M Dent & Sons, Ltd.

Staum, Myra J., and Melisa Brotons. 2000. The Effect of Music Amplitude on the Relaxation Response. *Journal of Music Therapy* 37 (1): 22–39.

Steblin, Rita. 1995. The Gender Stereotyping of Musical Instruments in the Western Tradition. *Canadian University Music Review* 16 (1): 128–144.

Taylor, Donald M. 2009. Support Structures Contributing to Instrument Choice and Achievement among Texas All-State Male Flutists. *Bulletin of the Council for Research in Music Education* 179 (Winter): 45–60.

Taylor, Jodie. 2012. Taking It in the Ear: On Musico-Sexual Synergies and the (Queer) Possibility That Music Is Sex. *Continuum* 26 (4): 603–614.

Treitler, Leo. 2011. *Reflections on Musical Meaning and its Representations*. Bloomington, IN: Indiana University Press.

Uematsu, Nobuo. *Final Fantasy VI: Grand Finale*. Milan Symphony Orchestra. NTT Publishing. PSCN-5004, 1994. Compact Disk.

Voorhees, Gerald. 2014. Neoliberal Masculinity: The Government of Play and Masculinity in E-Sports. In *Playing to Win: Sports, Video Games, and the Culture of Play*, ed. Robert A. Brookey and Thomas P. Oates, 63–91. Bloomington, IN: Indiana University Press.

Weisgram, Erica S., Megan Fulcher, and Lisa M. Dinella. 2014. Pink Gives Girls Permission; Exploring the Roles of Explicit Gender Lables and Gender-Typed Colors on Preschool Children's Toy Preferences. *Journal of Applied Developmental Psychology* 35 (5): 401–409.

Williams, Dmitri, Nicole Martins, Mia Consalvo, and James D. Ivory. 2009. The Virtual Census: Representations of Gender, Race and Age in Video Games. *New Media & Society* 11 (5): 815–834.

Games

Bethesda Game Studios. 2011. *The Elder Scrolls V: Skyrim*. [Microsoft Windows, PlayStation 3, Xbox 360]. Rockville, MD: Bethesda Softworks.

BioWare. 2009. *Dragon Age: Origins*. [Microsoft Windows, OSX, Playstation 3, Xbox 360]. Redwood City, CA: Electronic Arts.

———. 2014. *Dragon Age: Inquisition*. [Microsoft Windows, PlayStation 3, PlayStation 4, Xbox 360, Xbox One]. Redwood City, CA: Electronic Arts.

Core Design, et al. 1996. *Tomb Raider*. [Sega Saturn, PlayStation, MS-DOS]. London: Eidos Interactive.

Nintendo Creative Department. 1985. *Super Mario Bros. [NES]*. Kyoto: Nintendo.

Nintendo EAD. 1998. *The Legend of Zelda: Ocarina of Time*. [Nintendo 64, GameCube, IQue Player]. Kyoto: Nintendo.

Nintendo R&D1, et al. 1986. *Metroid*. [NES]. Kyoto: Nintendo.

Square Co., Ltd. 1994. *Final Fantasy VI*. [Super NES]. Tokyo: Square Co. Ltd.

The Game Designers Studio. 2004. *Final Fantasy: Crystal Chronicles*. [Nintendo GameCube]. Kyoto: Nintendo.

11

Tools of the Game: The Gendered Discourses of Peripheral Advertising

Sam Srauy and Valerie Palmer-Mehta

Once considered a niche product, video games are now a mainstay in US culture. As game developer Tobias Batton states, video games are "the most powerful entertainment medium" of the twenty-first century and they "show no signs of relinquishing the mantle" (Correa 2013, para. 1). Underscoring this point, the Entertainment Software Association (2015) reports that 155 million Americans play video games, while 80% of homes possess technology that enables play (2). The video game player, however, has not enjoyed a similar surge in reputation in the broader culture, despite the meaningful benefits conferred on those who inhabit the gamer identity within gaming cultures and the disadvantages that those outside of it endure. Indeed, Shaw (2012) notes that the stigma attached to the gamer identity can negatively affect some players' willingness to be identified as a gamer; this stigma also diminishes players' concerns regarding whether their particular social identities find representation in the form. Gamergate further complicates this picture by painting an image of male gamers as hostile misogynists on the front line of a broader cultural war. These issues point to the knotty, contested, and politically relevant terrain of identity within video game cultures and the importance of productively theorizing how identity is constructed in this space (Burrill 2008; Kafai et al. 2008; Shaw 2014).

Epicentral to video games and gaming cultures, but often overlooked, are the discourses that circulate around and promote them, providing another

S. Srauy (✉) • V. Palmer-Mehta
Oakland University, Rochester, MI, USA

© The Author(s) 2018
N. Taylor, G. Voorhees (eds.), *Masculinities in Play*, Palgrave Games in Context,
https://doi.org/10.1007/978-3-319-90581-5_11

important layer to our understanding of identity, which we view as intersectional. Newman and Vanderhoef (2013) argue that discourses such as specialty presses, marketing, and advertising contribute meaningfully to the gendering of gaming cultures (383), while Chess (2011) refers to advertising as a "cultural barometer" that lends insight into "larger issues of gender and video games" (230). Scharrer's (2004) content analysis of video game magazine advertising gestures toward the potential influence of such discourses in its finding that men outnumbered women in ads by three to one—inferring a masculine gamer identity. Despite the ongoing presence of women in gaming and feminist interventions into gaming cultures, even video game ads targeted directly to women in women's magazines tend to reinforce a gendered view of gaming. Chess (2011) found that such ads work to encourage women into gaming by promoting self-improvement, suggesting that women can improve their physical and mental self-care through games, thus reinforcing stereotypical gender preferences and intimating that technology and play are male domains.

Meanwhile, the ideological contours of the promotional discourses surrounding the peripherals that afford, animate, and bolster play have remained virtually unexplored. Keyboards and keypads, mice, controllers, and the like are critical peripherals for game play, constituting a unique cultural form. Computer games, defined as video games played on desktop or laptop computers, are programmed with the expectation that non-specialized peripherals are present. Yet, there is a profitable market for specialized peripherals that cater to gamers, particularly for computer-based, but also for general, gaming. The popularity of the gaming company Razer, which has a rumored valuation of $1 billion, has been built largely on peripherals, demonstrating peripherals' penetration of the marketplace.

In this chapter, we take as a case study the web advertising for Razer with a focus on how the company's keyboards and keypads, mice, and controllers are promoted to consumers on its website. Using ideological discourse analysis, we seek to identify how ideologies related to identity are structured into and articulated through the text and images of Razer peripheral advertising. We believe that commercial discourses surrounding peripherals constitute a key, but overlooked, site where an assumed and "legitimate" gaming subject is being struggled over. More specifically, based on our analysis, we suggest that Razer's peripherals are articulating a larger struggle in the industry between a historic connection of gaming with young, white males and an emerging recognition of the diversity of those who play video games. We argue that, while some language and imagery on the site point to an effort to be more inclusive, its overall ideological tone suggests a reification of the white male gamer identity through its discursive construction of a particular model of masculinity grounded in combat/war, mastery over the game, and the gaining of unfair advantages. We note that while the white male gamer enjoys a kind of primacy in the gaming industry, he cannot be said to constitute the ideal form of masculinity to which hegemonic masculinity typically refers. Consequently, we argue that this "complicit gamer masculinity," which has gained ascendancy in gamer cultures through an assemblage of forces—of which advertising is one—is part of what Demetriou (2001) calls the hybrid masculine bloc. The masculine bloc enables alternative masculinities, like the complicit gamer masculinity, to work in negotiation with and receive residual social power and benefit—what Connell (1996) has referred to as patriarchal dividends—from hegemonic masculinity, enabling white patriarchy further force and legitimation, and contributing to the broader culture wars.

To illuminate our argument, the chapter takes the following shape. We begin with a discussion of the performance of masculinity in gaming, particularly e-sports, to contextualize the issues under discussion. Next, we provide a note on our methodology before identifying the elements of the Razer peripheral website that can be interpreted as gesturing toward gender neutrality and gender blending. This is followed by a discussion of the manner by which the site promotes discourses of combat/war, mastery, and unfair advantages, which dovetail together to promote a particular complicit gamer masculinity. We conclude with some thoughts regarding the importance of studying peripheral advertising for capturing a more nuanced picture of how e-sports activates particular identities.

Performing Gaming Masculinity

A certain "image" attends the e-sports athlete; it is an identity grounded in a familiar articulation of straight, white masculinity: "He is tough and competitive; he is heterosexual (and typically white); he is lean; he performs with bravado and shows zero tolerance for flaws" (Witkowski 2013, 217). This familiar persona, Witkowski (2013) argues, "is the image of the North American digital sporting hero marketed to young male gamers engaging with electronic sports" (217). However strenuously this representation dominates the public imaginary of who and what constitutes a gamer, scholars have repeatedly noted that actual gamers, in e-sports and beyond, are more diverse than this image suggests (Nakamura 2012; Taylor 2009; Taylor 2012; Witkowski 2013), even though e-sports evinces a hypermasculine landscape that is not particularly conducive to the participation of women (Taylor 2009, 139–140). Despite the gendered hierarchy that dominates many gaming cultures, it must be noted that the configuration of masculinity itself within the context of e-sports is in flux, complex, and in need of further mapping.

Historically, gamer masculinity has been situated in relation to a geek or nerd masculinity that is tied to technological mastery, which serves as subcultural capital within the gaming environment. Mastery within gaming enables men whose bodies limit them in the broader culture to obtain esteem and power that may not be available to them. Access to status, authority, and control are realized through a cyberbody, which allows such men "to reaffirm their masculinity even outside the traditional masculine identity building institutions of sports and war" (Christensen 2006, para. 54). Although the disembodied self within cyberspace could open up possibilities for more fluid, creative performances of gender as well as a move toward gender bending, this potential is often dramatically undercut. Researchers such as Christensen (2006) have found that certain games, such as *Quake Online*, enable men to abandon the limitations of their real bodies and to adopt a cyberbody which they deploy to engage in aggressive, violent, hypermasculine behaviors while they verbally activate homophobic and misogynistic discourses. Cyber performances of hegemonic masculinity may be even more rigid than those enacted in reality, Christensen argues, because there are no safeguards or reform efforts in place to limit their damage (para. 56). Vanderhoef (2013) also identifies the gendered hierarchy that exists in the gaming landscape in his findings that "hardcore/core" gamers, who are coded as masculine, frequently levy vitriol at casual gamers, who are coded as feminine, in order to reify their hegemonic masculine status. This hardcore gamer masculinity is rooted in a "vulnerability [that] may stem from the low cultural status of the video game medium" which "historically [has] been infantilized and seen as immature" (Vanderhoef 2013, para. 36). Moreover, because gamers historically have been viewed in the broader culture as a marginalized masculinity that "mimics but does not match" hegemonic masculinity, this gamer masculinity can be viewed as "a fragile, defensive one that has relied repeatedly … on extreme violence, the sexualization of women, and strong, male homosocial bonds for its sense of power and personal legitimacy" (para. 37). While the gaming capital afforded to geek masculinity enables such men to gain ascendancy in gaming cultures, in part through the marginalization of Others, Taylor (2012) argues that geek culture also is going through a transformation that is rendering the culture "hip" in some circles, elevating its status to some extent in the broader culture. This complex, shifting configuration of geek culture indicates the subcultural capital and mutability of geek masculinity, as well as the idea that it "can be inflected up or down the power hierarchy" (Taylor 2012, 114).

Geek masculinity has predominated in studies of gaming masculinity; however, there exists a second trope within e-sports, T.L. Taylor (2012) argues, that of the "sportsperson (typically a man) and athleticism"—or, more simply—"athletic masculinity," which has a longer, more intimate, and more complete relationship to hegemonic masculinity (114) and a somewhat uneasy relationship with geek masculinity (115). In Trujillo's (1991) foundational description of hegemonic masculinity, physical force and control are featured as main elements of its performance, as the "male body comes to represent power, and power itself is masculinized as physical strength, force, speed, control, toughness and domination" (290). There are few locations where these elements dovetail together with more form and force than that of the realm of sports, conferring on those who inhabit this identity considerable cultural capital, which some e-sports players are bringing into the gaming environment. Taylor (2012) argues that, "inhabiting athleticism can form a powerful stance, offering access to a privileged form of masculinity that not only underpins notions of male dominance, but traffics in the valorization of strength, physical skills, and a kind of 'survival of the fittest' model of hierarchy" (114). Considering the regressive, but still present, belief in biological sex differences in athletics and the institutionalized "separate but equal" ideology explicated in Title IX (Milner and Braddock II 2016), it is perhaps no wonder that e-sports culture constructs male bodies as legitimate athletes while females are rendered as "inherently not … as good at computer games as men" (Taylor 2012, 117).

These two tropes of masculinity—among other performances—intermingle in e-sports, making mapping the performance of masculinity within this domain complex. Further complicating the effort "is the way in which hegemonic masculinity both at times infuses itself into the scene while the very embodied presence of the participants would undermine it" (Taylor 2012, 117). Consequently, just as who and what constitutes a gamer is a contested domain, so too is the performance of masculinity within e-sports in flux.

Rather than situating the male gamer identity squarely within a nerd culture or within athletic masculinity, we map the ideological contours of an emerging Razer peripheral gamer masculinity that appears to be a complex amalgamation of both. More specifically, we argue that, in Razer's web pages, while there is some effort toward including gender diversity through the use of a degree of gender-blending language and imagery, there is a subtle masculinizing of the discourse throughout the site, which works to entrench a particular iteration of masculinity grounded in combat/war, mastery over the game, and the gaining of unfair advantages. As we work to map the iteration of masculinity in the Razer peripheral advertising, we suggest that this "complicit" gamer identity participates, in its own way, in the hegemonic project through its contribution to what Demetriou (2001) terms the hybrid masculine bloc, as it works in negotiation with, and complicit to, hegemonic masculinity to support the patriarchal project in the broader culture. Demetriou works to expand Connell's conceptualization of hegemonic and alternative masculinities by positing that hegemonic masculinity functions as "a hybrid bloc that unites various and diverse practices in order to construct the best possible strategy for the reproduction of patriarchy" (348). Demetriou argues that they work in tandem and in negotiation—as a "strategic alliance"—to ensure the mutability and tenacity of patriarchal power in face of cultural change and challenges (347–348). Indeed, as Demetriou says, "it is its constant hybridization, its constant appropriation of diverse elements from various masculinities that makes the hegemonic bloc capable of reconfiguring itself and adapting to the specificities of new historical junctures" (348). In the sections that follow, we demonstrate the ways in which the complicit gamer masculinity is articulated on the site.

Razer: A Case Study

As a point of departure, we examined every web page pertaining to peripheral products on the Razer website.[1] More specifically, our initial examination included the web pages that advertised Razer mice, keyboards/keypads, audio, controllers, broadcaster, mouse mats, and licensed/team peripherals, which included a combination of the aforementioned peripherals. Due to the extensive nature of the website, we decided to narrow our focus for this case study to the advertising of those peripherals that arguably form the centerpiece of the peripheral gaming experience: the controllers, keypad/keyboards, and mice.

We employed ideological discourse analysis as our method of reading the texts and images on the site. Here we followed Van Dijk (1995) in viewing ideologies as "systems that are at the basis of the socio-political cognition of groups" and which "organize social group attitudes consisting of schematically organized general opinions about relevant social issues" and, by extension, identities (138). Focusing on ideology is particularly appropriate not only because gender and advertising are grounded in ideology, but also due to the fact that, as Burrill (2008) notes, "technology has evolved into a machine that is, in itself ideological" with the "means for its own reproduction" and "the means to cloak its own presence" (140). Like video games and peripherals themselves, the advertising on Razer's website is interactive and visually appealing, functioning as a compelling distraction to the ideological work being conducted there. We examined the manner through which Razer codes its site to appeal to what the company ostensibly perceives as its consumer, thus calling into being a particular gamer identity. In so doing, we contribute to the ongoing research in video game studies on the identity issues at play in gaming cultures by extending the research into the domain of peripheral advertising (Burrill 2008; Kafai et al. 2008; Shaw 2012, 2014).

Our case study of Razer advertising indicates that peripheral advertising discourses are an overlooked site where the cultural struggle regarding who constitutes a gamer is taking place. This struggle is manifest in the gendered nature of the Razer website. The discursive aggregate of the Razer peripheral web pages suggests that women are present, but marginal, in the gaming world and that Razer thinks white men constitute the driving force behind purchasing choices and thus constitute the primary gamer identity.

A Gesture Toward Gender Neutrality

Efforts toward gender neutrality can be found in descriptions of the peripherals. Much of the language promoting the mice, controllers, and keyboards focuses on comfort, design, performance, and technical specifications—elements any gamer, regardless of gender, would find desirable. Specifically, on the landing page for mice, the manufacturer prides itself on designing the first gaming mouse, the 1998 Razer Boomslang, reminding consumers that the mouse formed the basis of the company. As is expected from advertising, the page boasts that Razer takes the lead in developing quality, tournament-grade mice for the gaming industry. Interestingly, Razer employs gender-neutral pronouns on that page. In a move that violates noun-pronoun agreement, the company avoids providing a specific gender to the consumer: "The first thing *a gamer* understands when *they* put *their* hand on a Razer gaming mouse is not how powerful it is, but how nice it feels." Eschewing the singular pronoun "he" or "she" that the noun "gamer" requires, Razer opts for the more inclusive "they" and "their" broadening its audience to all genders. More frequently, however, Razer refers to "you" or "a gamer" instead of a gendered or plural pronoun in a move that seems to personalize and de-gender the shopping experience.

The peripheral web pages' imagery also represents a blend of the masculine and feminine. The website color scheme is arguably coded masculine; it possesses a vivid black background with grey and white text and the company logo, a three-headed snake, is depicted in a vibrant lime green. However, the snake imagery suggests a blending of the masculine and feminine. Indeed, depending on the culture and time period, snake imagery has been coded alternatively as masculine, feminine, a combination of both male and female (one morphing into the other), or androgynous. As Chevalier and Gheerbrant (1996) argue, the "ever ambivalent" serpent "toys with its own sexuality, it is both male and female, twins within the same body" (845). The Ouroboros mouse is a good example of this gender blending. The picture that headlines the Razer Ouroboros web page features a black, scaly snake wrapped around the mouse. The snake gestures toward the mouse's namesake, Ouroboros, which is a symbol depicting a serpent devouring its own tail. Although the Ouroboros has been represented by Plato (2000) in *Timaeus* as a male figure (18), others have viewed the serpent as embodying "opposing principles" such as the masculine and feminine forms found in the Chinese concepts of yin and yang (Chevalier and Gheerbrant 1996, 728). The Razer Naga Chroma mouse is situated a bit more clearly in the realm of the masculine, but with feminine possibilities. In the Indian tradition, Nāgas refer to male snake deities; the female form is referred to as Nāgi or Nāgini. Finally, the Razer Taipan mouse may be linked to the mythology of the rainbow serpent, which is prevalent among Native Australian peoples. The rainbow serpent, sometimes referred to as Taipan (Rose 2000, 306), does not have a definitive gender. As Sherman (2008) reports, "the Rainbow Serpent is said to be the mother of everything, but this deity is more often seen as either genderless or androgynous" (4).

While the color scheme and snake imagery oscillate between masculinity and femininity, it is the actual pictures on the site that work the hardest to reinforce a white male gaming identity. The Orochi mouse web page photo gallery features 11 images of people, all of which are white men. The nearly three-minute video titled "How to Perfectly Customize your Ouroboros [mouse]" features a white male instructing users on how to set up the mouse to fit their needs. As the company seeks to construct identification between itself and its consumer through its tagline "For Gamers By Gamers," the fact that the company's representative is a white male (by gamers) suggests that the consumer is also a white male (for gamers). On the landing page for Razer mice, under customizable ergonomics, a picture of a white masculine hand is used to demonstrate a thumb grip. Similarly, on the landing page for the keyboards, a white male hand is featured. The Wildcat Xbox One controller web page provides a picture of, and testimonial from, the national gaming champion, Tom Ryan, also a white male. Pictures of non-celebrities on the controller web pages also predominantly feature white males. The picture that headlines the Serval controller web page presents a white male's fingers using the controller and pictures in the image gallery at the bottom of that same page provide two images of a white male in his twenties engaging in play in a living room. Among those images is one picture of a white female's hands with fingernails painted forest green using a controller; there are no body or face images of women. The Turret controller also has a headlining picture of a white male's lap, arms, and hands on a lapboard and gaming mouse. Ultimately, the imagery on these pages reinforces a white male gaming identity, while also making a very modest gesture toward including white women as gamers.

It is interesting that none of the images featured people of color, considering the global nature of the company—it has regional headquarters in Singapore, Shanghai, and Taipai—and the diverse heritage of the Razer management team, including Chief Executive Officer, Min-Liang Tan, Senior Vice President of Sales and Marketing, Mike Dilmagani, and Chief Financial Officer, Edwin Chan. Further, Razer sponsors over 50 competitive gaming teams from 35 countries, and that diversity makes its way onto the Team Razer web page, which features men of varying ethnicities and nationalities. This diversity is strangely absent from the advertising images. This panoply of images suggests that the perceived or desired purchaser is a white male and that this is a male space that allows, but does not necessarily reward, a female presence.

A Move Toward Hegemonic Masculinity

While there is some effort toward gender diversity, there also is a subtle masculinizing of the discourse throughout the site, which we elucidate below through three themes—combat/war, mastery over the game, and unfair advantages. As Razer positions itself within the context of professional e-sports, it is perhaps unsurprising that underneath any fleeting gesture toward gender neutrality are the discourses of professional athleticism. Such discourses harken to traditional sports and relegate women to supporting roles such as cheerleader and booth babe, rather than legitimate e-sports competitors (Taylor et al. 2009). Simultaneously, there is a complex evocation of technological mastery that is tied to nerd masculinity. As these two tropes of gaming masculinity fuse together, a particular gaming identity emerges.

Combat/War

In many games, combat serves as the primary mechanic and backdrop of gameplay, which connotes a masculine space of play and conjures visions of male athleticism. As Connell (2000) notes, "though women have often manufactured weapons and serviced armies, it is historically rare for women to be in combat;" indeed, the "30 million members of the world's armed forces today are overwhelmingly male" while men simultaneously have a disproportionate presence in violent enforcement occupations such as police, prison, and security work (21). Violent forms of play reinforce and promote violence as markers of masculine identities (see Dawson 1994; Jansz 2005), exemplifying an ideal form of masculinity. Militarized activities constitute a long-held and widely recognized performance of masculinity—a militarized masculinity. As Higate and Hopton (2005) argue:

> Historically there has been a reciprocal relationship between militarism and masculinity ... militarism feeds into ideologies of masculinity through the eroticization of stoicism, risk taking, and even lethal violence ... However, the link ... reaches beyond the eroticization of masculinism through the glamorization of military culture and military actions. (434)

Dawson (1994) further notes that this use of combat as play has been historically nurtured in young boys through toys. Toy guns, tanks, and airplanes of yesteryear have ceded to new forms of interactions such as the free video games series released by the US Army, *America's Army*. In that game, in an attempt to advertise and recruit young people into the US Army, players—overwhelmingly young males—participate in battles as male characters (van der Graaf and Nieborg 2003, 331).

This militarized masculinity, and its valorization of battle/combat, finds form and force not only within video games and gaming cultures, but also in Razer advertising discourse itself. The tagline for the Razer Lycosa keyboard, for example, is "Nexus of Dominion," and the language of battle and domination is unmistakable as is the athletic "dexterity" required to enact such superiority: "Razer Lycosa is on an unstoppable mission to destroy and dominate. Execute complex combat maneuvers with swift dexterity. Launch your assaults timed to perfection. Annihilate your enemies and reign supreme on the battlefield. You now have the tactical advantage on every terrain, and your enemies' fates are in your hands." Similarly, the Razer DeathStalker Ultimate keyboard "delivers merciless power" which enables you to "execut[e] commands for your master plan faster than enemies can react." Further, the keyboard ensures gamers the ability to "deliver overwhelming destruction to your opponents." This theme of domination is not limited to mechanical keyboards. Even Razer's membrane keyboards are marketed as affording the ability to dominate one's enemies: "Your fingers can move quickly between the keys, ensuring your entire master plan for gaming domination is executed." Further, Razer's keypads allow a player to map keys to various commands or macros, thereby enabling an abbreviated device with which a player can efficiently interact. Razer couches these functions as a way to "expand your repertoire of game-destroying abilities even further." Indeed, even the use of the keys themselves are constructed as a way to "[a]rm yourself with 20 fully programmable mechanical keys for more skills, hotkeys, and macros right at your fingertips."

There also is a subtle overlay of discourses interspersed throughout the controller sections that speaks to a violent masculine norm and a militarized context. The Atrox Xbox One controller is marketed with the tagline, "Bred to Fight," celebrating and appealing to the cultivation of violence. Violence and domination in battle are reinforced when Razer tells consumers that the controller's internal storage compartments, "give you all the room you need when you take your weapon of fighting domination on the go." By suggesting that the controller itself is a weapon, which enables combat domination, Razer militarizes the equipment and gaming context. Conjuring nostalgia for what Razer calls the arcade "glory days," the Atrox Xbox One web page uses the language and space of play to further gesture toward a male gamer: "Hours spent at the arcade honed the gamer in you; for every ... combo you executed, every hit you took ... every ultra you unleashed in return—you became a better player." Couched in a masculinized discourse of battle—through the "execution" and "unleashing" of actions and the "hits" endured—this statement also appeals to what Newman and Vanderhoef (2013) call the traditionally masculine domain of the arcade, consolidating the masculine space of play.

The complicit gamer masculinity finds amplification in the Razer licensed products peripheral web pages. Razer's Goliathus Team Liquid Speed Edition mouse pad, for instance, is marked as having a "slick speed-enhancing surface" that "blends high acceleration with razor-sharp responsiveness" so that one can "amass an army, and take the competition down for the win." The texts that accompany licensed keyboards also show this focus on militarized masculinity where (ironically) battle/combat is the preferred method of peacekeeping. Razer is licensed to use the name and image of *Overwatch*, a multiplayer team shooter, for its accompanying keyboard, mouse, and mousepad. While the following description of *Overwatch* is inspired by the game's self-description, what must be understood is that co-branded or licensed products discursively tie products together (Blackett and Boad 1999). While the description is understood as referring to the game, the practice of cross-promotion implies that Razer seeks to make consumers see their peripherals as part and parcel of that game; consequently, Razer's marketing attempts to construct the Razer *Overwatch* peripherals as physical, tactile embodiments of the game and its gameplay. Each brand's identity is, however temporarily, reciprocally constructed in the co-branded product (Blackett and Boad 1999) as is seen in the following excerpt:

> In a time of global crisis, an international task force of heroes banded together to restore peace to a war-torn world: Overwatch. It ended the crisis and helped to maintain peace in the decades that followed, inspiring an era of exploration, innovation, and discovery. But after many years, Overwatch's influence waned, and it was eventually disbanded. Overwatch is gone … but the world still needs heroes. Fight for the future with the Overwatch Razer gaming peripherals.

Here we see the suggestion that peace is so elusive in this "war-torn world" that it necessitated a special supra-violent militaristic group to usher in peace through combat. Indeed, the site also suggests that as the influence of the fictional army Overwatch faded, so too did peace. Namely, peace was only possible in this game and, by extension, the keyboard and mouse—which operate as its physical instantiation—by the oppressive might of this militaristic force. Thus, in this advertising, the game and peripherals dovetail to suture together a violent masculine ideal.

Despite the fact that women play games almost as much as men (Entertainment Software Association 2015), Razer invokes a militarized masculine player. We recognize that men have no monopoly on violence or even militarized violence, but research repeatedly demonstrates that "men predominate in warlike conduct" in both the public and private spheres (Connell 2000, 21–22). Further, as Feather and Thomas (2013) aver, "achieving masculinity frequently, if not always, relies on acts of violence in one form or another" (1). Marketing material, like all forms of communication, must be understood within the context of its culture and its attendant cultural imagination. As the dominant imaginary of who constitutes a "gamer" is still linked to the iteration and performance of violent masculinity, so too is this marketing material.

Mastery Over the Game

In capitalistic Western societies, control is a key element by which masculinity is measured (Trujillo 1991); indeed, control over one's body, space, and abilities serve as markers of masculine potency. Canham (2009) found that a detriment to men's sense of masculinity is the loss of control over bodily, cognitive, and social abilities. Razer markets its keyboards toward this ideal as expressed in control and mastery over the device and, by extension, the game space. We chose the phrase "Mastery over the game" for its polysemy. In one case, we mean that Razer's advertising suggests that by using its products, a video game player would gain mastery over the video game itself. As they suggest, the macros, customizability, and "professional" grade engineering afford a heightened way for the player to interface with the game. It is this same construction of Razer as an "elite" product that permits Razer to position itself in the second case—as enabling the mastery over one's opponent in e-sports. As we pointed out earlier in this chapter, Razer also positions itself as a tool for professional gamers and those that would aspire to pro-gamer status. Razer employs a tried and true advertising strategy of endorsing pro-athletes (e-sports, in this case) to intimate that their goods are the products of choice in this arena. Finally, Razer's advertising can be read as mastery over customization. Simon (2007) argues that PC case modification—a form of modifying a peripheral—and overclocking CPUs function as both an outward show of geek masculine identity and technical expertise. In this sense, Razer also suggests that its devices are only for those with sufficient technical mastery to understand their complex gaming potential. In other words, Razer constructs its devices as those that afford the special elite geek—who can take "vanilla" technology and transform it into something excellent—mastery over the video game, mastery over opponents the player will face, and mastery over self-presentation.

Razer's keyboards evince this mastery over the game by permitting players to remap keys and program macros so that each keyboard layout is "unique" to the player—a layout that ostensibly gives a *unique* advantage for the player to dominate and control the game. Indeed, the Ouroboros mouse tutorial that features a white male instructing how to customize the "fit" also hails this ideal—that the ability to quickly customize the keyboard and mouse to a player's individual needs permits that player to dominate and control the battlefield. Further, the controllers are customizable too: "Built for serious gamers looking to take their Xbox 360 gaming to the next level, our controllers offer maximum customizability and features that go beyond standard controllers." The gamer keyboards even allow users to customize colors. Many keyboards targeted at the gamer market have lighted keys, and many of the newer ones, such as Razer's Chroma brand, have multicolor backlit keys:

> Made to give you all the freedom you need to set yourself apart, your Razer DeathStalker Chroma opens up a world of extreme personalization possibilities. From your own custom programmed palette of colors across 3 zones, to preloaded lighting effects, all set easily through Razer Synapse, the Razer DeathStalker Chroma lets you express yourself in a way that's unique only to you.

Wrapped in a discourse of freedom, the appeal is to an individualistic discourse ("set yourself apart"), but one that emerges from the ability to control the decorative lighting scheme ("extreme personalization"). This act of setting oneself apart is what Simon (2007) argues is the act of modifying peripherals and overclocking the CPU to express elite mastery over the gaming system. The use of "extreme" as a modifier discursively ties the idea of personalizing the keyboard to extreme acts and, thus, a hypermasculinity similar to those found in sports, extreme or otherwise (Messner et al. 2000). Moreover, as Taylor (2012) argues, e-sports, such as professional video games, are "real" sports with all of the trappings and rituals. Thus, control is understood as the domain of "elite" gamers (or e-sports athletes), not newbies—whom women are often misidentified as.

The emphasis on customizing the color scheme, while not directly tied to the ability to control the game, is emblematic of the desire to control the overall performance space and to strategically display one's superior performance capacity; in other words, such excessive customization provides another layer through which the player may be performatively marked as "elite" and thus male. With the Razer DeathStalker Ultimate, Tartarus Chroma, and Anansi gaming keyboards, through customization of colors, gamers can be sure that "this keyboard is yours and yours alone." Customizing lights and keystrokes may not seem illustrative of any form of complicit gamer masculinity. Yet, if we take keyboards as part and parcel of the computer gaming experience, these keyboards, along with the accompanying PC, "signify a game player's interest or technological projection of self-identity onto their game play platform" (Scacchi 2010, para. 18). If we consider that this ideal—customizability—is parallel to car culture, another bastion of masculinity, we see that customizing an engine to respond faster or lights to illuminate an aftermarket gauge is unmistakably hailed in the use of mechanical keys, "ultra-polling," custom information in liquid crystal displays (LCDs), custom lighting schemes for personalization, or custom keycaps (see Lumsden 2013). As Tragos (2009) noted post–World War II:

> [The] first thing most young men wanted was a car or motorcycle ... G.I.s had developed an innate sense of adaptation, so they hit the local junkyard for a jalopy. With some tools, ingenuity and a few old war buddies the metal-bending hot rod and chopper culture of America was born. Although car culture and motorcycle culture were different, they were parallel pursuits in handmade custom rides that were a means to maintaining camaraderie among men. (548)

As Tragos demonstrates, car and motorcycle cultures simultaneously provided the means through which to construct oneself into a larger masculine identity and reify the boundaries of a homosocial environment while expressing one's uniqueness through the act of customization. Similar to hot rodded cars, "these PCs embody a desire to achieve competitive game play advantage for some, or sheer display of performance or signification of performance potential" (Scacchi 2010, para. 17). Likewise, Razer's marketing material is evocative of that desire to be, at once, identified as a "gamer" and have space for an expression of "leet" (i.e., elite) technical mastery. As Taylor (2012) notes, "[b]eing able to engage with your machine and software at a detailed level for the purposes of play or competition is not simply about functionality, but part of a 'preferred subjectivity' at work" (92). This articulation of a preferred subjectivity by Razer can be read as a complicit gamer masculinity—an identity that is a part of the masculine bloc and which is poised to enjoy the patriarchal dividends provided by the adoption of practices shared by dominant masculinities.

Unfair Advantages

As indicated, Razer seemingly targets e-sports participants as its primary market. It is no surprise then that some of the attending advertisements draw on issues that surround sports—and sporting gear. Taylor (2012) outlines how e-sports and what are traditionally considered sports share similar discussions regarding the use of technological advancements to enhance performance:

> Whether it is a debate about the legitimacy of a new Speedo swimsuit, the use of high-altitude tents for training, or the allowance of a golf cart in a major tournament, traditional sports constantly negotiate the integration and boundary-monitoring of technologies and ongoing constructions of "pure" human agency. Though this boundary work may be more apparent in e-sports, it is not unique to it. (40)

The advantages provided by the accoutrements for any sporting activity raise some degree of questioning regarding the extent to which the participant is benefitted, fairly or unfairly, by the apparel or equipment utilized. Similar to how one might envision tennis athletes supplying their own racquets, Taylor (2012) notes that "tournament machines have discarded peripherals (sitting on the floor or stowed away by organizers) and most serious players use their own gear" (43) because the provided gear is deemed insufficient for advantaged play. Whether sporting equipment or gaming peripherals give one a competitive advantage or an "unfair advantage" is debatable, but it is clear that many participants—particularly those who consider themselves elite—desire that advantage.

Militarized language is replicated on the Turret game controller web page—where the advertising equates the controller to an armory—and it is accompanied by a discourse of advantages: "The key to securing victory every time, is having an arsenal of controls more impressive than your opponents." This positioning of the game controller as a tool of war hails discourses of combat discussed previously. However, while this "war" could be a fair one that the gamer achieves through skill and talent, the advertising for the controllers encourages the idea of securing unfair advantages by having "controls more impressive" than others and by promoting the Razer Sabertooth controller through the tagline, "Unlevel the playing field." Razer further glamorizes the violent masculine norm by asserting that the Sabertooth enables the gamer to "react to any … enemy instantaneously by putting more power right at your fingertips." By extending the play into the body, the discourse creates the context for an embodied, gendered gaming experience.

What is informative about the discourse of the Razer Turret and Sabertooth controllers is that there is a blurring between militarized masculinity and gaining an unfair advantage. One might readily identify militarized discourse as a reflection of a type of masculinity within the masculine bloc; however, connecting unfair advantages to that discourse may seem less apparent, unless one recognizes that advertising appeals not only to actual markets, but also to whoever is perceived to be the market (see Srauy 2014). Therefore, who is perceived to be the primary consumers of that unfair advantage is also instructive.

Consalvo (2007) makes a compelling case that particular forms of play, while affording an unfair advantage, do not necessarily constitute cheating per se. We take no position on what is or is not cheating. Rather, our point is that who is *imagined* to be interested in gaining an unfair advantage (of which cheating, however that is construed, is only one method) gestures to gendered hardcore/casual gamer discourses in game cultures. Consalvo (2007) notes that both women and men have a propensity to "cheat" while playing video games. However, cheating or seeking unfair advantages have attendant gendered discourses of who is or is not "hardcore" enough to desire these advantages. In other words, to the extent that men are imagined to be hardcore gamers, they also are imagined as those most likely to desire the benefits unfair advantages confer. Consalvo problematizes how the practice of cheating is gendered:

I believe it would be overly simplistic to ascribe this [cheating] behavior or practice to a particular gender or gendered construction of gameplay … [i]nterests that we initially ascribe to women or girl gamers have changed as they gained more experience playing games, or changed as research moved from studying girls to adult women. Sometimes, it seems, scholars *conflate what girls and women want and do with what are actually newbie player practices and interests.* (Consalvo 2007, 124, our emphasis)

While Consalvo specifically addresses the assumptions of scholars, her observation is instructive to the gaming community as a whole. As other scholars note, it is the *imaginary* of who plays "real" or "hardcore" games that is important (see Taylor 2008; Shaw 2012). That imaginary discursively structures, and often inhibits, people's ability to enjoin communities and play styles (Taylor 2008). Because of the conflation of women and newbie game players, women are discursively constructed as playing and enjoying only "casual games," and thus there is less social support for playing hardcore games (Consalvo 2007). Therefore, while unfair advantages themselves are not necessarily coded as male, "cheating" is coded as the domain of hardcore gamers because cheating can potentially mark a player as "prestigious" or "elite," which does mark the player as male (Consalvo 2007). Thus, it is not that "cheating" or unfair advantages necessarily marks you as masculine. Rather it marks you as "hardcore" enough to play a game in which you might desire these technological assistances and the various "kinds of power and gaming capital" they confer (Consalvo 2007, 123). And, being a "hardcore" game player marks you as masculine. It is in this way that we see Razer's use of "gaining an unfair advantage" language to suggest that its devices appeal to hardcore (and thus male) players.

The landing page for the controller section in general enshrouds each subsequent controller subsection with the suggestion that the controllers provide an unfair advantage: "Razer brings proven PC technology like Hyperresponse buttons to a line of customizable Xbox/PC controllers that give you *the unfair console gaming advantage*" (our emphasis). The implication is that there is something more elite and technologically sophisticated about PC gaming technology that would give a console gamer an unfair advantage and thus greater mastery over the gaming situation. Razer's advertising practices, which already are coded masculine, subtly articulate a dominant masculine discourse through a framing of its keyboards as a specific tool used by gamers to gain an unfair advantage. On the keyboard landing page, a large heading in capital letters exclaims "Razer keyboards—at the center of control." Underneath, the statement continues: "As the centerpiece to your gaming setup, each and every Razer keyboard is designed to deliver total satisfying control right to your fingertips. Right to the brim with the latest in bleeding-edge tech and features, you're getting the unfair advantage for fist-pumping epic wins."

Because this heading is on the main landing page, the implication is that the "bleeding-edge tech and features" that enable an "unfair advantage" are universal to all Razer keyboards instead of any specific model. The same is true of its mice. The Naga Chroma, Naga Epic Chroma, and Naga Hex, for example, are all promoted with the tagline, "Get IMBA," a modern colloquialism that means that something is so good that it makes the game unfair. Additionally, Razer's marketing strategy is to brand itself squarely as a peripheral manufacturer for gamers. Its web page is marked with the brand's catchphrase, "For gamers. By gamers," which hails those who identify as gamers and appropriates that identity for its corporate culture. It is, in effect, an articulation that Razer and those who use Razer peripherals are real, hardcore gamers—an identity that is coded masculine.

Interestingly, what Razer most frequently promotes in its marking material is the ability to record macros—the ability to automate a series of discrete keystrokes to one button so that when the button is pressed, the game registers the action. All Razer keyboards and keypads have the ability to record macros in situ. By marshaling the idea of "unfair advantage" and promoting the macro function of its keyboards, Razer simultaneously marks its understanding of a gamer as someone who might use macros (i.e., a "hardcore player") as a desirable unfair advantage strategy. Some Razer keyboards also feature extra macro keys that are designed specifically for macros: "Serious gamers know the value of macros—simplifying long, complex sequences of commands in-game to the touch of a single keystroke. Setting up a macro is really easy on a Razer keyboard." The phrase "serious gamers know the value of macros," gestures toward the complexity of many games' key combinations for various abilities. Serious (i.e., elite/hardcore) gamers, the marketing material tells us, would recognize the technological mastery and advantage in reducing keystrokes.

Razer also points to other ways of gaining unfair advantages. Razer's flagship keyboard, DeathStalker Ultimate, has an integrated LCD screen. The marketing material states that it can be used for finding walkthroughs: "Get stuck on a level, watch a walkthrough on YouTube, or even browse the Internet for tips, without ever having to Alt-Tab out of the game." Whether walkthroughs constitute a form of cheating is undertheorized (Consalvo 2003). However, if one views walkthroughs as cheating, as do some players, then DeathStalker's LCD screen further appeals to a discourse of unfair advantage.

Peripheral Advertising as Tools of Gender

Razer's web pages evince a larger struggle in game cultures—namely, the struggle over who constitutes a gamer and what that gamer in the broader cultural imaginary means. We have argued that the imagined white male gamer is better understood as a form of complicit masculinity that is constitutive of the masculine bloc. This complicit gamer masculinity is articulated in Razer's web pages as an expert (elite) game player who can dominate and destroy his opponent using peripherals that give him an unfair advantage. Moreover, this masculinity employs the peripherals' mastery potential—the potential to control one's opponent—toward an individualistic ideal through customization of the device.

Interestingly, we found that the keyboard advertising featured the most masculinized discourses in terms of both frequency and intensity, emerging as the most overtly masculinized of the three studied. There was more subtlety and gender neutrality to the mice and controllers, yet they still interspersed masculine codes. This might be explained by how the devices are used. Generally speaking, mice and keyboards are used together for PC games, whereas controllers are used for console games. That means part of the difference may lie in how these differing platforms are understood in game cultures. Cultural and scholarly debates suggest that PC gamers are perceived as more hardcore than console gamers; what seems to be the delineating factor (when game titles are not considered) is that PCs require more technical skills, are more customizable, and are capable of more detailed graphics—a colloquial benchmark of a "good" game (Srauy 2014). The emphasis on customizability and required technical skills for PC gaming is congruent with how we see Razer situating its gamer keyboards—that is, the purview of "elite" game players. Again, newbie—non-elite game players—are often coded as feminine (Consalvo 2007). This is, perhaps, unsurprising since past scholarship has noted that PCs have been culturally constructed as a masculine sphere (see Kendall 2002; Turkle 1984, 2005). In this context, as Sherry Turkle (2005) notes, "the computer becomes a personal and cultural symbol of what a woman is not" (33). Web page texts surrounding mice may be less gendered because Razer might assume that mice would be used with keyboards—the typical way that we interact with PCs—which are already masculinized. Razer's attempt to neutralize gendered text in *controllers*, on the other hand, may be seen as an attempt to appeal to the widening demographics of who plays games—elite and non-elite game players.

Although who constitutes a gamer can be narrowly defined, the population of game players has diversified steadily. Razer's discourse collides with reality and reinforces a vision of gamers and, by extension, gaming capital, as inherently white and male, which contributes to, as Nakamura (2012) argues, a cultural context in which women and people of color have to justify their presence and defend their credibility as gamers: "[T]he more gaming capital becomes identified with white masculinity, the more bitter the battle over its distribution, possession, and circulation will become" (3–4). Razer's brand identity as a peripheral manufacturer is centered around a specialized "gamer"—still imagined in their advertising as white and male, which works to consolidate gaming capital and gamer identity around a particular performance of white masculinity.

On the other hand, increasing diversity in game cultures means that Razer risks alienating potential customers, a risk they ostensibly are broaching tenuously. This issue is illuminated in the tension between Razer's naming strategies, color scheme, web page copy, and images that it employs. Its attempt at inclusive web page copy and naming is unbalanced by its traditional use of themes that appeal to this gamer imaginary, which suggests that Razer is addressing, to some extent, the broadening of the market, but in a way that does not ruffle the "male backchannel" of gaming discourse (Nakamura 2012, 3). Thus, peripheral marketing discourses, in this case study, subtly functioned to reify the binaries that exist in e-sports while opening a small space for acknowledging the diversity of gamers. Perhaps companies like Razer are also concerned about the anticipated backlash that comes when gaming cultures are stretched to include Others. If so, this would seem to underscore the continuing importance of challenging business as usual "by documenting, archiving, analyzing, and responding to sexism, racism, ageism, and homophobia in games and game spaces" (Huntemann 2013), which, we argue, should also include peripheral advertising, where the reification of the "isms" that permeate game cultures might be all the more persuasive for its subtlety.

Note

1. Our analysis is based on website content that we viewed between October 2015 and February 2016.

Bibliography

Blackett, Tom, and Robert W. Boad. 1999. *Co-Branding: The Science of Alliance.* Basingstoke: Palgrave Macmillan.

Burrill, Derek A. 2008. *Die Tryin': Videogames, Masculinity, Culture.* New York: Peter Lang.

Canham, Sarah L. 2009. The Interaction of Masculinity and Control and Its Impact on the Experience of Suffering for an Older Man. *Journal of Aging Studies* 23 (2): 90–96. https://doi.org/10.1016/j.jaging.2008.12.003.

Chess, Shira. 2011. A 36-24-36 Cerebrum: Productivity, Gender, and Video Game Advertising. *Critical Studies in Media Communication* 28 (3): 230–252.

Chevalier, Jean, and Alain Gheerbrant. 1996. *The Penguin Dictionary of Symbols.* London: Penguin Books.

Christensen, Natasha Chen. 2006. Geeks at Play: Doing Masculinity in an Online Gaming Site. *Reconstruction* 6 (1). http://reconstruction.eserver.org/Issues/061/christensen.shtml.

Connell, R.W. 1996. Politics of Changing Men. *Arena Journal* 6: 53.

———. 2000. Arms and the Man: Using the New Research on Masculinity to Understand Violence and Promote Peace in the Contemporary World. In *Male Roles, Masculinities and Violence: A Culture of Peace Perspective,* ed. Ingebord Breines, R.W. Connell, and Ingrid Eide, 21–34. Paris: UNESCO.

Consalvo, Mia. 2003. Zelda 64 and Video Game Fans: A Walkthrough of Games, Intertextuality, and Narrative. *Television & New Media* 4 (3): 321–334. https://doi.org/10.1177/1527476403253993.

———. 2007. *Cheating: Gaining Advantage in Videogames.* Cambridge, MA: MIT Press.

Correa, Christopher. 2013. Why Video Games Are More Addictive and Bigger than Movies Ever Will Be. *Forbes Magazine,* April 11. http://www.forbes.com/sites/christophercorrea/2013/04/11/why-video-games-are-addictive-and-bigger-than-movies-will-ever-be/#637a430430bc. Accessed 16 May 2016.

Dawson, Graham. 1994. *Soldier Heroes: British Adventure, Empire and the Imagining of Masculinities.* New York: Routledge.

Demetriou, Demetrakis Z. 2001. Connell's Concept of Hegemonic Masculinity: A Critique. *Theory and Society* 30 (3): 337–361. https://doi.org/10.1023/A:1017596718715.

Entertainment Software Association. 2015. 2015 Sales, Demographics and Usage Data. http://www.theesa.com/wp-content/uploads/2015/04/ESA-Essential-Facts-2015.pdf. Accessed 16 May 2016.

Feather, Jennifer, and Catherine Thomas. 2013. *Violent Masculinities: Male Aggression in Early Modern Texts and Culture.* New York: Palgrave Macmillan.

Higate, Paul, and John Hopton. 2005. War, Militarism, and Masculinities. In *Handbook of Studies on Men and Masculinities*, ed. Michael S. Kimmel, Jeff Hearn, and R.W. Connell, 432–447. Thousand Oaks, CA: Sage Publications.

Huntemann, Nina. 2013. Introduction: Feminist Discourses in Games/Game Studies. *Ada: A Journal of Gender, New Media, & Technology* 2. https://doi.org/10.7264/N37D2S2F.

Jansz, Jeroen. 2005. The Emotional Appeal of Violent Video Games for Adolescent Males. *Communication Theory* 15 (3): 219–241. https://doi.org/10.1111/j.1468-2885.2005.tb00334.x.

Kafai, Yasmin B., Carrie Heeter, Jill Denner, and Jennifer Y. Sun. 2008. *Beyond Barbie & Mortal Kombat: New Perspectives on Gender and Gaming*. Cambridge, MA: MIT Press.

Kendall, Lori. 2002. *Hanging Out in the Virtual Pub: Masculinities and Relationships Online*. Berkeley: University of California Press.

Lumsden, Karen. 2013. *Boy Racer Culture: Youth, Masculinity and Deviance*. New York: Routledge.

Messner, Michael A., Michele Dunbar, and Darnell Hunt. 2000. The Televised Sports Manhood Formula. *Journal of Sport & Social Issues* 24 (4): 380–394. https://doi.org/10.1177/0193723500244006.

Milner, Adrienne N., and Jomills Henry Braddock II. 2016. *Sex Segregation in Sports: Why Separate Is Not Equal: Why Separate Is Not Equal*. Santa Barbara, CA: Praeger.

Nakamura, Lisa. 2012. Queer Female of Color: The Highest Difficulty Setting There Is? Gaming Rhetoric as Gender Capital. *Ada: Journal of Gender, New Media, and Technology* 1. https://doi.org/10.7264/N37P8W9V.

Newman, Michael Z., and John Vanderhoef. 2013. Masculinity. In *The Routledge Companion to Video Game Studies*. New York: Routledge.

Plato. 2000. *Timaeus*. Trans. Donald J. Zeyl. Indianapolis, IN: Hacket Publishing.

Rose, Carol. 2000. *Giants, Monsters, and Dragons: An Encyclopedia of Folklore, Legend, and Myth*. New York: W.W. Norton & Company.

Scacchi, Walt. 2010. Computer Game Mods, Modders, Modding, and the Mod Scene. *First Monday* 15 (5). https://doi.org/10.5210/fm.v15i5.2965.

Scharrer, Erica. 2004. Virtual Violence: Gender and Aggression in Video Game Advertisements. *Mass Communication and Society* 7 (4): 393–412. https://doi.org/10.1207/s15327825mcs0704_2.

Shaw, Adrienne. 2012. Do You Identify as a Gamer? Gender, Race, Sexuality, and Gamer Identity. *New Media & Society* 14 (1): 28–44. https://doi.org/10.1177/1461444811410394.

———. 2014. *Gaming at the Edge: Sexuality and Gender at the Margins of Gamer Culture*. Minneapolis: University of Minnesota Press.

Sherman, Josepha. 2008. *Storytelling: An Encyclopedia of Mythology and Folklore*. London: Routledge.

Simon, Bart. 2007. Geek Chic Machine Aesthetics, Digital Gaming, and the Cultural Politics of the Case Mod. *Games and Culture* 2 (3): 175–193.

Srauy, Sambo. 2014. *Speaking About Race: Biopower and Racism in the Videogame Landscape.* PhD diss., Temple University. http://gradworks.umi.com/36/23/3623267.html. Accessed 1 May 2016.

Taylor, T.L. 2008. Becoming a Player: Networks, Structure, and Imagined Futures. In *Beyond Barbie & Mortal Kombat: New Perspectives on Gender and Gaming*, ed. Yasmin B. Kafai, Carrie Heeter, Jill Denner, and Jennifer Y. Sun, 51–65. Cambridge, MA: The MIT Press.

Taylor, Nicholas. 2009. *Power Play: Digital Gaming Goes Pro.* PhD Dissertation, York University, Toronto.

Taylor, T.L. 2012. *Raising the Stakes: E-Sports and the Professionalization of Computer Gaming.* Cambridge, MA: MIT Press.

Taylor, Nicholas, Jen Jenson, and Suzanne de Castell. 2009. Cheerleaders/Booth Babes/Halo Hoes: Pro-Gaming, Gender and Jobs for the Boys. *Digital Creativity* 20 (4): 239–252.

Tragos, Peter. 2009. Monster Masculinity: Honey, I'll Be In The Garage Reasserting My Manhood. *The Journal of Popular Culture* 42 (3): 541–553. https://doi.org/10.1111/j.1540-5931.2009.00695.x.

Trujillo, Nick. 1991. Hegemonic Masculinity on the Mound: Media Representations of Nolan Ryan and American Sports Culture. *Critical Studies in Mass Communication* 8 (3): 290–308.

Turkle, Sherry. 1984. *The Second Self: Computers and the Human Spirit.* New York: Simon and Schuster.

———. 2005. Computational Reticence: Why Women Fear the Intimate Machine. In *Technology and Women's Voices: Keeping in Touch*, ed. Cheris Kramarae, 33–49. New York: Routledge.

Van der Graaf, Shenja, and David B. Nieborg. 2003. Together We Brand: America's Army. In *Level Up: Digital Games Research Conference*, ed. Marinka Copier and Joost Raessens, 324–338. Utrecht, Holland: DiGRA.

Van Dijk, Teun A. 1995. Ideological Discourse Analysis. *New Courant* 4 (1): 135–161.

Vanderhoef, John. 2013. Casual Threats: The Feminization of Casual Video Games. *Ada: A Journal of Gender, New Media & Technology* 2. https://doi.org/10.7264/N3V40S4D.

Witkowski, Emma. 2013. Negotiations of Hegemonic Sports Masculinities at LANS. In *Sports Videogames*, ed. Mia Consalvo, Konstantin Mitgutsch, and Abe Stein, 217–235. New York: Routledge.

Part III

The Right Man for the Job: Gaming and Social Futures

12

Performing Neoliberal Masculinity: Reconfiguring Hegemonic Masculinity in Professional Gaming

Gerald Voorhees and Alexandra Orlando

This chapter examines reconfigurations of masculinity in the culture of competitive, professionalized first-person shooter (hereafter, FPS) games. Our arguments center on a close study of the Cloud9 *Counter-Strike: Global Offensive* (hereafter, CS:GO) team's performances both at tournaments and in the streams and other media with which they promote and market their brand. Cloud9 is an eSports organization that sponsors groups of players across eight of the most popular competitive games. Arguably, the most unique of all of Cloud9's teams is their *Counter-Strike: Global Offensive* division. Recognizing the Cloud9 CS:GO team's prominence in competitive FPS, we treat them as a "representative anecdote," a case study if you will, not only for success in this community but also as exemplary of how masculinities are performed in this particular eSports scene.[1]

We build from the work on geek and jock masculinities undertaken by T.L. Taylor and Nick Taylor by first enlarging the tropology of figures of masculinity being enacted by professional players. While the Cloud9 CS:GO team's gameplay evidences the imbrication of technological mastery and sportive, militarized masculinity, among the team members we also find an outsider, an everyman, a team mother, a boyish joker, and a dandy. And rather than see these various figures of masculinity in opposition, we attempt to show that eSports inculcates a neoliberal form of masculinity that borrows facets of hegemonic, subordinate, and even counterhegemonic formations of

G. Voorhees (✉) • A. Orlando
University of Waterloo, Waterloo, ON, Canada

© The Author(s) 2018
N. Taylor, G. Voorhees (eds.), *Masculinities in Play*, Palgrave Games in Context,
https://doi.org/10.1007/978-3-319-90581-5_12

211

masculinity for the purpose of competitive effectiveness and marketability. This melange of practices and attributes is neoliberal in its utter lack of coherence to any values beyond success within the competitive FPS community and corresponding financial success for the team's investors and players, and it illustrates how professional(ized) gaming contributes to the production of the masculine neoliberal subject. Finally, we argue that mainstream North American culture endeavors to domesticate this neoliberal form of masculinity by eroticizing it and in this way subordinating it to hegemonic masculinity. In their promotional videos and streams, the Cloud9 CS:GO team constructs their masculinities in ways that not only fetishize the sexuality of the male body but also enact homoerotic discourses and tensions, putting them in a decidedly subordinate position vis-à-vis the heteronormative foundations of hegemonic masculinities.

This chapter begins with a brief overview of game studies research on eSports and masculinities in eSports, in order to better situate our intervention. The next section will analyze the Cloud9 CS:GO team's performances of masculinity both in and outside the game by looking first at the neoliberal assemblage of masculinities and second at the eroticization of this configuration of masculinity. We conclude by arguing that these configurations of masculinity function to re-entrench the toxic, hegemonic form of masculinity characteristic of game culture, but nevertheless open possibilities to resist more pathological formations of manhood.

Masculinities in/and eSports

Current eSports research has laid the groundwork for establishing the industry as an important topic of sociological study, sports research, and cultural studies, paving the way for those who have worked to trace the rapid evolution of the industry. At the most fundamental level, Witkowski (2012) and others (Voorhees 2012; Taylor 2012) have worked to establish the "sportiveness" of eSport, and a couple of edited volumes have attempted to address eSports in relation to a larger of body sports-themed games (Brookey and Oates 2014; Consalvo et al. 2013). There are writings concerning the Korean eSports industry, where the culture of eSports is most ingrained into the culture and infrastructure (Jin 2010); Chinese eSports, which are only recently but rapidly becoming mainstream (Szablewicz 2011); and the North American industry, which is home to smaller, grassroots followings of many game genres (Taylor et al. 2009; Taylor 2012; Harper 2014). Additionally, while there are works that look at eSports from a global context (Hutchins 2008; Jonasson and Thiborg 2010) work on emerging regions such as Brazil, India, and Taiwan and even the industry nuances between regions in Europe have yet to circulate widely in North America. All-encompassing forays like those discussed here, which attempt to describe national eSports industries, are essential to introducing the topic into multidisciplinary discourses, but miss the nuances of genre- and even game-specific writing.

This work has, thankfully, begun and somewhat unsurprisingly these more locally oriented studies of eSports have much to say about masculinity and misogyny. While scholarship on gender in gaming tends to not discuss the imbedded toxic masculinity that oppresses women and regulates men on a day-to-day basis (Cassell and Jenkins 1998; Kafai 2008) and more recent studies have begun to take a survey approach to the gender disparity in gaming communities (Ratan et al. 2015; Bryce and Rutter 2003), studies of specific eSports scenes offer more incisive analysis. Todd Harper's *The Culture of Digital Fighting Games*, for instance, is one of a few texts to examine the culture of the fighting game scene. Harper argues that misogyny and racism are so engrained in the culture that, despite having one of the most diverse groups of players and organizers in the industry, the scene would be fundamentally different without these pathological elements. Harper, furthermore, makes it clear that intersectionality plays a role in how minority groups in the industry suffer at the hands of hegemonic masculinity. Likewise, Nick Taylor has scrutinized the culture and practices characteristic of FPS games in North America, calling attention to the standardization of gameplay and communication patterns used by competitive players in this scene (Taylor 2011; Taylor 2012). While Taylor highlights fascinating moments of homoeroticism, his analysis emphasizes the construction of hypermasculine practices, discursive and embodied, that police the boundaries of the notions of masculinity acceptable in the scene.

There are, nevertheless, significant shortcomings to research on the gendered cultures of games, which tend to veer toward examinations of male players and masculinities, suggesting that female players are the outlier, struggling in a masculinized world where harassment and sexualization are rampant (Taylor et al. 2009; Taylor 2012; Ratan et al. 2013). Some scholars, additionally, have focused on gender representation in games themselves as a way to reflect the treatment of women and men in the field (Rehak 2003; Shaw 2014). Additionally, more writing needs to be done to address the easy bifurcation of geek and sports masculinity, which is prominent in both T.L. Taylor's and Nick Taylor's work on eSports (though Nick Taylor's more recent studies of *The Walking Dead* have troubled this binary) and Robin Johnson's (2011) studies of science-fiction shooting games, as the industry evolves and new marketing strategies are established and cultural practices normalized.

This chapter aims to intervene in the conversation concerning gender, and more specifically, masculinity, and game cultures. This chapter will endeavor to do some of the work of decentering hegemonic masculinities by defamiliarizing and pushing seemingly conventional forms of masculinity to the margins. We do so by examining not game representations but rather how eSports competitors perform their masculinities, often in stylized ways, in public forums designed to promote the activity and to build relations with fans. The performances of masculinity we consider flaunt the binary of geek versus jock masculinity, enthusiastically enacting an array of masculinities, some of which are subordinate to or even denigrated by the hegemonic masculinity operative in games, which valorizes physical power, violence, domination, and aggression, a construction Kline et al. (2003) call "militarized masculinity." Indeed, it is our contention that within eSports this neoliberal masculinity (rather than militarized masculinity) enjoys the position of "hegemonic masculinity" (Connell 1995). It is with this "local level," where "hegemonic patterns of masculinity are embedded in specific social environments, such as formal organizations," that this inquiry is aimed (Connell and Messerschmidt 2005, 839).

Homo Economicus *and Neoliberal Masculinity*

In Michel Foucault's theorization, neoliberalism extends the line of economic theory that stretches from Adam Smith's concept of the *laissez faire* to the Chicago School (the origin of neoliberal economics) into the multifaceted arenas of everyday life. To wit, neoliberalism is a "massive expansion of the field and scope of economics" into "[e]verything for which human beings attempt to realize their ends, from marriage, to crime, to expenditures on children, [which] can be understood 'economically' according to a particular calculation of cost for benefit" (Read 2009, 28). Government "becomes a sort of enterprise whose task is to universalize competition and invent market-shaped systems of action for individuals, groups and institutions" (Lemke 2001, 197). In this neoliberal condition, the boundary between society and government, in the political-juridical sense, becomes porous as both domains are reconfigured by the influence of economic rationality and in this way subject to neoliberal governmentality, a concept Foucault deploys in order to explain "The ensemble formed by the institutions, procedures, analyses and reflections, the calculations and tactics that allow the exercise of this very specific albeit complex form of power" (Foucault 1991, 192).

The diffusion of neoliberal rationality throughout everyday life turns culture into a form of government (from an analytical standpoint). This necessarily entails an understanding of culture as discursive, or even rhetorical, as well as material. As "a distinctive set of knowledges, expertise, techniques and apparatuses which—through the roles they play as technologies of sign systems connected to technologies of power and working through the technologies of the self—act on, and are aligned to, the social in distinctive ways," culture is coterminous with governmentality (Bennett 2003, 60). A far cry from Matthew Arnold's notion of culture as the civilized and civilizing qualities cultivated by a social system and even from Raymond William's germinal idea of culture as shared symbolic systems, thinking through the relation between culture and governmentality means approaching culture as a "grid of intelligibility" (Biesecker 1995, 354). This is to say that people act in accordance to what makes sense in a particular situation given what they know and how they understand the probable effectivity of their possible actions. In this way, power governs; disciplinary technologies and technologies of the self, "which permit individuals to effect by their own means or with the help of others a certain number of operations on their own bodies and souls, thoughts, conduct, and way of being," operate in and according to the same cultural logic (Foucault 1988, 19).

While Foucault's *corpus* tackles several technologies of the self, Greek philosophy and Christianity for instance, the construct of governmentality most relevant to contemporary society is neoliberalism. Within the regime of neoliberal reason, "both persons and states are construed on the model of the contemporary firm, both persons and states are expected to comport themselves in ways that maximize their capital value in the present and enhance their future value, and both persons and states do so through practices of entrepreneurialism, self-investment, and/or attracting investors" (Brown 2015, 22). Significantly, the subject of neoliberalism, the subject that ascribes to the mandates of neoliberalism, is "an entrepreneur of every aspect of their life" (Nguyen 2016, 5). "A free and autonomous 'atom' of self-interest who is fully responsible for navigating the social realm using rational choice and cost-benefit calculation *to the express exclusion* of all other values and interests," *homo economicus* is the figure of the subject that emerges within the social conditions of neoliberalism (original emphasis, Hamann 2009, 38). Literally "economic man," and possessing of the "common abstract essence" of the population, *homo economicus* is the sort of individual who navigates the possibilities enabled by the material and cultural milieu in search of the most advantageous probabilities. For this subject, neoliberalism is an ethical imperative to think through the cost and benefit of each potential action with an eye toward developing the self as "human capital," a measure that accounts for both one's inborn qualities and the skills and abilities acquired through life choices (Lemke 2001, 199). As Nguyen (2016) explains, this subject of neoliberalism is fundamentally distinct from the subject of liberalism in that *homo economicus* has no inherent obligation to the state or civil society but rather contributes to the commonweal through the selfish pursuit of individual self-interest (5). To wit, as both a technology of power and a technology of the self, complete with its own ethical imperatives for the subject to cultivate their self, neoliberalism precipitates the transformation of an array of human relations—including, we will argue, masculinities—into means to develop the economic viability of the self.

Game studies has given some attention to how the game industry functions within the neoliberal world system (e.g. Dyer-Witheford and de Peuter 2009) and how games have capitalized on neoliberal models of labor (e.g. Hong 2013; Taylor et al. 2015), but focused primarily on how games enable and even encourage players to enact the conduct of *homo economicus*. The relationship between ludic structures and neoliberal logics is highlighted in Baerg's (2012) analysis of risk and risk management in digital role-playing games and treated as a basis for the institutionalization of a player-generated disciplinary apparatus in Silverman and Simon's (2009) study of *World of Warcraft*. More empirical studies, meanwhile, have examined how play practices have taken up the mandate of neoliberal technologies of the self to engender and refine more productive bodies (Whitson 2013; Millington 2009). Still others have reconnected these micro-level analyses of players using games to facilitate their own subjectivation to the macro-level entrenchment of neoliberalism in the political and economic structures endorsed by the state (Zhang 2013; Szablewicz 2011). Notably, both Szablewicz and Zhang's work considers how digital gameplay is understood in the People's Republic of China, a country transitioning from socialism to neoliberalism, and they each locate the professionalization of play as the catalyst for its mainstream acceptance. Szablewicz and Zhang clearly demonstrate that the professionalization of play enables the discursive construction of gaming as prosocial to the extent that it encourages players to compete to not simply win but to better themselves as players. As Voorhees (2012) has argued, the neoliberal imperative of the professionalization of play in eSports, and the cultural zeitgeist of professionalization that inflects the play of hobbyists, "is a means of bringing into being *homo economicus* by incentivizing, through high-stakes competition, a way of being dictated by rational choice and cost-benefit analysis" (68).

Furthermore, according to Voorhees this contributes to the constitution of a "neoliberal masculinity" that embraces aspects of hegemonic, subordinate but complicit, and counterhegemonic configurations of masculinity. This is not because eSports embraces a culture of tolerance. Far from it (as Taylor and Harper, above, have shown). Rather, playful boyishness, militarized violence, and intellectualization are accepted and worked together into neoliberal masculinity because they, in combination, constitute the most effective approach to professional play, and quite possibly to marketing too. This chapter builds from these theorizations of neoliberalism and *homo economicus*, generally, and from the conception of neoliberal masculinity in particular.

On Cloud9: Performing Neoliberal Masculinities

Our examination of the Cloud9 CS:GO team illustrates how neoliberal masculinity is performed in the context of team-based games. Unlike Voorhees' analysis, which is agnostic in regard to either team-based or single-player eSports, this chapter endeavors to show how neoliberal masculinity is configured across a group of players. In particular, we argue that different figures of masculinity—hegemonic, subordinate, and oppositional—are cited and thus reconstituted by different members of the team, but that as a team Cloud9 operates as a coherent melange to perform neoliberal masculinity. Though interpersonal relationships do develop between team members, the team is constituted solely on the principle that the different members of the group contribute to its competitive effectivity and to its marketability.

At the time of the writing of this chapter, there are five players on the CS:GO roster, each of whom performs a different style of masculinity. The team's makeup is similar to that of a boy band in so far as they have individually created a canon that makes them marketable on their own and as a group. However, where a boy band is deliberately assembled and each of its band members preened to conform to marketable young heterosexual male ideals by a cadre of marketing executives, managers, and A&R representatives, Cloud9's CS:GO players do this work largely on their own, giving their fans icons to aspire to not only in terms of skill in the game but also in appearance. These differences are prized not for the sake of diversity but because they materialize in-game as sets of practices that complement and increase the effectiveness of one another. In the following pages, we create a composite of the masculinities each player performs, as well as discussing how they collectively perform neoliberal masculinity.

Ryan "fREAKAZOiD" Abadir represents the most poignant example of hegemonic, militarized masculinity. Outside of matches he is known as an amateur bodybuilder who leads the other team members through his gym routine, which other members of the team have cited as one of the keys to their gaming success. Furthermore, fREAKAZOiD dresses in a manner that draws attention to his buff physique, often wearing tank tops that show off his muscular arms in promotional videos and in private streams. This image of violent, sportive masculinity has stuck to fREAKAZOiD and likely contributed to a controversial, disputed charge of bullying a rival player that resulted in a steep fine. His performance of militarized masculinity is echoed in-game too, where casters commonly describe his play as "hyper aggressive." This is in line with his role on the team. fREAKAZOiD is what is commonly referred to as an "entry fragger" which is typically the most threatening role in the game, the first one into the fight and likely either the first to kill or be killed. This role requires the quickest reflexes, the greatest ability to follow orders, and, arguably, the least creativity. However, fREAKAZOiD is also loud and expressive, often shouting to celebrate a challenging kill or play well-executed by teammates, and a playful joker who is just as likely to hoist a teammate overhead as a trophy. In this way, his performance of militarized masculinity is colored by his embrace of "digital boyhood" (Burrill 2008, 15).

Within the context of hegemonic masculinity, the quiet Tyler "Skadoodle" Latham is the counterpart to fREAKAZOiD's exuberance but, more importantly, he exemplifies the individualism enshrined by hegemonic masculinity (Trujillo 1991, 291). He presents himself as the strong silent type, a loner that often refuses to smile or give extensive answers in interviews. His silence may be, in apart, a result of social awkwardness but it is also an integral part of his performance of masculinity. He has constructed the persona of a cold, hard killer, a guy who is too tough for words. Eschewing most non-instrumental communication, his is the masculinity of a lone wolf. Fittingly, Skadoodle's role in-game is the "AWPer" (named for the game's sniper rifle), the person who stands farthest back from the fight for longer distance kills. This allows him to contribute to the overall effort without typically being in the middle of the action. Indeed, highlight reels featuring Skadoodle are filled with scenarios in which all of his teammates are out of the match and he defeats three, four, or even five (a full complement) opponents single-handedly. Both in-game and out Skadoodle is an outsider and a loner.

This is somewhat similar to the role of "lurker" that Jordan "n0thing" Gilbert, the joker and resident "mother" of the team, plays. However, unlike the AWPer, the lurker is concerned not only with finding and maintaining the right position but also with collecting and managing information about the opposing team's movements and positions. In this way, the lurker is far from a loner and instead is an integral node in their team's communication network, keeping their team apprised of what others are up to. Though the domain is certainly different, this bears some similarity to the function of a kin-keeper, a familial role that is typically gendered feminine and generally taken on by women, and that involves coordination and communication within the family (Rosenthal 1985). His profile video on Valve's YouTube channel, uniquely, situates n0thing as strongly filial, emphasizing ties to his brother and parents. Given that n0thing is also known for cooking meals and treats while the team is traveling, his performance of masculinity is rife with communication, care, and nurturing both during gameplay and in videos and other promotional materials. Indeed, also known for inventing his own hype dance, "the flashbang," and encouraging teammates to join in its performance, n0thing also plays the part of a "cheerleader." Significantly, Taylor et al.'s (2009) study of women's participation in eSports articulates this function to the actual girlfriends and mothers (of players) at events.

The sole Canadian on the team, Mike "shroud" Grzesiek is also the only player to have experience training and playing in Europe. Despite his pedigree, he is arguably the most approachable and personable member of the team, perhaps because his dedication to and success as a Twitch streamer, which places him in a position to more frequently and directly interact with fans and the community. That shroud is surrounded by the bigger personalities of his teammates also contributes to the positive perception of him, with enthusiasts calling him "good guy shroud," playing on the "good guy Greg" meme, and praising him for being a "nice guy," on Reddit and elsewhere. In game, shroud plays the part of a "support," a player who primarily aids the entry fragger. Outside of professional play the role is largely shunned because it is about setting up rather than executing highlights and amazing plays, and as such it does not generally do well in regard to player rankings. Of course, the position is vital but it can seem otherwise and be overlooked because the "support" does not exhibit command, perform extreme aggression, highlight its individuality, or enact feminized communication labor. However, there is reason to argue that the "support" role, generally, is gendered feminine in game culture. Miller and Summers (2007) discern a tendency for the supporting characters, those in supplemental or helper roles, to be gendered feminine. This is supported by Ratan et al. (2015), who found that among League of Legends players, women tended to play roles supporting male players.

Though Sean "sgares" Gares retired just before the writing of this chapter, he was the face and the voice of the team, both in and out of gameplay. Fans commonly asked for advice about how he styles his hair and he is perceived as the dandy of the group. He is the player that others point to when asked about who is the most successful romantically or the most handsome (questions that come up frequently). But sgares is not just a pretty face, he also plays the part of the figurative brain of the team. sgares is the "strat caller," the team's leader and decision-maker. In this role, sgares sets the strategy for each match during the initial moments of gameplay and identifies and sets into action effective tactical responses as the matches unfolded. This role, more than any other in the professional CS:GO scene, is premised on control and is actualized in the repeated performance of mastery of the game. Where each position requires a mastery of a particular domain of embodied cognition, the "strat caller" must account for and successfully coordinate the efforts of the entirety of the team. The managerial quality is, in Western culture, often identified with the faculty of reason (Seigel 2005, 304). And Wajcman (1991) and Connell (1995) each make a distinct and compelling case for understanding constructions of masculinity premised on reason as subordinate but nevertheless complicit with hegemonic masculinities.

Each of the five members of the Cloud9 CS:GO team performs their own brand of masculinity. fREAKAZOiD enacts the most characteristic performance of militarized masculinity: the violent, aggressive, and physical figure that is still, in many contexts, the hegemonic construct. This is, oddly, complemented by sgares' physical attractiveness, and contrasted with sgares' deliberate, intelligent leadership over the rest of the team. Skadoodle's radical individualism is a return to core components of hegemonic masculinity, and exemplifies the "strong, silent type." This is offset by n0thing's strongly communicative and emotionally expressive performance, both in his gameplay role and in his antics in streams and video materials. Among this group, shroud, the easy-going nice guy whose role is support, is sometimes overlooked. When compared directly, there are clear distinctions to be drawn between them.

But it is important to note that while each of the Cloud9 players is practicing a distinct form(ation) of masculinity, they are all drawing from culturally relevant precedents, stereotypes, and representations. Some, like fREAKAZOiD's militarized masculinity, seem to be taken more whole-cloth from a description of hegemonic masculinity in North American popular culture generally, but even then it is tinged with the affect of digital boyhood. Others enact complex and contradictory practices that blend elements of hegemonic, complicit, and subordinate masculinities, like n0thing, who, like the rest of his team, is proficient with the simulated violence at the core of the game, as well as the technology and techniques for playing his role effectively, but also enacts a good deal of communication and caring for his team. This latter performance of masculinity is firmly in line with the neoliberal masculinity that, Voorhees (2012) argues, is becoming hegemonic in eSports, and game cultures more broadly.

However, we maintain that it is more vital to note that when taken as a whole the team exemplifies the compromises that neoliberalism demands of masculinities. There is no necessary allegiance to the patriarchal order that enshrines more conventional forms of hegemonic masculinity. In fact, communication, care, and support are valued as essential elements to the success of the team. These activities and practices, traditionally feminized in the game cultures (Harvey and Fisher 2013; Parker et al. 2017), are integrated into the spectacle of masculinities characteristic of professional FPS players. Of course, the coordination of hegemonic, complicit, and subordinate masculinities to maintain patriarchal domination is by no means novel; it is a historical pattern that Connell (1995) explains in her foundational work. Rather, what is notable is the way that in eSports militarized masculinity, which occupies the hegemonic position in the wider spheres of games culture and popular culture, is subordinated to a "geek" masculinity, one based on knowledge and intellectual mastery. In this configuration, typically marginalized expressions of masculinity—those that are nurturing or supportive—are granted access to patriarchal power that is in other contexts unavailable.

Coming Down from Cloud9

This is indicative of the emergence of a distinct form of hegemonic masculinity in the context of professional(ized) digital gameplay and culture, a neoliberal masculinity. And while it shares some touchstones with the militarized construction of hegemonic masculinity operative in North American public culture, outside of specific contexts, neoliberal masculinity is both complicit with and subordinate to hegemonic masculinity. But within the domain of eSports, neoliberal masculinity—the fluid, adaptable, and impious figure of manliness, the *bricoleur* that draws from anything that works—is dominant.

This form of masculinity, at first blush, appears to be progressive.

Traditionally feminized practices like communication and support, while marginalized in other aspects of game culture, are valued in eSports and professional(ized) gameplay. Intellect, rather than the physical body, is recognized as vital, bypassing one of the foundations of hegemonic masculinity (Connell 1995, 52–53). Furthermore, the very playing field is constituted by information, and the activity of gameplay is preoccupied with the management and response to information. As Johnson (2011) argues, the technomasculinities often articulated to games and game cultures are premised on the mastery and management of information, and are subordinated to militarized masculinities in public culture. But, as GamerGate should remind us (Connell made a strong case for this 30 years ago), subordinate masculinities are every bit as invested in accessing and wielding the privileges of the patriarchal order, and will use symbolic and physical violence to protect it (Nakamura 2012).

After all, technomasculinities may be centered on knowledge, but they are still premised upon domination and mastery (Burrill 2008). And while techno-masculinities may de-center militarized masculinity, they still work to exclude and marginalize women by naturalizing the association between technology and men (Kocurek 2015).

In fact, there is no evidence and little reason to believe the neoliberal masculinity is in any way ethically or instrumentally (that is to say, politically) better than the hegemonic masculinity that reigns in North American public culture. Certainly, it could be argued that neoliberal masculinity at least marks a malleable spot in an otherwise rigidly fixed masculine order. Though this is "only" a symbolic victory, it does make available symbolic resources for others who may come after. Still, this has little material benefit to anyone other than the men who can gain access to patriarchal power through this new configuration of masculinities. Indeed, as Shugart's (2008) analysis of the emergence of "metrosexual" masculinity shows, seemingly progressive masculinities do not challenge the structure of gender relations but rather illustrate the resilience of patriarchy.

Coming full circle, there is no better example of this than the homoerotic talking, touching, and looking that passes between the members of the Cloud9 CS:GO team, and between the team and their fans. Though Connell (1992) makes it clear that the increased intelligibility of gayness—and we would add queerness generally—does open possibilities for subverting the patriarchal gender order, in the context of sports, homoeroticism has a troubled history of shoring up patriarchal power (c.f. Taylor and Chess in this volume). And Western sports industries have developed nuanced strategies, some employing homoeroticism, for the commodification of the bodies of male players (Miller 2002). This is not to suggest that homoeroticism in (e)sports is not a valid or common affect. Only that it can't be embraced uncritically.

So when the players are asked questions about team dynamics and relationships in videos produced by the gaming accessory and peripheral companies that sponsor the team, homoeroticism is openly displayed. One series of "20 Questions"-style videos asks players, "Who is your favourite teammate?" and "If you could go on a date with any teammate who would it be and why?" During n0thing's 20 Questions video, sgares comes from off camera to kiss him on the cheek after responding to the question "Who on the team are you closest with?" During the kiss a small heart animation was added: "We have a special relationship as you can see." Skadoodle is asked "Who would you date out of all your teammates?" but his answer, given without pause, is the same: "sgares." But when sgares is asked, "Who has the biggest bromance on the team?" he describes shroud and n0thing "almost naked in bed watching demos together." And later, when asked about his current love interests, sgares responds, "Definitely Jordan (n0thing). He sings to me, he massages me at LANs ... cooks for me." These questions, some of which are selected from fan submissions, are not unusual, nor is it uncommon to see team members putting their arm around each other, touching suggestively for the viewers, and looking directly at the camera during suggestive moments. Only fREAKA-ZOiD refuses to discursively engage with this circulation of desire, and when asked to describe teammates responds with jokes, "smelly" or likens them to family, describing them as a "long lost cousin," a "big brother as a father figure," and a cool "step-brother." Still, fREAKAZOiD contributes to the homoerotic dynamic in other ways; his muscular physique is featured prominently in the introductory portion of his 20 Questions video and in 3 of the 20 questions. Another question asks why other players, and especially n0thing, are not allowed to touch him, and instead of a kiss on the cheek the video shows him roughhousing with a teammate. Even in these circumspect ways and despite his ostensible refusal, fREAKAZOiD is caught up in the performance, representation, and circulation of homoerotic desires.

And according to the team members, this desire also circulates between the players and their fans. Players tell stories about fans to asking to have their nipples signed because "[they] seem like a cool team" and several instances in which fans have asked for them to take their shirts off and give them to them. While they tell fans that it is not appropriate to hug or drape a sweaty arm around players, they also emphasize that the attention is appreciated in the right context. For instance, sgares posted a photograph on Twitter that features him next to a male fan with one arm around him and another holding a sign (signed by six other professional gamers) that reads: "I'm gay for Sean." sgares commented, "This made me smile today," and another pro replied, "At least he's man enough to admit it. The entire NA [North American] pro scene feels this way." Homoerotic practices and desires become normalized through the team's actions in these types of promotional videos and in-person interactions with team.

But normalized to what effect? It would be inaccurate to claim that heteronormativity is not a prevailing cultural force in most areas of games culture, and indefensible to suggest that the Cloud9 CS:GO team's homoerotic performances reflect a deliberately progressive communication or branding strategy. Even within the team and among their fans, for all the erotic looks, touches, and language there is more that anchors their masculinities in heterosexism and outright homophobia.

The players all attempt to enact various images of hegemonic masculinity rather than the stereotypical image of the gamer: awkward, lanky bodies, shaggy unkempt hair, and pimply faces. And each individual player's performance of masculinity, though in some cases inflected with traditionally feminine qualities, is also grounded in the clear citation of (or reference to) normative masculinities. And though fREAKAZOiD may best exemplify it, all the players, at times, on Cloud9's CS:GO team display toxic elements of sportive masculinity such as the emphasis on going to the gym as part of a training routine, telling sexist "your mom" jokes, and giving problematic, even misogynistic, advice on dating "grills." Furthermore, by promoting a "healthy lifestyle" coterminous with a gaming career, including a regime of exercise and diet, the Cloud9 team claims that "everybody" can be a successful gamer but actually work to ensure that the bodies typically privileged in other spaces find privilege in professional gaming too. By helping to entrench sportive masculinity in these spaces, even as one of several facets of a neoliberal masculinity, they carry forward the same ideals that disparage women and other minority groups and make it more difficult for them to participate in the culture.

In lieu of a proper conclusion, there is no better example of the ambiguous, and somewhat tense, relationship between patriarchy and the seemingly progressive elements of neoliberal masculinities than the following scene from a live-streamed "Ask Me Anything" session for Reddit. Cloud9's CS:GO team manager reads a question off his laptop: "'Since you guys are spending a lot of time together, does it ever heat up a bit?' And I don't think he means that sexually, before things get weird." The player to his right, n0thing, responds by first replying to the coach, "I think that's the only thing he meant, and I wanna say 'shame on you'" before looking to the camera and responding to the fan's question: "Of course things get heated up." Everyone laughs and the conversation quickly moves on to describe a few occasions when the players have gotten into fights with one another. This instance is a wonderful illustration of the promise and peril of the neoliberal masculinity inculcated through professional(ized) gameplay. Not because it is an aberration in an otherwise heteronormative exchange, but rather because this moment exemplifies the dialect of progressive and oppressive qualities of neoliberal masculinity. Homoerotic relations, with a laugh, are sublimated into talk about fights, familiar ground for militarized masculinities.

Note

1. Kenneth Burke (1969) argued that criticism often "involves the search for a 'representative anecdote,' to be used as a form in conformity with which the vocabulary is constructed" (59). This is to say, an specific example that so crystalizes a textual of social formation that it can be employed as the basis for comparison, generalization, and critique.

Bibliography

Baerg, Andrew. 2012. Risky Business: Neoliberal Rationality and the Computer RPG. In *Dungeons, Dragons, and Digital Denizens: The Digital Role-Playing Game*, ed. Gerald Voorhees, Josh Call, and Katie Whitlock, 153–173. New York: Continuum.

Bennett, Tony. 2003. Culture and Governmentality. In *Foucault, Cultural Studies and Governmentality*, ed. Jack Bratich, Jeremy Packer, and Cameron McCarthy, 47–65. Albany, NY: State University of New York.

Biesecker, Barbara. 1995. Michel Foucault and the Question of Rhetoric. *Philosophy and Rhetoric* 2: 351–364.

Brookey, Robert Alan, and Thomas Patrick Oates, eds. 2014. *Playing to Win: Sports, Video Games, and the Culture of Play*. Indianapolis, IN: Indiana University Press.

Brown, Wendy. 2015. *Undoing the Demos: Neoliberalism's Stealth Revolution*. New York: Zone Books.

Bryce, Jo, and Jason Rutter. 2003. Gender Dynamics and the Social and Spatial Organization of Computer Gaming. *Leisure Studies* 22 (1): 1–15.

Burke, Kenneth. 1969. *Grammar of Motives*. Berkeley, CA: University of California Press.

Burrill, Derek A. 2008. *Die Tryin': Videogames, Masculinity, Culture*. New York: Peter Lang.

Cassell, Justine, and Henry Jenkins. 1998. *From Barbie to Mortal Kombat: Gender and Computer Games*. Cambridge, MA: MIT.

Connell, Raewyn. 1992. A Very Straight Gay: Masculinity, Homosexual Experience, and the Dynamics of Gender. *American Sociological Review* 57 (6): 735–751.

———. 1995. *Masculinities*. Cambridge: Polity Press.

Connell, R., and James W. Messerschmidt. 2005. Hegemonic Masculinity: Rethinking the Concept. *Gender & Society* 19 (6): 829–859.

Consalvo, Mia, Konstantin Mitgutsch, and Abraham Stein, eds. 2013. *Sports Videogames*. New York: Routledge.

Dyer-Witheford, Nick, and Greig de Peuter. 2009. *Games of Empire: Global Capitalism and Video Games*. Minneapolis, MN: University of Minnesota Press.

Foucault, Michel. 1991. Governmentality. In *The Foucault Effect: Studies in Governmentality*, ed. Graham Burchell, Colin Gordon, and Peter Miller, 87–104. Chicago, IL: University of Chicago Press.

———. 1988. Technologies of the Self. In *Technologies of the Self: A Seminar with Michel Foucault*, ed. Martin Luther, Huck Guttman, and Patrick Hutton, 16–48. Amherst, MA: University of Massachusetts Press.

Hamann, Trent H. 2009. Neoliberalism, Governmentality, and Ethics. *Foucault Studies* 6: 37–59.

Harper, Todd. 2014. *The Culture of Digital Fighting Games: Performance and Practice*. New York: Routledge.

Harvey, Alison, and Stephanie Fisher. 2013. Making a Name in Games. *Information, Communication & Society* 16 (3): 362–380.

Hong, Renyi. 2013. Game Modding, Prosumerism and Neoliberal Labor Practices. *International Journal of Communication* 7: 984–1002.

Hutchins, Brett. 2008. Signs of Meta-change in Second Modernity: The Growth of e-Sport and the World Cyber Games. *New Media & Society* 10 (6): 851–869.

Jin, Dal Yong. 2010. *Korea's Online Gaming Empire*. Cambridge, MA: The MIT Press.

Johnson, Robin S. 2011. Masculinities in Play: Examining Hegemonic and Technomasculinity in *Resident Evil 5* and *Dead Space. American Men's Studies Annual Review* 2: 122–142.

Jonasson, Kelly, and Jesper Thiborg. 2010. Electronic Sport and Its Impact on Future Sports. *Sport in Society: Cultures, Commerce, Media, Politics* 13 (2): 287–299.

Kafai, Yasmin B. 2008. *Beyond Barbie and Mortal Kombat: New Perspectives on Gender and Gaming*. Cambridge, MA: MIT.

Kline, Steven, Nick Dyer-Witheford, and Greg de Peuter. 2003. *Digital Play: The Interaction of Technology, Culture and Marketing*. Montreal, QC: McGill-Queen's University Press.

Kocurek, Carley. 2015. *Coin Operated Americans: Rebooting Boyhood at the Video Arcade*. St Paul, MN: University of Minnesota Press.

Lemke, Thomas. 2001. 'The Birth of Bio-politics': Michel Foucault's Lecture at the College de France on Neo-liberal Governmentality. *Economy and Society* 30 (2): 190–207.

Miller, Monica, and Alice Summers. 2007. Gender Differences in Video Game Characters' Roles, Appearances, and Attire as Portrayed in Video Game Magazines. *Sex Roles* 57 (9–10): 733–742.

Miller, Toby. 2002. *Sportsex*. Philadelphia, PA: Temple University Press.

Millington, Brad. 2009. Wii Has Never Been Modern: 'Active' Video Games and the 'Conduct of Conduct'. *New Media & Society* 11 (4): 621–640.

Nakamura, Lisa. 2012. Queer Female of Color: The Highest Difficulty Setting There Is? Gaming Rhetoric as Gender Capital. *Ada: A Journal of Gender, New Media, and Technology* 1. https://doi.org/10.7264/N37P8W9V.

Nguyen, Kim. 2016. Rhetoric in Neoliberalism. In *Rhetoric and Neoliberalism*, ed. Kim Nguyen, 1–14. New York: Palgrave Macmillan.

Parker, Felan, Jeniffer Whitson, and Bart Simon. 2017. Mega Booth: The Cultural Intermediation of Indie Games. *New Media & Society*. https://doi.org/10.1177/1461444817711403.

Ratan, Rabindra, Nick Taylor, Jameson Hogan, Tracy Kennedy, and Dimitri Williams. 2015. Stand by Your Man: An Examination of Gender Disparity in League of Legends. *Games and Culture* 10 (5): 438–462.

Read, Jason. 2009. A Genealogy of Homo-Economicus: Neoliberalism and the Production of Subjectivity. *Foucault Studies* 6: 25–36.

Rehak, Bob. 2003. Playing at Being: Psychoanalysis and the Avatar. In *The Video Game Theory Reader*, ed. M.J.P. Wolf and B. Perron, 103–127. New York: Routledge.

Rosenthal, Carolyn. 1985. Kinkeeping in the Familial Division of Labor. *Journal of Marriage and the Family* 47 (4): 965–974.

Seigel, Jerrod. 2005. *The Idea of the Self: Thought and Experience in Western Europe Since the Seventeenth Century*. New York: Cambridge University Press.

Shaw, Adrienne. 2014. *Gaming at the Edge: Sexuality and Gender at the Margins of Gamer Culture*. Minneapolis, MN: University of Minnesota Press.

Shugart, Helene. 2008. Managing Masculinities: The Metrosexual Moment. *Communication and Critical/Cultural Studies* 5 (3): 280–300.

Silverman, Mark, and Bart Simon. 2009. Discipline and Dragon Kill Points in the Online Power Game. *Games and Culture* 4 (4): 353–378.

Szablewicz, Marcella. 2011. From Addicts to Athletes: Participation in the Discursive Construction of Digital Games in Urban China. In *Selected Papers of Internet Research*, ed. Association of Internet Researchers. http://spir.aoir.org/papers/szablewicz.pdf.

Taylor, Nicholas. 2011. Play Globally, Act Locally: The Standardization of Pro Halo 3 Gaming. *International Journal of Gender, Science and Technology* 3 (1): 228–242.

Taylor, Nicholas, Jen Jenson, and Suzanne De Castell. 2009. Cheerleaders/Booth Babes/ Halo Hoes: Pro-gaming, Gender and Jobs for the Boys. *Digital Creativity NDCR* 20 (4): 239–252.

Taylor, Nicholas, Kelly Bergstrom, Jen Jenson, and Suzanne de Castell. 2015. Alienated Playbour: Relations of Production in EVE Online. *Games and Culture* 10 (4): 365–388.

Taylor, T.L. 2012. *Raising the Stakes: E-Sports and the Professionalization of Computer Gaming*. Cambridge, MA: MIT.

Trujillo, Nick. 1991. Hegemonic Masculinity on the Mound: Media Representations of Nolan Ryan and American Sports Culture. *Critical Studies in Mass Communication* 8 (3): 290–308.

Voorhees, Gerald. 2012. Neoliberal Masculinity: The Government of Play and Masculinity in eSports. In *Playing to Win: Sports, Video Games, and the Culture of Play*, ed. Robert Brookey and Thomas Oates, 63–91. Indianapolis, IN: Indiana University Press.

Wajcman, Judy. 1991. *Feminism Confronts Technology*. Cambridge: Polity Press.

Whitson, Jennifer. 2013. Gaming the Quantified Self. *Surveillance and Society* 11 (1/2): 163–176.

Witkowski, Emma. 2012. On the Digital Playing Field How We "Do Sport" With Networked Computer Games. *Games and Culture* 7 (5): 349–374.

Zhang, Lin. 2013. Productive vs. Pathological. The Contested Space of Video Games in Post-Reform China (1980s–2012). *International Journal of Communication* 7: 2391–2411.

13

Masculinity's New Battle Arena in International e-Sports: The Games Begin

Lily Zhu

In April 2014, a Chinese-based *League of Legends* (*League*) team, LMQ, permanently moved to the United States, and qualified for the North American Championship Series, sparking questions of nationality and global representation. Could a team full of Chinese-born citizens ever truly represent North America (NA) in international tournaments? Or were they "North America" in name only, forever a reminder of foreign encroachment? For a vocal set of e-sports fans, there could be no national pride, for if LMQ won, it would still be a victory for China; as GG08 (see Zhu 1) writes, "imagine if they actually won worlds … it'd pretty much just be china winning … not NA." Formal discussions of green cards, citizenship, and nationhood gave way to disputes over less tangible measures of identity, such as arbitrary standards of "sincerity" and compatibility with American ideals. While plenty of *League* players did welcome LMQ as an "American Dream" Cinderella story, the team's arrival nevertheless exposed a racial divide that persists to this day (see Fig. 13.1).

In this chapter, I trace the progress of a reactionary rhetoric in the *League* community, generated by North American and European perceptions of Asian dominance in e-sports. Because five out of the past six World Championships have featured South Korean, Chinese, or Taiwanese finalists, fans have often treated the event, and the state of the competitive scene as a whole, as a battle of East versus West, with North American and European players putting aside differences for the sake of a common goal: defeating the

L. Zhu (✉)
University of Texas, Austin, TX, USA

© The Author(s) 2018
N. Taylor, G. Voorhees (eds.), *Masculinities in Play*, Palgrave Games in Context,
https://doi.org/10.1007/978-3-319-90581-5_13

Fig. 13.1 Reactions to LMQ's relocation from China to the United States

undefeatable giants of East Asia.[1] The hemispheric division exceeds simple patriotic fervor, and has spawned a racialized discourse that eschews body-dependent manifestations of masculinity[2] only so another troubling model can be constructed in their place. By studying player and audience responses to world championships, team playstyles, and player trades, we can see how the feminization and roboticization of East Asian opponents reflects an attempt to mitigate the threat that these individuals and teams offer to Euro-American hegemony, in a virtual domain where the male body—its over-whelming presence, its potential to force submission through physical strength—no longer dictates the terms of masculinity in quite the same way. In "Let's Get Physical," I study the rhetoric of physical emasculation that e-sports participants have co-opted and modified to dismiss the individual as an outlier, and in "Man versus Goliath," I study the correlating rhetoric of dehumanization that allows the large-scale, group erasure of East Asian differ-ence. Though digital masculinity—that is, masculinity expressed through digital means—overwrites some remnants of nineteenth-century race theory (e.g. the "sick man of Asia" trope David Scott references in *China and the International System* [2008]), it does so at the risk of spawning equally dichot-omous, if updated, conceptions of East and West that encourage an ethnic antagonism veiled as nationalism. e-Sports thus functions as a point of cul-tural friction and exchange: where global diversity meets monolithic impulses.

My project is a case study of *League* culture and relies on forum posts and team publicity statements as primary sources. Though I address a range of competitive games, I choose to focus on *League*, a MOBA with increasing numbers of external investors and consumers, a structural emphasis on player leagues, and a professional scene less consistently regulated and systemized than those of contemporaries (e.g. *Defense of the Ancients 2*). For instance, the president (Marc Merrill) and other high-profile employees of Riot Games, *League*'s developer, frequently post on Reddit about a variety of issues and in response to player concerns voiced through the venue. The line between public and private has yet to be clearly defined in this game space: fans play with and against professionals; retired professionals become game analysts and interviewers; and Riot employees interact directly with their consumers. The sources I've compiled for this project reflect the same sense of fluidity. In the *League* community, news articles and academic statistics hold just as much weight (perhaps less) as the real-time, unpolished interactions published on Reddit and the official *League* forum. I approach these e-sports artifacts with critical discourse analysis and Pierre Bourdieu's work[3] on embodied practices in mind because nonacademic voices have directly impacted ongoing policy changes and influenced the competitive climate.[4] *League* is a game that is—for good or ill—particularly sensitive to its player base, reproducing and embodying the underlying sociocultural struggles of its consumers through the policies Riot Games enacts in response.

Let's Get Physical

The focus on dexterity elements[5] rather than on strength has led some to conclude that competitive gaming is an egalitarian space, where differences in gender and sex are made irrelevant. Ralf Reichert, CEO of the Electronic Sports League (ESL), stated that "there is no reason why a female gamer should not be able to compete with a male one, and surpass him in terms of skill" (Gera 2014). As egalitarian as this may sound, the prioritization of strategy over brute force has done little to diversify e-sports, which remains a masculine domain with a skewed gender distribution. Rather, masculinity, stripped of its *traditional* connection to the body, has been redefined according to intellectual patterns of dominance and toxicity that continue to intersect with a player's physical form.[6]

The objective diminution of physical barriers to entry into the competitive scene does not signal the community's lack of interest in physical markers; in fact, the verbal abuse that is frequently leveraged against opponents is anchored in a preoccupation with the body—with how a player's size, race, sex (and sexuality), and able-bodiedness are represented through his/her successes and failures in the game space. In "A Silent Team Is a Dead Team: Communicative Norms in Competitive FPS Play" (2012a), Nick Taylor discusses e-sport's engagement with "verbal antagonism," "which traffics in the kinds of homophobia, misogyny, and hyper-masculinization commonly associated with professional sports" (257). Interestingly, were you to ask any casual or amateur e-sports participants about the presence of such gendered behavior, they would likely respond that it is more a vocalization of psychological play or frustrated insecurity than anything else. Kwak and Blackburn (2015) state that "computer-mediated communication" is particularly susceptible to a "hostility and aggressiveness" that "players themselves sometimes fail to recognize … as toxic" (209). When expectations fail to be met or failure seems imminent, players "… grow increasingly aggressive, eventually lashing out with purely abusive language" (215). Competitive gaming enthusiasts refashion standard, masculine locker-room expressions as strategy, or at the very least, a byproduct of passionate, intellectual investment. What does it say, though, about those claims that video games free us from cultural biases against certain bodies when the goal to "tilt" an opponent or to defend one's own ego relies on reinforcing the primacy of the physical form? Toxic language circumvents the perceived emasculation of virtual loss by associating manifestations of masculinity and power with phenotypic qualities *unrelated* to the play at hand.

With the rising popularity of competitive gaming, there has been a return to, and privileging of, bodies that have shaped conceptions of masculinity in recent history. A player's body—not the eyes, hands, fingers, and fine motor skills necessary for e-sports, but the body in its entirety—has the potential to debunk demeaning stereotypes of the marginalized, unhealthy gamer, and to elevate games in terms of artistic merit, activity, and social interaction (Kowet et al. 2014). Several idealized, male figures have thrown their weight behind e-sports, increasing the urgency of making e-sports events and professionals fit (literally and metaphorically) for public consumption. Former American football player Christ Kluwe (2014) drew from his background as an athlete and gamer to indict #GamerGate while celebrating the assimilation of games into popular culture; his article is an expletive-laden diatribe that notes the very hostile, masculine nature of verbal interactions in game culture. Gordon Hayward, an NBA basketball player for the Utah Jazz, featured in a video interview for *League*, touting the similarities between physical sports and e-sports as he plays informal *League* matches with the professional team Curse (Dorsey 2014). And Rick Fox, retired basketball player for the Los Angeles Lakers, purchased a North American *League* team in December 2015, rebranded it as Echo Fox, and plans to expand it into *Counter-Strike: Global Offensive* (Mueller 2016).

What is notable about these events is that while they serve to validate the legitimacy of e-sports as an actual sport, they do so through the filter of a distinctly Euro-American masculinity, one that has historically exoticized and effeminized Asian bodies. Asian studies scholars have long discussed the roots of "stereotypical representations and images of a feminized and emasculated Asian American masculinity" (Eng 2001, 33), tracing its lineage through the immigration of Chinese railroad workers (Cheung 2007) and further back through the effects of, and justifications for, the nineteenth-century British imperialism. Modern globalization has guaranteed the international ubiquity of this effeminized (East) Asian masculinity. Take, for instance, Jeremy Lin's experience in (and prior to) the NBA. Jason Whitlock (2012) of Foxsports. com tweeted, "Some lucky lady in NYC is gonna feel a couple inches of pain tonight" following Lin's high-scoring performance against the Lakers. Former NBA athlete Rex Walters attributed the lack of collegiate and professional interest in Jeremy Lin prior to his draft to this same stereotype: "It's the Asian thing .... people who don't think stereotypes exist are crazy. If he's white, he's either a good shooter or heady. If he's Asian, he's good at math. We're not taking him" (Reilly 2012). Both comments expose an artificial hierarchy of bodily characteristics where height and build are certainly important, but not as important as racial markers in determining gaming skill and social success. When an Asian male undermines these expectations, he becomes a spectacle, a subject of confusion and discomfort who must be simplified.

The virtual realm is not emancipated from gender or race, and like physical sports, places an undue burden on those who are visually othered. On February 21, 2016, following the impressive performance of Balls (An Le) in C9's *League* match against TSM, a Redditor—"Skiipie"[7]—began a top-voted thread that banters about Le's sexual and physical abilities. A posted picture of An Le jokingly flexing his bicep for a female fan led to a sub-thread comparing Le to another Asian American team member's success with the "hunnies" (barteks10 2016), though the eventual conclusion was that "Hai" (Hai Lam) remained the "Whiz Khalifa of E-sports" (Promasterchief 2016). While the fans' gentle ribbing is clearly supportive and affectionate, it is dictated by regulatory curiosity toward a foreign masculinity that has been desexualized in the Western hemisphere. This racial component is never addressed outright, but becomes more explicit lower down in the thread, when "GhostshipDemos" contributes another photo of Le, this time of his face and chest during a workout session. The photo generates a series of comments that reveals discomfort, defensiveness, and stereotypical rationalizations having little to do with the intellectual activity of e-sports. I have transcribed the Reddit thread below, while maintaining the original nested format:

- GhostshipDemos: http://i.imgur.com/NMyZPMs.jpg

  - HEBushido: I wasn't gonna say Balls is that jacked, but damn those cheat striations are nuts. Is he southeast Asian? I know a dude who's Thai who isn't big, but he's strong as fuck.

    - Banana_Fetish: That feel when you're a 6'5" 200 lb white dude whos been lifting for 5 years and your bench is still 60 lbs below 5'3" Balls.

      - Aspiring_Physicist: 200 at 6'5 is pretty skinny still … especially if you've been lifting for 5 years.

        - Banana_Fetish: I had meningitis and was on a fluid only diet for quite a while, I'm currently trying to regain what I lost, I agree, 200 is quite small, I was sitting around 215.

          - Aspiring_Physicist: Gotcha. I wasn't trying to take a shot at you, just pointing out that you could eat more and probably see some strength gains. Congrats on being healthy again!

        - Pachinginator: He has to bench literally twice the distance balls does …. being tall and having long arms makes lifting a lot harder for bench especially

          - Aspiring_Physicist: Trust me I know. I wasn't taking shots at him.

        - Turboswag: Not everyone lifts to get big tho

      - Bearrison_Ford: Don't feel bad, it's way easier for short people to lift than it is for tall people.

[removed: section on the relevance of height to lifting ability]

  - Kalesvol: yeah. hes Vietnamese.

    - HEBushido: That explains it. He looks like Tony Jaa right there.

  - My_elo_is_potato: He is Vietnamese.
  - KumonRoguing: Low body fat shows muscles well.

Based on the succession of comments,[8] Le's body is on display not because it is *a* body or even a *male* body, but because it is an East Asian (male) body. "Banana_Fetish" admiringly and somewhat jokingly writes, "That feel when you're a 6'5" 200 lb *white* dude whos [sic] been lifting for 5 years and your bench is still 60 lbs below 5'3" Balls."[9] While

"Banana_Fetish" intends to indirectly compliment Le, his insertion of "white" is telling. "Banana_Fetish" considers his own racial and/or ethnic identity to be deeply relevant to this conversation. Being "white" is listed as an *addition* to—not synonym for—height and weight. Regardless of whether his embarrassment is feigned, "Banana_Fetish" and other commenters normalize the inclusion of whiteness in a thread that is ostensibly about size differentials. It is so defaulted as to be invisible, the subject of no replies or debate; yes, whiteness is associated with masculine achievement, and yes, Le's superiority in this respect has disturbed that foundation. The whiteness of "Banana_Fetish" is tied to his weightlifting achievements not just in his mind, but the mind of others too. Le's performance calls into question the role of whiteness in setting the standard for international, physical masculinity.

As this thread continues, it quickly veers from admiration to qualified praise that renders Le's body a racial outlier—anomalous and therefore dismissible in the Euro-American construction of Asian masculinities. A commenter notes that "Banana_Fetish" is weak for his size (and by proxy, his race), a point which "Banana_Fetish" concedes with additional information (meningitis).[10] In other words, the failure of Banana_Fetish to equal or exceed Le's lifting statistics is not representative of those in the same group as "Banana_Fetish" (i.e. "white dude[s]"), nor can his failure be used to reconceptualize Le's place in Asian masculinities. "HEBushido" asks if Le is "southeast Asian," to which "Kalesvoi" replies in the affirmative—an affirmative that offers comfort: "That explains it." "Explains" what? Le's disconcerting show of strength? Le's destabilization of masculine expectations? Le's performance is reframed through a rare sensitivity to the array of ethnicities and peoples in Asia, a rhetorical move made not out of respect, but out of the desire to exclude. The monolithic treatment of Asians is temporarily halted so that any threat An Le could potentially offer to masculinity is made anomalous. It is imperative that Le be separated from the rest of Asia (still monolithic) so that the stereotype of general Asian male docility can be protected. Le's abilities are the result of a particular region and a particular minority group that is too specific to function as the impetus for a paradigm shift. Paradoxically, the recognition of Asian diversity, of Le's Vietnamese background as distinct, is what maintains the Redditors' confidence in regressive understandings of Asian physique as a whole.

The increasing relevance of male bodies in determining competitive worth in e-sports is symptomatic of general anxiety towards the intrusion of markedly different people into a history of Euro-American homogeneity.

As with traditional sports,[11] the East Asian body must once more face speculation and juxtaposition against the international standard of (western) masculinity.

Man Versus Goliath

By discounting the Asian bodies that would otherwise demand attention and consideration, it becomes easier for the e-sports community to dehumanize and erase entire ethnicities. The international viability of e-sports is dependent on a perception of racial and ethnic homogeneity that regulates and contains "Asian" presence within the simple narrative of East versus West—of those robotic, voracious consumers versus those daring entrepreneurs who designed the game(s) in the first place, and now seek to reclaim their rightful places as creators *and* e-sports champions. The variety of Asian nations and individuals involved in the competitive sphere are akin to *League* "bots," difficult AI opponents to be overcome rather than appreciated as global participants in the creative process.

Over the years, it has become an ironic fact and a sore point that though massively popular games are produced and distributed in the western hemisphere, their competitive scenes are co-opted by East Asian nations such as China and South Korea. Whether it is *Starcraft II* (Blizzard Entertainment 2010), *Defense of the Ancients II,* or *League,* many e-sports and real-time strategy (RTS) games are developed by American companies, and released first in North America and Europe. At the same time, the increasingly profitable e-sports industries in North America and Europe are dependent on the economic and cultural infrastructures previously set in place by gaming giants like South Korea and China—a fact most gamers openly acknowledge (D. Devil 2011). In his article for *Venture Beat,* Jay Eum (2015) expresses a sentiment common to fans and professionals alike: "the games may be American, but the associations and tournaments with the longest history, and the most dominant teams and players are overwhelmingly Asian." While the opposition of "American" and "Asian" seems insignificant here, it is an unintentional shift that reflects a greater dialogic trend—fostered by players of all nationalities and ethnicities—pitting individual Western nations against the perceived cultural and ethnic collective of Asia. Prior to this statement, Eum had been detailing South Korea's early, pivotal role in revolutionizing the landscape of e-sports; and yet, the moment historical background must transition to a comparison of South Korean and

American gaming culture in present day, Eum abruptly replaces "South Korean" with "Asian." The discussion of America's receptiveness to competitive gaming is not subsumed within "North America" or the "West," but South Korea is made synonymous with "Asia"—an entire continent. Eum is unaware of his linguistic slippage, referring to South Korea once as "that Asian nation" (the United States is never "that North American nation"), and titling the 2015 article "The Next Multibillion Dollar Tech Trend from Asia" despite referencing one other Asian nation (Japan,[12] and only as a contrast to South Korea). According to this common style of e-sports journalism, in the face of Euro-American diversity, Asia is a homogeneous monolith, a vast region wherein one nation is equivalent and interchangeable with any other nation.

Western culture and Eastern culture are poised in opposition, with the former portrayed as conducive to production and innovation, and the latter as ... not. Keith Sawyer (2011) argues that the "creativity beliefs" of the "Western world" are "rooted in a broader set of cultural assumptions known as *individualism*"—of being exceptional, unique, and separate (2028–2029). Because individualism is equated to fragmentation, cultures in the "West" can remain distinct from each other even as they are home to an overarching set of ideologies. On the other side of the binary are "cultures at the collectivist end" (Sawyer 2029)—cultures, we can safely assume, that are non-Western, that are proponents of the unexceptional, and that are therefore monolithic. Within this paradigm, an individualistic United States will not be mistaken for an individualistic Germany, but a collectivist South Korea can be substituted with a collectivist China which can be substituted with a collectivist Taiwan. The current dichotomy of creative individualism and unimaginative collectivism originates from a long, imperial history of Asian exclusion, and is driven by a similar impulse to minimize the racial/cultural/national threats that Asian achievements imply:

> Takaki (1992) writes of how white workers in nineteenth-century US, when accusing Chinese workers of posing unfair competition, described them as 'human machines' and 'steam engines' that could work endlessly. Echoing these accusations, current hostilities towards Asians often focus on their inhuman, robot-like and one-dimensional qualities .... (Kibria 1998, 953–954)

The relegation of young, Asian gamers to this same inhuman and erosive category of "robot" takes on an additional intonation when we contextualize creation in Western masculinity. Sandra Gilbert and Susan Gubar begin the first chapter of *The Madwoman in the Attic* (2000) with the evocative question, "Is a pen a metaphorical penis?" They trace a history of sexist thought that linked (and still links) "the creative gift" to males, and authorship—by virtue of its etymology—to fathers (3–4). To dictate ownership of creativity and creative potential is to define the boundaries of masculinity, in this case, along troubling lines of the nineteenth-century "whiteness" (Kibria). In a discourse where they are denied creative abilities, Asian nations are essentially being stripped of manhood, of virility, and of masculinity.

The susceptibility of Asian nations to generalizations by European and North American countries[13] is exacerbated by the neutering of Asian masculinities. Discussions of work ethic are routed through robotics[14] and mechanics, diminishing the human, sympathetic component of play and castrating the Asian male gamers who enact those same plays. The former Senior Editor for Fnatic (a premiere European e-sports organization whose team won the first *League* championship) writes, "[the] level of sacrifice that is required to become the best, is almost second nature to the Asian teams, as it is something they have grown up with since birth" (Carson 2011). Carson touches on the "strict collectivist environment" and what would be "for many kids in western society … almost unreasonable": the sacrifice of time ("14 hours a day"), family, friends, and "general freedom." Carson's language is, if anything, honorific; yet his reductive description of "Asia" as a singular entity further isolates Asian gamers from "the rest of the world." Their willingness to forgo creature comforts, to forgo society even, in favor of gaming practice is treated as unrealistic, unattainable, and inhuman. Rote gameplay is dominated by an invasion of hive-minded, homogenized Asian drones who are not quite male, and, as I will soon show, not quite American either.

The emasculation of Asian players sublimates anxieties manifesting from a threatened, Euro-American masculinity into xenophobic nationalism. Rather than confronting the ways in which South Korea and China destabilize confidence in a specific type of aggressive, male power—largely derived from, and bolstered by, imperialist race theories—players and fans are free to reframe the conversation in terms of nationalism and patriotism. With help from the underdog trope, "Asia" serves as an immovable, technically skilled behemoth that ultimately dominates the landscape of professional gaming. Until the World championships every year, the primary, heated rivalry is North America versus Europe; with a quick Google, you can find no shortage of "EU > NA" jokes—but enter South Korea, enter China, and the map reorients itself. Now, North America and Europe must band together[15] to topple the Goliath that is Asia.

To return to the beginning of my chapter then, the explosive responses to LMQ's 2014 entrance into the American *League* scene are the underlying dynamics of international e-sports laid bare. While LMQ competed its way from the bottom NA tier all the way up to the North American *League of Legends* Championship Series, many fans felt that this alone did not fully address what it means to represent the United States and NA. Of course, neither did learning English, streaming personal team moments, or sharing stories to the public. When friendlier, progressive voices cited the American dream, this also failed to placate those who claimed that a formerly Chinese team full of Chinese nationals could never be North American. This resentment bled into various playoffs, when LMQ was repeatedly "booed" for defeating other NA teams. During one memorable case, the audience for LMQ's match against Complexity Black began chanting "USA USA"—which in itself was, sadly, not unusual for LMQ—when "Brokenshard" (Ram Djemal) defeated an LMQ player. The sportscaster, "Phreak" (David Turley), ironically and laughingly comments, "They are USA chants for the Israeli jungler" (LoL Esports 2014, 11:00). His observation immediately cut short the jingoistic shouts as it was intended to; however, it also highlights the hypocritical racism at play. How is an Israeli national any more "USA"-worthy than a Chinese national who may or may not apply for American citizenship (a fact that was indeterminate at the time)? What does Ram Djemal have that Zhou Qi-Lin does not?

Because the members of LMQ are treated as inherently othered, with humanity and masculinity erased, they cannot be comfortably assimilated into the American identity. Whereas Djemal's passing whiteness preserves his status as person, "Asian" foreignness defines all of LMQ as alien. Complexity Black is/was hardly the only *League* team with non-American players. There is, for instance, Evil Geniuses (EG), whose starting roster during this same period of time featured a single American: Eugene Park; however, the distinct lack of American nationals on EG did not catalyze a debate over tournament eligibility rules and concerns over representation. North American teams composed primarily of Asian American players are legitimate. NA teams that undergo extensive "boot camp" training sessions in East Asia are still NA. NA teams with European players face the occasional snide remark from other Europeans, and little else. It is when standard (re: Western) conceptions of masculinity cannot be directly credited for an athlete's abilities and e-sports dominance, when alternate, drastically different cultures of masculinity prove just as effective at earning recognition and respect, that a default to the Asian monolith narrative is triggered (see Fig. 13.2).

Fig. 13.2 Swedish player Dennis Johnsen changes his in-game name to "Taipeichingchong"

The damaging effects of such a dehumanizing process were made abundantly clear in the months after the LMQ debacle. During the 2014 World Championships, a Danish professional player Dennis Johnsen changed his in-game name from "Svenskeren" to "Taipeichingchong" while on the Taiwanese server, chatting with a Taiwanese fan. In doing so, Johnsen invokes an old, racial insult[16] that at once condemns "DiexOxO" for being part of an unintelligible culture, and mocks "DiexOxO" for his ignorance of the humiliation he is suffering. It is telling that while under the world spotlight, Johnsen did not seem to consider the consequences of such an action against one of the championship's host countries. Yes. Dennis Johnsen, who would soon be in Taipei, Taiwan, for the playoffs, had no qualms about using his public account to insult a Taiwanese fan. Part of this can be attributed to teenaged folly, but I argue that a larger part is the result of masculinity—of a privileged, Euro-American masculinity that has little understanding of, and respect for, Asian masculinities. The interaction shown in Zhu 2 indicates that Johnsen reads a normal display of fan worship as East Asian submission and docility, perceiving himself to be the aggressor who has stripped masculine pride and power from "DiexOxO." The backlash that immediately followed was thus unexpected. Unsurprisingly, the "Official apology from SK Gaming [Johnsen's organization]" registers confusion and fails to confront the lack of humanity with which Johnsen viewed the Taiwanese fan: "We want to sincerely apologise officially for our players [sic] actions and as an organisation to anyone who felt or feels offended .... Even though we understand Svenskerens [sic] actions today were not meant to harm or disrespect anyone, they caused people feeling [sic] offended and therefore go against one of the core arguments SK Gaming is standing [sic] for" (Müller 2014). There is a sense of bewilderment, as though the writer is wondering why an ostensibly quiet group of people might have reacted so negatively, and why that reaction could be warranted.

League's tumultuous year concluded with little fanfare. LMQ tied for the 12th place at Worlds and was rebranded as Team Impulse. Dennis Johnsen faced a temporary fine and suspension—and now plays for an American team (this despite the amount of American fans who roundly condemned Johnsen's actions). In other words, while these incidents might have exposed festering issues of masculinity and race, they did not motivate any immediate changes. "Asia" is still the goliath of competitive gaming and its players, neutered, emotionless drones.

Conclusion

LMQ's presence in North America correlates with the late 2014 implementation of a new "interregional movement policy" (Allen 2014). Teams can now have no more than two "non-resident" starters so that the majority (three) of the starting members will be "local." Proof of residency requires government documents of some kind, and regular habitation within that region. This policy is a product of multiple factors, not just LMQ and teams like Evil Geniuses. Rather, the global nature of competitive gaming has led to player trading on an international scale rarely seen in other sports. In an effort to foster local talent, Riot Games is curtailing such movements, which most directly impacts South Korean drafts (the most coveted) and the regions that depend on them. The United States is among those countries that have strengthened their e-sports position through East Asian drafts. There are benefits to the policy, of course. Countries with greater funding (such as the United States) cannot create an unbeatable team simply by luring the best players from around the world with outrageous salaries; and regional e-sports culture can be strengthened and promoted. However, less restricted trade could have, over time, helped dissolve the national/ethnic boundaries that encourage international antagonism; importing players raises regional standards to match global ones, as some have argued in the case of LMQ; most importantly, international player trades involve the open exchange of disparate skills, strategies, and cultures. The updated "interregional movement policy" limits cross-pollination, and implies that there is an insurmountable difference dividing local/regional playstyles from foreign ones. As I have shown, even when this policy did not exist, North America displayed a disproportionate discomfort toward East Asian player presence (as opposed to European presence). The 2014 "interregional movement policy" reinforces the either/or dilemma, suggesting that there is either the active preservation of local gameplay or the absolute surrender to foreign influences.

The discourse that motivated Riot to institute the "interregional movement policy" has shifted into a new, more introspective phase that may yet be reflected in future game changes. On October 29, the 2016 League of Legends season ended with SK Telecom T1 (a South Korean team) defending its title as the reigning World Champion against Samsung Galaxy (another South Korean team). North America's and Europe's teams performed poorly despite repeated claims—made mostly in jest by fans and professionals—that "the gap is closing." While this infamous "gap" dividing East and West has been standard fare in popular discussions of League's competitive scene for years, Season 6 involved Redditors explicitly confronting the problematic behaviors and rhetoric that stemmed from such divisive depictions of League's professional teams. In very highly upvoted Reddit threads,[17] contributors initiated discussions ranging from the disrespectful booing of a South Korean team competing in the United States (Kim 2016) to the lovability of the rookie South Korean player, "Peanut" (IM_12_YRS_OLD 2016). Most noticeably, a Redditor chose to comment on the sense of resentment and injured pride that was tainting the North American and European fan reactions to the progression of the tournament matches. Prior to the South Korean versus South Korean final, a Redditor posted that (s)he is "happy with Koreans dominating, as long as we get to see high quality league of legends," acknowledging that others may find the matches "boring because they want western teams to do well" (Tarp96 2016). While commenters did not come to an agreement as to whether stagnation in the competitive scene would hurt public interest in League of Legends as an e-sport, or whether the dearth of EU/NA representation does indeed make tournaments lesser in some way, the mere fact that fans are addressing the issue at all is telling. With a 77% approval rating and 3369 total upvote points, Tarp96's post implies that the Euro-American community of e-sports enthusiasts is in a better place to move beyond reductive binaries, or, to at least fruitfully debate them.

Because the landscape of competitive gaming evolves as rapidly as the games themselves do, it is important to keep in mind that neither is a static text and that the external narratives that emerge are constantly in flux. Players are replaced, teams dissolve, and strategies become obsolete.[18] Even the representative pride common to most sports and games played on a global scale is complicated by the medium itself; game servers[19] are currently located in regions, not in individual nations, player names and avatars are fluid— available for constant customization, and the nature of digital play reshapes standard borders and spatial barriers. Without these standard markers of difference, electronic sports (e-sports) battle lines are drawn and modified according to the protean system of competitive play unique to video games, one which hybridizes and confuses culture, nationality, regionalism, and ethnicity. The competitive scene is expanding so quickly and broadly that international gaming enacts sociopolitical forces which are not apparent in physical sports limited by popularity and geographical scope (e.g. soccer, basketball, rugby, baseball). E-sports clearly has the potential to be more geographically diverse and influential than any other global competition.

Notes

1. While it is certainly considered a badge of honor for a North American team to defeat a European one (and vice versa)—fans can become quite heated— community discussions indicate that there is a compulsive desire among Western players to ensure that there is no East Asia versus East Asia World final. See my section, "Man versus Goliath."

2. The professionalization of competitive gaming has encouraged the development of a masculinity that is not as reliant on physical prowess and athleticism. In Chap. 2 of *Raising the Stakes: E-Sports and the Professionalization of Computer Gaming* (2012b), T.L. Taylor writes that "overt demonstrations of physical activity" have traditionally intersected with masculinity, but that this status quo is being challenged by digital play (36).

3. My general methodology aligns with Norman Fairclough's textually oriented discourse analysis as found in *Discourse and Social Change* (1993) and focuses on the intersections of speech and (sociocultural) practice. Bourdieu's text, *Distinction: A Social Critique of the Judgment of Taste* (2010), is particularly relevant when we consider the ambivalent rhetoric directed toward minority gamers, discourses that dictate what is and isn't appropriate to admire in players and play marked by otherness.

4. Video game interactivity does not just encompass the technical ability to modify digital environments, but the player's potential to participate in the creative process. Player feedback influences "patches," software updates that can fix bugs and introduce new content. Characters can be "nerfed" (weakened) if they're considered too powerful, lore can be rewritten in response to cultural critiques, and mechanics can be refined to balance the play. Unlike other forms of art, video games are dynamic and participatory, allowing players to access and create certain types of knowledge that developers could not

have predicted (Take *Dwarf Fortress* [2006], for example, an indie simulation game whose emergent gameplay leads to infinite scenarios and outcomes), and which scholars cannot understand based only on distant observations of game and gameplay. This is especially true in terms of competitive gaming, where players dictate metagame trends and the nature of the competitive sphere. Without the same type of physical barriers present in other sports, e-sports fans can be both viewers and players, as much drivers of competitive gaming as professionals, sponsors, and game developers are.

5. "eSports, although intellectually demanding, also rely on physical skills. Within eSports the demand for rapid and accurate coordination between the hand and the eye stands out as a gainful skill" (Jonasson and Thiborg 2010, 290).

6. As Michael Newman noted in "The Name of the Game is Jocktronics" (2015), "Video games developed in these early years into a form of boy culture, drawing on a tradition of masculine play and leisure-time amusement" (25). Although competitive video games are still fighting for mainstream recognition and respect as skill-based sports rather than cheap simulations of one, their underlying relationship to the formation of adolescent masculinity was never in question.

7. For the integrity of this historical record, and to best represent the choice that is implicit in handle names, I have decided to preserve the commenters' original usernames. Handle names are self-constructed representations of these gamers, constructs they defend and maintain in pseudo-anonymous, but incredibly public, domains. They are as much a part of the threads as their posts' contents.

8. Transcribed from the same thread (Skiipie 2016) in chronological order.

9. Emphasis mine.

10. My transcription of this thread does not include a lengthy detour into size as various Redditors argue whether Le's compact build enables him to do what "Banana_Fetish" might find difficult.

11. Yomee Lee's article, "From Forever Foreigners to Model Minority: Asian American Men in Sports" (2016), describes how the "model minority" stereotype reinforces "ideological assaults on Asian American men as effeminate, emasculated, and androgynous de-sexualized uni-dimensional caricatures" (24).

12. Eum notes that Japan's lack of interest in e-sports parallels the stagnation of the US market.

13. See Edward Said's scholarship on orientalism and imperialism.

14. Interestingly, the image of automatons has long been present in gaming controversies. "Scripters"—players who illegally utilize code/third-party programs to cheat—are an unavoidable element in most multiplayer games, competitive or otherwise. Cheats can range from auto-leveling an account, auto-farming (i.e. accumulating gold and resources while the player is absent), or modifying accuracy and predictive abilities (this is most common in competitive games).

Having played against a few scripters myself in *League*, I can say that it is a prevalent and frustrating problem. Lisa Nakamura's article, "Don't Hate the Player, Hate the Game: The Racialization of Labor in World of Warcraft" (2009), discusses the racialized antagonism directed at "gold farmers," players who sell curated, game accounts in return for physical currency. In these cases, however, the racism stems from player beliefs that cheaters are only ever morally bereft Asians. On the other hand, *League of Legends* players who do not script and are *still* compared to "bots" encounter a form of racial bias that targets their masculinity and denigrates their skills.

15. To be clear, the relationship between North American and European fans is (playfully) contentious. It is considered somewhat shameful for a European team to make it further in a tournament than a North American one, and vice versa.

16. "Ching chong" is both a specific insult directed toward those of Chinese descent and a general insult directed toward any (East) Asian who might be Chinese.

17. Users can "upvote" Reddit posts to indicate their interest/approval, which in turn is converted into an approval rating (the number of upvotes versus downvotes). A post has reached a wide audience if it receives upvotes (or downvotes) in the upper hundreds and low thousands.

18. For more on the "dynamic nature" of e-sports (Taylor 29), see *Raising the Stakes*.

19. Game servers maintain a specific version of a multiplayer game world, shared only with other members of that server.

Bibliography

Adams, Tarn. 2006. *Dwarf Fortress*. Bay 12 Games.

Allen, Nick. 2014. Interregional Movement Policy: Official Rule. *League of Legends*, September 13. http://2015.na.lolesports.com/articles/interregional-movement-policy-official-rule.

barteks10. 2016. *Team SoloMid vs. Cloud 9/NA LCS 2016 Spring—Week 6/Post-Match Discussion [HAI in the Background is Like Where are My Hunnies, Fuck My Life]*, February 21. Message. https://www.reddit.com/r/leagueoflegends/comments/46sh5g/team_solomid_vs_cloud_9_na_lcs_2016_spring_week_6/d07iaoq.

Blizzard Entertainment. 2010. *StarCraft II: Wings of Liberty*. Irvine, CA: Blizzard Entertainment.

Bourdieu, Pierre. 2010. *Distinction: A Social Critique of the Judgement of Taste*. London: Routledge.

Carson, Cameron. 2011. Do Asian Teams Really Dominate Western Teams? *Fnatic*, March 13. http://www.fnatic.com/content/8569.

Cheung, Floyd. 2007. Anxious and Ambivalent Representations: Nineteenth-Century Images of Chinese American Men. *The Journal of American Culture* 30 (3): 293–309.

D.Devil. 2011. eSports: A Short History of Nearly Everything. *TeamLiquid*, July 31. http://www.teamliquid.net/forum/starcraft-2/249860-esports-a-short-history-of-nearly-everything.

Dorsey, Patrick. 2014. Gordon Hayward Says He's Better Than LeBron … at 'League of Legends' *ESPN*, October 15. http://espn.go.com/espn/story/_/page/instan-tawesome-141014/gordon-hayward-says-better-lebron-james-league-legends.

Eng, David. 2001. *Racial Castration: Managing Masculinity in Asian America.* Durham: Duke UP.

Eum, Jay. 2015. The Next Multibillion Dollar Tech Trend from Asia: E-sports. *VentureBeat*, March 29. http://venturebeat.com/2015/03/29/the-next-multibil-lion-dollar-tech-trend-from-asia-e-sports/.

Fairclough, Norman. 1993. *Discourse and Social Change.* Cambridge: Polity Press.

Gera, Emily. 2014. Where are the Women in eSports. *Polygon*, May 27. http://www.polygon.com/2014/5/27/5723446/women-in-esports-professional-gaming-riot-games-blizzard-starcraft-lol.

GhostshipDemos. 2016. *Team SoloMid vs. Cloud 9/NA LCS 2016 Spring—Week 6/ Post-Match Discussion [http://i.imgur.com/NMyZPMs.jpg]*, February 21. Message. https://www.reddit.com/r/leagueoflegends/comments/46sh5g/team_solomid_vs_cloud_9_na_lcs_2016_spring_week_6/d07j29r/.

Gilbert, Sandra, and Susan Gubar. 2000. *The Madwoman in the Attic: The Woman Writer and the Nineteenth-Century Literary Imagination.* New Haven: Yale UP.

IM_12_YRS_OLD. 2016. *Peanut Appreciation Thread*, October 21. https://www.reddit.com/r/leagueoflegends/comments/58rfr7/peanut_appreciation_thread/.

Jonasson, Kalle, and Jesper Thiborg. 2010. Electronic Sport and Its Impact on Future Sport. *Sport in Society* 13 (2): 287–299.

Kibria, Nazli. 1998. The Contested Meanings of 'Asian American': Racial Dilemmas in the Contemporary US. *Ethnic and Racial Studies* 21 (5): 939–958.

Kim, Andrew. 2016. Crown Talks to Korean Casters About Being Booed, CuVee's Haircut and SSG's Chances to Win the Summoner's Cup. *Slingshot*, October 14. https://slingshotsports.com/2016/10/14/crown-on-being-booed-cuvees-haircut-ssgs-chances-to-win-the-summoners-cup/.

Kluwe, Chris. 2014. Why #Gamergaters Piss Me The F*** Off. *Medium*, October 21. https://thecauldron.si.com/why-gamergaters-piss-me-the-f-off-a7e4c7f6d8a6#.lc64tqdtx.

Kowert, Rachel, Ruth Festl, and Thorsten Quandt. 2014. Unpopular, Overweight, and Socially Inept: Reconsidering the Stereotype of Online Gamers. *Cyberpsychology, Behavior, and Social Networking* 17 (3): 141–146.

Kwak, Haewoon, and Jeremy Blackburn. 2015. Linguistic Analysis of Toxic Behavior in an Online Video Game. *Lecture Notes in Computer Science (Including Subseries Lecture Notes in Artificial Intelligence and Lecture Notes in Bioinformatics)* 8852: 209–217.

Lee, Yomee. 2016. From Forever Foreigners to Model Minority: Asian American Men in Sports. *Physical Culture and Sport Studies and Research* 72 (1): 23–32.

LoL Esports VODs KazaGamez. 2014. LMQ vs Complexity Black Grand Final Game 1 NA Challenger Series *YouTube*, February 16. https://youtu.be/KyqhV9U6-SQ?t=11m.

Mueller, Saira. 2016. Rick Fox: Echo Fox Beat Several Teams in Fight to Sign Sean Gares—Just Like with Froggen. *The Daily Dot*, January 27. http://www.dailydot.com/esports/echo-fox-counter-strike-global-offensive-roster-m0e-sgares/.

Müller-Rodic, Alexander T. 2014. Official Apology from SK Gaming. *SK Gaming*, September 16. http://www.sk-gaming.com/content/1666237-Official_apology_from_SK_Gaming.

Nakamura, Lisa. 2009. Don't Hate the Player, Hate the Game: The Racialization of Labor in World of Warcraft. *Critical Studies in Media Communication* 26 (2): 128–144.

Newman, Michael Z. 2015. The Name of the Game Is Jocktronics: Sport and Masculinity in Early Video Games. In *Playing to Win*, ed. Thomas P. Oates and Robert Alan Brookey, 23–44. Bloomington: Indiana University Press.

Promasterchief. 2016. *Team SoloMid vs. Cloud 9/NA LCS 2016 Spring—Week 6/Post-Match Discussion [He Looks Like the Wiz Khalifa of E-sports in this]*, February 21. Message. https://www.reddit.com/r/leagueoflegends/comments/46sh5g/team_solomid_vs_cloud_9_na_lcs_2016_spring_week_6/d07iaoq.

Reilly, Rick. 2012. How Do You Like Me Now? *ESPN*, February 15. http://espn.go.com/espn/story/_/id/7574087/overlooking-jeremy-lin.

Sawyer, Keith. 2011. The Western Cultural Model of Creativity: Its Influence on Intellectual Property Law. *The Notre Dame Law Review* 86 (5): 2027–2056.

Scott, David. 2008. *China and the International System, 1840–1949: Power, Presence, and Perceptions in a Century of Humiliation*. Albany: SUNY Press.

Skiipie. 2016. Team SoloMid vs. Cloud 9/NA LCS 2016 Spring—Week 6/Post-Match Discussion [https://twitter.com/ShorterACE/status/650713370287468544], February 21. Message. https://www.reddit.com/r/leagueoflegends/comments/46sh5g/team_solomid_vs_cloud_9_na_lcs_2016_spring_week_6/d07iaoq.

Tarp96. 2016. *I Am Happy with Koreans Dominating, as Long as We Get to See High Quality League of Legends*, October 22. https://www.reddit.com/r/leagueoflegends/comments/58tecn/i_am_happy_with_koreans_dominating_as_long_as_we/.

Taylor, Nick. 2012a. A Silent Team is a Dead Team: Communicative Norms in Competitive FPS Play. In *Guns, Grenades, and Grunts: First-Person Shooter Games*, ed. Gerald A. Voorhees, Joshua Call, and Katie Whitlock. London: Continuum.

Taylor, T.L. 2012b. *Raising the Stakes: E-Sports and the Professionalization of Computer Gaming*. Cambridge, MA: MIT Press.

Whitlock, Jason. 2012. *Twitter Post*, February 10, 10:52pm. http://i.kinja-img.com/gawker-media/image/upload/s%2D%2DM6m3_xTU%2D%2D/18j4mb3rz8a42png.png.

14

Technomasculinity and Its Influence in Video Game Production

Robin Johnson

Video games emerged in part from military-funded research, and there are ongoing links between military simulation research, military recruitment efforts, and the video game industry (Halter 2007; Huntemann and Payne 2010). The overall culture of video games was defined in gendered terms as the promotion of a "militarized masculinity" early in its ascendance into a prominent media industry (Kline et al. 2003) with many game design practices and game narratives focused on scenarios of war, conquest, and combat. More than a decade later, game studies scholars continue to call attention to a "toxic gamer culture" where incidents of sexism have "become more virulent and concentrated in the past couple of years" (Consalvo 2012).

Major game development studios and multinational publishers still compete to win the "core" demographic of hardcore male gamers (Kline et al. 2003) even though there has been an increase in gender diversity among players associated with the rise of the casual game market (Evans 2016). Militarized masculinity is not only confined to the first-person shooter. It spans genres. And the profit-based structure of video games makes it risky to develop more gender-inclusive games. Dovey and Kennedy (2006) write that gender exerts "a powerful structuring force upon the distinctiveness of computer game culture" (36).

Along with militarized masculine content, there is also a reproduction of male game employees from the ranks of the hardcore game players, who reproduce the kinds of games they grew up playing. This chapter is situated

R. Johnson (✉)
University of Idaho, Moscow, ID, USA

© The Author(s) 2018
N. Taylor, G. Voorhees (eds.), *Masculinities in Play*, Palgrave Games in Context,
https://doi.org/10.1007/978-3-319-90581-5_14

within the above historical and cultural understanding of masculinity and video game culture. However, its focus is on a different type of masculinity that is also important but less apparent. The type of masculinity discussed is one that associates men with advanced computer knowledge and proficiency, and it is one part of a structure of hegemonic masculinity (Connell 1987) that also incorporates the more apparent militarized masculinity.

This technically oriented masculinity (or "technomasculinity" to borrow a term from Sidneyeve Matrix's 2006 book, *Cyberpop*) also affects video game production and culture. Through in-depth interviews with game workers, this chapter argues that technomasculinity is expressed by video game workers in their accounts of early socialization into computer proficiency, current working practices, and passion for gaming. Ultimately, the two types of masculinity affecting the culture make entry into the video game industry and retention problematic for women and men who express other types of masculinities.

In-depth interviews were conducted as part of a larger ethnographic study of gender in the work and culture at Dynevolve,[1] a mid-size game development studio in the United States. The studio is well established in the industry, having made commercially and critically successful "AAA" titles over its 15-year history. The studio employs about 75 people, of which more than 95 percent are men, who were working on four game projects when the interviews were conducted at the work site between 2008 and 2010. Twenty game employees, or about 25 percent of those employed at the studio, were interviewed for the study. Interview lengths ranged from 50 to 90 minutes and addressed the subjects' relationship with video games and computer technology throughout their lives, current work practices and rituals, and video game culture.

The in-depth interview is a methodological practice that forms an evolving, constructed interpretation between the interviewer and interviewee with an aim to document and understand people's experiences and practices beyond mere descriptions (Josselson 2013). Interviews are used to understand an interview subjects' experiences, to inquire about the past or gather information about things or events that cannot be observed directly, and to verify social processes (Lindlof and Taylor 2011). Although this method cannot be used to generalize the experiences of everyone in a particular population such as video game employees, an interpretive analysis of multiple interviews can discover common understandings, stories, or ideas that emerge from those who are interviewed that resonate among individuals of the larger population.

Additionally, one of the above-mentioned themes, subjects' relationship with video games and computer technology throughout their lives, is relatively more stable as a phenomenon than current work practices or game culture, although the other two have not radically changed over the last half-decade.

For example, mainstream news outlets covered the largely gender-based #Gamergate controversy in 2014 that documented aspects of video game culture that remain stubbornly misogynist and androcentric, as Nick Wingfield noted in a *New York Times* article on October 16, 2014, while video game creation is still organized around three broad areas of software programming, game design, and art. The data collected was reviewed and included only if it was still relevant to contemporary video game production and culture. The analysis of in-depth interviews revealed three themes that contribute to the expression of technomasculinity by male video game employees. The three structures are the familial passing of computer interest and competency to sons, the sexual division of labor in the field of skilled computer work, and a passion for playing video games.

In the video game and other software industries, the types of knowledge work that demonstrate the mastery of computer skills in terms of programming and aesthetics that are cherished in the post-industrial West have been gendered occupational categories (Rakow 1988). In the field of video games, the circuits of production, marketing, and technology have all contributed to defining video games as a medium largely designed by and for men (Kline et al. 2003). This is not to say that women do not play video games nor work on aspects of production (Consalvo 2008; Royse et al. 2007), but when we are discussing the overall culture, most video games can be seen as sites for the production of contemporary masculinity (Walkerdine 2006).

Academic studies using in-depth interviews or ethnographic methods to understand the social and cultural aspects of video game production include Casey O'Donnell's (2014) look at creative working practices in the industry, Mia Consalvo's (2008) interviews with female game employees, Adrienne Shaw's (2009) analysis of the production of GLBT content, and the analyses of masculine culture and social boundaries of a game studio (Johnson 2014; Johnson 2013). This chapter supplements this work by analyzing discourses by game employees to see how gender dynamics play out in accounts of video games and computer technology in their lives and work.

Gender Order and Configuration

Gender is socially organized in the West in a hierarchized binary differentiating men and women along supposedly natural or biological masculine and feminine traits. However, masculinity and femininity are better understood as "configurations of gender practice" that are always in process of being configured (Connell 2005). Gender is a primary part of an individual's identity, and gendered practices or performativity generate schemes of perception about men and women, their differences, and their relative positions and worth in the social world (Bourdieu 1977; Butler 1990). Gender shapes people's conception of themselves throughout their lives but is also unstable when its symbolic configuration combines with other sets of discourses in any individual life, including institutions such as the workplace and family socialization (Krais 2006; Connell 2005).

Judy Wajcman (2004) writes that the association between technology, masculinity, and what we think of as skilled work is still fundamental to the way in which the gendered division of labor is being reproduced today. Men have traditionally held both a monopoly on technology and the definitions of what constitutes skilled, technological work (Cockburn 1985). Computer aptitude at the developmental and functional level are "basic measures of masculine status and self-esteem," while "the least technical jobs" involving routing symbol manipulation and end-user computer work are seen as more "suitable for women" (Wajcman 2004, 27).

This fusion of computer technology and masculinity into technomasculinity has become an alternative masculinity that is one part of the hegemonic masculine ideal that also includes masculinity traditionally associated with military command:

> Historically there has been an important division between forms of masculinity organized around direct domination ... and forms organized around technical knowledge. The latter have challenged the former for hegemony in the gender order of advanced capitalist societies, without complete success. (Connell 2005, 165)

In the interviews with game workers that comprise the data for this chapter, questions about the role of computer technology and video games in the lives and work of game employees revealed three themes that note a more technically oriented expression of masculinity than one based on direct domination. These interconnected themes include gendered explanations of family socialization, the sexual division of labor working with and modifying computer hardware and software, and the development of a passion for playing video games. The interviews with game employees do not reveal a fixed or "essential" masculine identity because that is not how gender is configured. However, technomasculinity is an important factor (among others) that symbolically interacts with the militarized masculinity and, as the literature above informs us, is a dominant form of masculinity idealized in the products created by the video game industry.

Technomasculinity and Game Employees

This section focuses on the game employees' explanations of their lives ranging from family dynamics, education, leisure activities, and labor practices. The analysis of their discourses maps out gender and technomasculinity as they are talked about in stories elicited from interviews about socialization, education, leisure, and work. Family socialization channels boys rather than girls toward interests in computers, science, and technology, which has been noted in other research on gender and occupational choices (Committee on Maximizing the Potential of Women in Academic Science and Engineering 2007). The careers of fathers and other male family members play another key role in developing gendered interests. The sexual division of labor is "an allocation of particular types of work to particular categories of people" (Connell 1987, 99) that predisposes more men than women to see software development and computer knowledge as a viable and desirable career choice. Finally, the game industry provides its own gendered influences based on the interview subjects' stories about developing a "passion" or love of games.

Family Socialization and Dynamics

According to in-depth interviews, fathers typically introduce computers and programming to their sons rather than their daughters. Larry, a digital artist who specializes in physical terrain and environments, remembers his father taking him to his government job and allowing him to play simple computer games like *Rodent's Revenge*. Marco, a young sound programmer who is also in a band that plays covers of video game songs, said that he "was always into computers as a kid. I'm sure you hear this from a lot of the older guys, but I also had a crappy computer with DOS and Basic on it. I had a book that my dad gave to me. He said, 'Here's a programming book. You might like this.' I was just hooked from that moment on." When asked what his father did, he said that his "whole family" is engineers. "They are all hard core engineers, my grandfather, my uncle. I'm the only programmer, really, but it's a math kind of thing I fell into." Marco's conception of his "whole family" of engineers consists of the men and does not extend to wives, mothers, grandmothers, aunts, or sisters.

Chris, a male designer in his early 20s, had a similar experience with his father.

Chris: I first started learning to program at about eight because my father is also a programmer at a company. He would bring stuff home and show me stuff. … I started programming because it seemed cool, and

I could do things. Most of what I know about programming is self-taught. That's because I spent a lot of time when I was younger making my own games and playing around with things. And that is what developed my love for this industry.

Chris has a bachelor's degree in History, and it is not typical that someone with his educational background also knows high level programming such as the C++ programming language. He said he learned part of it on his own but supplemented that knowledge with a few classes in high school and college. Chris doesn't measure up to someone with a computer science degree, but he did manage to learn a fair amount of C++ in the three years he has worked at Dynevolve.

Other game workers acquired their computer skills through recreational play that was frowned on by their mothers. For example, after high school, Carl, a producer who worked his way up the career ladder through quality assurance, was compelled by his mother to find a job because he was spending more time playing computer games than going to school. "I left high school and got my GED," Carl recalled. "At community college I was just staying up all night playing video games like *Warcraft II* all the time. I was bombing out of college, and my mom basically told me that I either needed to get a job or she was going to throw me out of the house."

Carl started searching for computer jobs in the area and saw that a well-known designer who created many of the games he enjoyed had just formed Dynevolve.

Carl: So back in the winter of 1996, I put on a suit, and I came here and asked for a job. They said, 'No, you don't have enough experience, but there is a company down the street. You could probably go there to get some experience.' I was heartbroken. I ended up applying for the job there, and a few months later, I got an interview. They hired me on the spot actually, which was pretty nice. That resulted in me not getting thrown out of my parents' house and proving to my mother that staying up all night playing video games did not hurt but actually helped me. That was pretty cool.

As the lead game designer for the latest franchise game at the studio, Chris receives (and often argues over) gameplay suggestions from fans, testers, and co-workers. In these discussions, he is usually able to quickly determine a good idea from a bad one because he played the game so much that his mother complained.

Chris: What helps me is that I've probably played more [of Dynevolve's franchise game series] than anyone else, which is both good and bad. It's good because I got a job, but had I not then it would have been a problem. My mom wasn't too much of a fan of the game until I got hired, and she was suddenly a big fan. It's funny how that works. I've had lots and lots of experience with this genre, with this game series in particular. … You become aware over time the things that people like and dislike, and the issues that might arise from these ideas.

Although fathers got most of the respondents into technology and computers at an early age, the father-son relationship is not a requirement. Ron, a personable young artist at the studio, praised his mother and older sister for getting him into computers. His mother is an architect, and he said that she would take him to work where he developed experience using 3D software. Ron would help out the architects using AutoCAD software when he was just 13 years old, performing menial tasks such as labeling room numbers and storage buildings. "I learned from the guys in the office how to be professional at a really young age," Ron said. "My mom was a professional too. She tried to teach me as much as she could." Ron's older sister also provided him an opportunity to explore the field of 3D modeling.

Ron: I got an internship really young at a small firm in Stanford where I grew up called Ball & Chain Studios. I did that because my sister dated one of the artists there. So my sister dated this guy and said, 'You know, my brother is into video games. How about you give him a summer internship?' I got to work with them, but I don't think I was a real help to them. They let me use their computers when they weren't using them. I got to model Star Wars figures, X-Wings, and fighters in 3D, and I thought it was awesome.

The digital artists' lifestyle incorporated elements of technomasculinity that left a lasting impression on Ron. He loved the studio's culture and setting. "I loved working at a CG house where you could wear flip-flops, shorts, sandals and T-shirts to work," Ron said. The office was in an old Victorian house that had been renovated to accommodate computer technology. "I loved the juxtaposition of old Victorian architecture with high-tech wiring and computer screens everywhere," Ron said. "And they had a giant TV with Nintendo 64, so whenever the guys were rendering something in 3D they would take a break and play Mario Kart. Awesome! What could be cooler than that?"

Sexual Division of Labor in Highly Skilled Computer Work

The sexual division of labor in terms of highly skilled computer work is often traced to a general disjuncture between women and computer technology. Computer technology is culturally associated with men through practices such as "tinkering" or hacking. This perpetuates a gendered dichotomy between working *on* rather than solely *with* technology (Croissant 2000). Sixteen of the men interviewed told stories of receiving or buying computers of their own before turning 18. Two (Foster and Vincent) talked about developing an interest in computers at college after taking computer art classes

When Carl struggled to maintain his college enrollment and was told by his mother to get a job or else, he looked for computer work. When asked about what qualified him for computer work without a college education, he said that he and his brother saved their money to buy a computer, building it from parts.

Carl: So I knew how to assemble a computer. I knew how to use DOS, and I was using BBS back before the internet. Using that knowledge to play games and download games. I was even selling copies of shareware games at flea markets as a kid. I knew how to use a computer and make games run on it. ... The knowledge that I had was I loved computers. They made sense to me. I loved games. ... I just really liked computers.

Todd, a producer, spent his youth as an Army brat and early adult years building and understanding computer hardware. His hobby was "digging" into hardware and figuring out how things work like motherboards and memory. Todd was interested in computers as finite systems that need to be logical and reasonable in terms of how they are made and how memory and electricity is used. He recalled the pleasure in building his first computer and figuring out performance bottlenecks, which he would fix in the subsequent computers he built. "That was when I was into the PC ... playing a lot of first person shooters and [strategy] games," Todd said.

Foster, a senior artist at the studio, originally went to art school wanting to become a gallery artist but switched to computer art:

Foster: So I took a few classes in computer graphics, and they felt great because I grew up playing video games, and I played a lot of computer games. And to me, working on a computer making art felt a lot like playing video games and drawing at the same time. It was a really good experience. It felt really powerful. ... Working on a computer felt very freeing.

As Foster's experience indicates, the playing video games and developing computer skills and knowledge go hand in hand.

The Passion of Gaming

It's no coincidence that video games played a prominent role in shoring up interest and career choices in computers and technology. But the passion, love, and obsession with games expressed by video game workers transcend the category of computer interest. David, a digital animator who only had been working in the industry for a few months, changed careers from high-paying computer engineering work so he could work in the industry.

David: I was a huge video game buff. I knew that I wanted to do something technology based. Where I am from, South Jersey, it's all fields so even finding somewhere to work on computers was difficult. A lot of people didn't know computers. Most people didn't have computers in their homes. I reserved the thought that if you work in video games or movies you were like a god at what you do. It was something almost impossible to get into.

Instead of choosing video games as a first career, David got a degree in computer engineering. He held a job with the federal government on an anti-bioterrorism team. The work made him unhappy. It didn't take him long to finish his tasks, so much of his time at work was down time, which was looked at suspiciously by the managers. David took a job in the private sector, and then it dawned on him that it wasn't the government set up that made him unhappy. It was computer engineering. "I started to go to a school called Animation Mentor, which is an online animation school," David said. "From there, it's history. I really loved that school. I would send anybody there. They gave me everything I needed to know to learn the art of animation." After he finished training, David put his demo reel together and tried to find work. "I primarily wanted to work for gaming because that's what I always loved and spend most of my free time," he said.

Dennis, a midlevel designer, was beginning to wind down from working crunch time, an intense period of production on a project in which he was lead designer. During the interview, his thoughts would drift back to the few remaining bugs and tweaks lingering in the game before it was scheduled to be shipped out to the publisher. Growing up, he was really interested with the rules and strategies of games.

Dennis: I've always had an obsession with video games. Not even video games but games in general. ... A friend had invited me over to play Monopoly, and I did this huge analysis of it. I always beat him at

Monopoly, and we started talking about basic game mechanics and strategies and why I made the choices that I did. He told me about a startup company that tested video games and said I would be perfect for it. I didn't even realize there was a job that could be had. This was about ten or twelve years ago. I went and interviewed, and I saw that the person interviewing me had a bunch of books and board games that I recognized. I went through the different mechanics and why they worked the way they did and got hired based on my knowledge of games.

Dennis moved up to a lead tester position and then made his move to Dynevolve, which was fortunately in the same building. He first did some freelance work, coming in and testing games for bugs when the studio needed extra laborers. Dennis used the time to get to know people there and to let them know his passion for games. When he was laid off from his lead testing position, he got contract work as a producer at Dynevolve. But his real interest was in game design. "Luckily [Dynevolve] needed some help designing. They had outsourced an expansion pack to another company, and the design didn't turn out well," Dennis said. "So I redesigned all the scenarios for that, and then my contract ran out. They hired me on after that. ... I wasn't trained to work here. It was more or less my obsession that led me."

Software programmers who were interviewed said that it is hard to break into the industry without prior experience working on a commercial game title. For some game workers, the practice of "modding" displays a passion for games, and sometimes these independent mods are used as demos for recruitment into the industry. Modding is the practice of making modifications or "mods" to a game. Mods "range from changes in the physics of the virtual world to total conversions in game play that can lead to changes in story line and game type" (Postigo 2007, 301). Marco did a fair amount of modding growing up, although he doesn't consider himself a modder. He did little mods of *Doom* and *Duke Nukem* levels and also worked on a bigger mod project at the end of college.

Marco: I did a project called Pirates v. Ninjas. That was really fun. I'm still working on it to this day, actually. It was a senior software engineer project, but really it was an excuse to write some game code. ... Although, it has gotten out of hand recently. Every now and then I will pick it up and keep working on it. Last weekend I added this big physics system. ... I showed this game off during my interview here. I had made something that is kind of completed. A day or two before the interview, I was up all night working on it to polish it and make it not suck in places. It was to show that I have worked on games before. It was mine, but I have some experience. Everyone wants all this experience. It's very hard to get a job as a game programmer if you have never worked on a commercial title before. It's a big catch-22 sometimes.

Modding was one of the primary reasons why Chris was hired at the studio. When he interned at Dynevolve as a programmer, he was one of the first to test the modding tools the studio was creating for the (then) latest installment of the studio's franchise game. He previously had modded several scenarios and maps on an earlier game in the series. Chris shares his mods with other gamers, but he said he does it more for his personal enjoyment.

Chris: It was primarily because I just thought it was fun. Most of the time when you make a mod, it usually doesn't get finished. You just work on something until it stops being fun, and you drop it and do something else because you don't have to [finish]. It was something that was beneficial to the community as well because all of the modding efforts are done through the external community. So when you make something, you post a thread and say, 'Hey, take a look at this. I made a map. Have fun, or whatever.' You may do it for your own satisfaction but other people can have access and play. One scenario I made … about WWI ended up with 30,000 downloads. Quite a few people played it even though I did it in my spare time because I thought it would be fun.

Family and educational socialization, the division of labor, and passion for games all contributed to a distinctly technomasculine aspect of the employees' lives. Although beyond the scope of this chapter, technomasculinity plays a part in informing work practices and symbolic activities in creating video games (Johnson 2014).

Technomasculinity and Its Relation to Militarized Masculinity

Technomasculinity was found to comprise one aspect of the lives of the male employees interviewed, but it may sometimes run counter to the culture of idealized militarized masculinity in the industry. There is a tension between the two because militarized masculinity is placed in a binary position of power in relation to technomasculinity. Militarized masculinity as it is expressed in the wider culture of video games tends to subordinate technomasculinity, devaluing its cultural capital proficient in technical knowledge to the type of masculinity that values tough, dominant men of action and physical acumen. Because of this, part of the game workers' very identities are subordinated in recreating militarized masculinity as the ideal.

The implication of the tension between the two types of masculinity in video game production is that it manifests itself as a reproductive element of the overall hegemonic gender structure. Game employees negotiate and configure their subjectivity as we all do throughout our lives. Working in a tech-oriented industry that also elevates a heroic, militarized masculinity creates an active site of identity negotiation. This also affects the working environment and identities of those who do not express technomasculinity.

It will not be effortless to change the industry. Mia Consalvo (2008) argues that we cannot "simply add more women to the industry and make it better—there are particular constraints currently built into organizational, everyday work practices that make it difficult for most workers, and in particular female workers, to survive and potentially thrive in this industry" (179).

The more an individual is subconsciously attuned to technomasculinity and idealizations of militarized masculinity, the more likely he or she will be employed, fit in, get all the references and jokes, play the right games, stay late hours working without realizing the time, join in the rituals, and progress in seniority. Those who do not will most likely struggle in some or all areas of work. This is a significant constraint and not only because the culture tends toward a stagnating homogeneity. It is a constraint precisely because the dynamic is gendered, and this provides a significant inheritance of cultural capital to men.

Note

1. Dynevolve and all employees' names are pseudonyms.

Bibliography

Bourdieu, Pierre. 1977. *Outline of a Theory of Practice*. Trans. Richard Nice. New York: Cambridge University Press.
Butler, Judith. 1990. *Gender Trouble: Feminism and the Subversion of Identity*. New York: Routledge.

Cockburn, Cynthia. 1985. *Machinery of Dominance: Men, Women and Technical Know-How*. London: Pluto Press.

Committee on Maximizing the Potential of Women in Academic Science and Engineering. 2007. *Beyond Bias and Barriers: Fulfilling the Potential of Women in Academic Science and Engineering*. Washington, DC: National Academies Press.

Connell, R.W. 1987. *Gender and Power*. Stanford, CA: Stanford University Press.

———. 2005. *Masculinities*. 2nd ed. Los Angeles: University of California Press.

Consalvo, Mia. 2008. Crunched by Passion: Women Game Developers and Workplace Challenges. In *Beyond Barbie and Mortal Kombat: New Perspectives on Gender and Gaming*, ed. Yasmin B. Kafai, Carrie Heeter, Jill Denner, and Jennifer Y. Sun, 177–192. Cambridge: MIT Press.

———. 2012. Confronting Toxic Gamer Culture: A Challenge for Feminist Game Studies Scholars. *Ada: A Journal of Gender, New Media & Technology* 1. https://doi.org/10.7264/N33X84KH. Accessed 15 Dec 2014.

Croissant, Jennifer. 2000. Engendering Technology: Culture, Gender and Work. In *Research in Science and Technology Studies: Gender and Work*, ed. Shirley Gorenstein, 189–208. Stamford, CT: JAI Press.

Dovey, John, and Helen Kennedy. 2006. *Game Cultures: Computer Games as New Media*. Berkshire: Open University Press.

Evans, Elizabeth. 2016. The Economics of Free: Freemium Games, Branding and the Impatience Economy. *Convergence: The International Journal of Research into New Media Technologies* 22 (6): 563–580.

Halter, Ed. 2007. *From Sun Tzu to Xbox: War and Video Games*. New York: Thunder Mouth Press.

Huntemann, Nina, and Matthew Payne. 2010. Introduction. In *Joystick Soldiers: The Politics of Play in Military Video Games*, ed. Nina Huntemann and Matthew Payne, 1–18. New York: Routledge.

Johnson, Robin. 2013. Towards Greater Production Diversity: Examining Social Boundaries at a Video Game Studio. *Games and Culture* 8 (3): 136–160.

———. 2014. Hiding in Plain Sight: Reproducing Masculine Culture at a Video Game Studio. *Communication, Culture & Critique* 7 (4): 578–594.

Josselson, Ruthellen. 2013. *Interviewing for Qualitative Inquiry*. New York: Guilford Press.

Kline, Stephen, Nick Dyer-Witheford, and Graig de Peuter. 2003. *Digital Play: The Interaction of Technology, Culture and Marketing*. Ithaca, NY: McGill-Queen's University Press.

Krais, Beate. 2006. Gender, Sociological Theory and Bourdieu's Sociology of Practice. *Theory, Culture & Society* 23 (6): 119–134.

Lindlof, Thomas, and Bryan C. Taylor. 2011. *Qualitative Communication Research Methods*. 3rd ed. Thousand Oaks, CA: Sage.

O'Donnell, Casey. 2014. *Developer's Dilemma*. Cambridge: MIT Press.

Postigo, Hector. 2007. Of Mods and Modders: Chasing Down the Value of Fan-based Digital Game Modifications. *Games & Culture* 2 (4): 300–313.

Rakow, Lana F. 1988. Gendered Technology, Gendered Practice. *Critical Studies in Mass Communication* 5 (1): 57–71.

Royse, Pam, Joon Lee, Baasanjav Undrahbuyan, Mark Hopson, and Mia Consalvo. 2007. Women and Games: Technologies of the Gendered Self. *New Media & Society* 9 (4): 555–576.

Shaw, Adrienne. 2009. Putting the Gay in Games: Cultural Production and GLBT Content in Video Games. *Games and Culture* 4 (3): 228–253.

Wajcman, Judy. 2004. *TechnoFeminism*. Malden, MA: Polity Press.

Walkerdine, Valerie. 2006. Playing the Game. *Feminist Media Studies* 6 (4): 519–537.

15

Not So Straight Shooters: Queering the Cyborg Body in Masculinized Gaming

Nicholas Taylor and Shira Chess

It is late at night on Saturday, the second day of a massive, weekend-long LAN party held at a horse-racing track in south England, in a small town halfway between London and Bristol, in the summer of 2010. Taylor, there to conduct fieldwork, finds himself in one of the private rooms made available to groups of LAN attendees.

Like an inverted Laud Humphreys, Taylor had spent that afternoon loitering in between the men's washroom and the closed door to one of these private rooms, hoping to catch someone walking out of the washroom so they could invite him into their play space. Though these rooms are normally rented out to corporate-sponsored e-sports teams at a higher cost than seating on the lower two floors, the one Taylor was eventually invited into had been reserved by a group of 15 or so friends, who migrated together from one online game to the next. During that first afternoon visit, most of the group had been at their respective computers, playing World of Warcraft *(WoW), eating junk food, and transitioning from energy drinks, coffee, and tea to beer.*

It is now around 2 a.m.; only half of the group from the afternoon is here, all young men. The air is thick with the odour of bodies, junk food, chips, and beer. There is no illumination except for the glows of screens. Group play has fragmented and transformed into a more heterogeneous mix of activities: some single-player

N. Taylor (✉)
North Carolina State University, Raleigh, NC, USA

S. Chess
University of Georgia, Athens, GA, USA

© The Author(s) 2018
N. Taylor, G. Voorhees (eds.), *Masculinities in Play*, Palgrave Games in Context,
https://doi.org/10.1007/978-3-319-90581-5_15

gameplay, a couple of people playing WoW. Five are crowded around one young man's screen.

As two of the onlookers explain, the player is on Chatroulette, a social media application allowing for random hookups mediated by webcams. In the place of a live webcam feed, this player has found a way to load in a looping video feed of a young blonde woman in a lacy bra suggestively posing in front of a webcam; this is what other rouletters see when matched up with this player's profile. We watch as the player drops in and out of various rooms until he finds a suitable mark, and begins encouraging his interlocutor to undress. From here, things progress the way this fantasy of the straight cybersex hookup dictates—the man on the other end, titillated by the video of the young blonde woman and the male player's typed encouragements, pulls down his pants and, in the words of one of the onlookers, "starts wanking it." At this point the player abruptly stops the fake video feed, and he and his friends lean into the webcam and jeer at the mark; as they shout "faggot!" and "you fucking wanker!" the mark fumbles with his clothes and the keyboard, and after a few agonizing seconds, cuts the connection. The crowd of onlookers are in hysterics, high-fiving each other. The player turns around in his chair to beam at us triumphantly. A few moments pass and he starts the process again.

What's going on here? The conceptual vocabulary of contemporary game studies offers little that might help us better understand this instance of digitally mediated sexual aggression perpetrated by straight white males at a LAN party. And yet, acts of homoeroticism and verbalized and/or digitized sexual aggression between men are endemic to many gaming communities. This encompasses avatars teabagging each other in *Halo*, to the mundane use of "rape" in competitive gaming, to straight men engaging in homosexual cybersex online (Smith and Fels 2012).[1] Moreover, LAN parties, like the arcades of the 1980s and 1990s (Alloway and Gilbert 1998; Kocurek 2015), present-day e-sports tournaments (Taylor et al. 2009; Witkowski 2013), and man caves (Nettleton 2016), are intensely homosocial spaces (Sedgwick 1995). Such contexts frequently place predominantly straight white male bodies, often in heightened states of arousal, in close proximity. As in other homosocial contexts (Ward 2015), we would therefore expect to see the continuum, that Eve Sedgwick posited, between male bonding and homosexual contact become re-established through digital play between straight white men—however ritualized and digitally mediated that contact may be.

This chapter offers a "diffractive" consideration (Barad 2003) of posthumanist and cyberfeminist theory, masculinity studies, and research on gender and gaming that views digital play between straight white men as a form of homosexual contact via cyborg bodies, one that is mediated by the material and semiotic apparatuses of gaming, but no less real because of that.[2] One goal here is to better understand and account for practices of homoeroticism, homophobia, and sexual aggression that transpire between predominantly straight white male game players, encompassing acts of verbal communication ("rape" and other violent sexual metaphors), in-game actions (teabagging), and gamified practices at gaming events like the Chatroulette interaction described above. We would also like to suggest that perhaps less explicitly homoerotic instances of male-to-male touching and proximity—self-reported straight men sitting closer together on a couch while playing than they might do while watching TV or movies, and hugging after a victorious match— might be seen in similar terms.

Circuits, Cyborgs, and Straight White Guys

Like other forms of homosexual contact in frat houses, locker rooms, army barracks, and so on, erotic congress between straight white male bodies during play is framed (and legitimized) by violent, misogynistic and/or homophobic ritual—to poach conventional video game theory, a sort of "magic circle" of homosexual contact in which the everyday rules of heteromasculinity are suspended. Unlike the forms of ritualized homosexual contact described in other male-dominated domains, however, gameplay also involves forms of machinic intimacy that must be addressed—accounting for a cyborg body that is stimulated by and stimulating other cyborg bodies. Our chapter therefore portrays the instance of Chatroulette described above (and by extension, similar forms of game-based homosexual contact), as the visible and audible outcomes of technoeroticized and homoerotized affects as they circulate between bodies, controllers, screens, and in-game agents.

We construct this account by engaging in theorizations of the erotics associated, on the one hand, with homosocial masculine domains, and on the other, with gaming hardware; drawing from materialist[3] and posthumanist theories of media, our account views gameplay as a hybridized circuit in which both human and non-human bodies are constantly being jerked, pressed, and penetrated. Of course, this runs antithetical to straight white masculinity, with its emphasis on hard, impenetrable bodies (Messner 2002), and to our dominant narratives of gaming as the exercise of agency, control, and mastery, with the straight white male body positioned as the default subject (Fron et al. 2007; Leonard 2005).

We focus on straight white male gamers for two main reasons: first, because this intersection carries the most privilege yet, in accounts of gender and gaming and their confluences, arguably bears the least scrutiny; second,

because, as the history of gender as an institution that both shapes and is constituted through games and gaming practice bears out, attempts to curtail,
undermine, trivialize, threaten, and demean efforts at making games more
inclusive are by and large carried out by and on behalf of straight white male
gamers. This is a history that includes everything from the early interpellation
of arcade players by marketers, movies, and games themselves (Kocurek 2015),
to the reactionary activities of the gamergate hate group (Cross 2014), to the
ongoing efforts to link competitive spectatorial gaming to a masculinized
world of professional sports (Taylor 2012). In focusing on straight while male
gaming bodies, we are not suggesting that this is the only site in which we
might locate a materialist erotics of play; quite the opposite. Rather, our inten-
tion here is to draw attention to the overlapping of intersectional privileges—
the privilege to so naturally and unquestioningly lay claim to gaming as both
a hobby and identity, coupled with the power to engage in homoerotic intimacy while still maintaining a heteronormative identity.

This chapter does not explicitly address the more widespread and well-
publicized instances of aggression, often sexualized, aimed at women and
sexual minorities who have spoken out against misogyny and homophobia in
gaming (Chess and Shaw 2015; Consalvo 2012). Our aim is to better understand acts of homoeroticism and sexual aggression between male players. That
said, our analysis of the material and affective aspects of straight white male
gaming practices does have ramifications for how we understand the virulent
and vitriolic forms of harassment carried out by predominantly straight white
male game players towards those who want to make the contexts and practices
of play more inclusive.

Hard Bodies: Gaming and Masculinity

Current research on masculinity and gaming focuses mainly on the discourses
of masculinity enacted by particular games (Kirkland 2009), and on the
exclusionary tactics and politics of male-dominated gaming cultures (Gray
2012; Salter and Blodgett 2012; Taylor et al. 2009). While the former examines games' enactments of certain aspects of hegemonic masculinity—patriarchy, militarism, fatherhood, and violence—with the understanding that these
interpellate particular player subjectivities, the latter documents the misogynistic vitriol of a predominantly male subset of intensive gamers actively oriented towards the marginalization and harassment of women and queers who
play. There is as well a small but vital body of ethnographic work that attends
to the embodied aspects of competitive gameplay in the masculinized domain

of e-sports (Harper 2014; Taylor 2012; Witkowski 2013), though here, the emphasis is less on the (homo)erotic dimensions of e-sports and instead on the ways the body, and the player's awareness of it, is transformed and extended through intensive, highly skilled gaming.

Beyond the Gaze

Existing work on homoeroticism and gaming is informed primarily by critical cinema and literature studies, and centrally concerns the "male gaze" and the avatar as the locus of desire. Mia Consalvo's (2003) work on *Final Fantasy IX*, and the "erotic triangle" formed between Zidane, ambiguously presented but "insistently heterosexual" playable character; Princess Garnet, his love interest; and the presumably male, heterosexual player who "identifies" with Zidane and, by virtue of the protagonist's own explicitly straight orientation, re-affirms his own sexual orientation through play. Gerald Voorhees' (2014) analysis offers a compelling case for positioning desire, not identification, as the primary affective state governing player/avatar relations; and in this volume, he considers how we might extend the homoerotic male gaze to acts of game spectatorship, not just play.

These works are immensely productive, in that they point to the ways games create opportunities for complex, potentially queering practices of interpretation and play, with homoerotic pleasure and desire situated alongside (and within) hypermasculinized enactments of game-based masculinity. That said, this research has focused primarily on the hermeneutic properties of game texts, and has not yet broached questions of how desire might operate within masculinized play contexts. In order to do so, we turn first to theorizations of homosexual contact in other domains which, like gaming, are historically male-dominated and operate (ostensibly) according to the "heterosexual imperative" (Rich 1980).

Playing It Straight

In *Not Gay: Sex Between Straight White Men*, Jane Ward (2015) documents the surprising prevalence of sexual contact between heterosexually identified white men. She argues that "homosexual contact is a ubiquitous feature of the culture of straight white men", and that contrary to a conventional notion of heterosexuality that sees it as the absence of homosexuality, homosexual contact seems "to thrive in hyper-heterosexual environments" such as frat houses, sports, and the military. Ward's careful reconstruction of the complex histories and contemporary interplay between heterosexuality, homosexuality, masculinity, and whiteness shows the ways in which heterosexuality has, throughout its relatively brief history as "natural" sexual orientation, always involved ritualized spaces and practices through which white men could have sex with each other without identitarian consequences. These contexts include pre–World War II men's clubs in North American cities; post-war biker bars and saloons frequented by men who were so ruggedly, violently straight that they could engage regularly in "rebellious" homosexual acts; public bathrooms in white, conservative suburbs as documented in Laud Humphreys' (1970) *Tearoom Trade*; hazing rituals, both in the military and in frat houses; and in the Craigslist advertisements by "str8 dudes" looking for opportunities for mutual masturbation (and more) with other white "chill bros" (132).

Ward's analysis of the persistent role of homosexual contact in white male heterosexuality offers a number of implications for our understandings of het-eromasculinity. Among these is the realization that male sexual desire is much more fluid than we typically acknowledge, undermining the popular science that views it as rigid (particularly in comparison to female sexuality). Furthermore, Ward points out that conventional, "hetero-exceptionalist" (99) understandings of homosexual contact between straight men perpetually try to frame it as about anything *but* pleasure and desire, instead seeing it dictated by instrumental reasons (earning money, proving one's toughness, demon-strating one's dominance over other males, having no other outlet for sexual release, etc.). As with heterosexual sex, Ward argues, extrinsic and intrinsic motivations for straight white male homosexuality are never mutually exclu-sive; heterosexual sex is just as likely to be driven by instrumental reasons and, inversely, sexual activity between straight-identified white men is just as likely to involve pleasure and desire, no matter how obligatory practices like hazing may be portrayed as through their ritualistic framing. All this underscores Ward's claim at the outset of the book: that heterosexuality, far from being a "natural" disposition for straight-identified white men, is a tenuous, fraught project—one marked not so much by the absence of homosexual contact as by the continual investment in heterosexual rituals and practices, character-ized by misogyny and homophobia.

"Know How I Know You're Gay?": Beyond Homosociality

Ward's research provides a productive framework by which we can situate digital play between straight white men alongside other homosocial domains. Of course, the concept of homosociality is most closely associated with the work of Eve Sedgwick (1995). Her exploration of the paradoxical pairing of (straight white) male bonding, with its often overtly homoerotic overtones, and homophobia and misogyny, has been immensely productive in accounting for the fraught relationship between heteromasculinity and male intimacy. Sedgwick saw a broken link between homosocial contexts and homosexual contact, however erotically charged those contexts might be. Contemporary investigations of homoeroticism, on the other hand, examine the various ways this link is re-established via ritualized and often violent forms of heteroerotic homosexual encounters—particularly in the hypermasculinized domains of fraternities (Mechling 2008), prisons (Sabo et al. 2001), sports (Messner 2001; Pronger 1999), and the military (Belkin 2012; Zeeland 1996).

Looking more closely at these domains, Aaron Belkin (2012) and Brian Pronger (1999) write how men's bodies, whether in the barracks or the locker room respectively, are constantly penetrated by other men—either symbolically and/or physically. They argue that hypermasculine subjectivity in these institutions is constituted on the one hand through sexual aggression towards other men—and surviving this sexual aggression, by mannishly *sticking it out*—and on the other through a violent rejection of queerness and femininity. The result is that men in these contexts get to both literally and figuratively fuck each other, always behind closed doors, while still preserving their heteronormative status; after all, their story most often goes, they had to do it.[4]

Addressing homosexual contact in these various contexts, Ward notes that they are persistently linked to extenuating circumstances—men in these situations are seen as having no other choice but to have sex with each other (as in prisons), or compelled into it because they need the money, or it initiates them into the group, or they were forced into it, or they were drunk. As Ward points out, *pleasure* and *desire* are conspicuous in their absence from the list of reasons straight white men (and the theorists that write about them) offer for these behaviours. Indeed, in the cases she examines most closely (hazing rituals in college dorms and paramilitary barracks), men go out of their way to produce elaborate ritualized scenarios in which they *must* engage in homosexual contact—suggesting, for her, that such efforts are *always about* pleasure, however unacknowledged that pleasure does (and must) remain, and even as the legitimizing frameworks make it about something else.

At this point, it seems unremarkable to describe heteromasculinized contexts such as arcades, LAN parties, and man caves as "homosocial" spaces. These contexts share all the features of the domains Sedgwick examines— characterized by forms of male bonding that are at once homoerotic and homophobic. Indeed, if we were to attend exclusively to the representational elements of the aggressively homoerotic exchanges we account for in this chapter (teabagging, Chatroulette, and so on) our analysis might end here: straight white men's gameplay traffics heavily in symbolic forms of male-on-male contact that is often at once violent and eroticized.

However, we wish to push this analysis further by attending more closely to the *material* and corporeal dimensions of play between straight white men. Specifically, we offer a materialist account of the erotics associated with gaming devices, in order to argue that the bodily pleasures of straight white men's play involve a complex amalgam of homoeroticism and technoeroticism, a circuit in which sexual contact is at once corporally experienced as play upon the penetrated and penetrating body, even as it is remediated on a representational plane as hypermasculine violence.

From Boys to Toys: The Techno-erotics of Gaming

Seth Giddings and Helen Kennedy's (2008) micro-ethnographic account of their co-operative play in *Lego Star Wars* pushes against some of our conventional understandings regarding the relationship between player agency and pleasure. Rather than situating the player as the most important source of agency in digital games, and seeing this agency as games' primary source of pleasure, they argue that much of our enjoyment of games comes during moments where we have little or no agency—where we are not so much controlling, as being controlled by other human and non-human agents. They write:

> At the very least we can argue that 'mastery' is only one pleasure among many, that activity and passivity are not opposites in videogame play but fluctuations in the circuit, and thus that a new conceptual language is needed to attend to both the operations of nonhuman agency and the human pleasures of lack of agency, of being controlled, of being acted upon. (30)

While representation-focused reflections on the role of desire in digital games have been offered for some time (most often explored via the relationship between player and avatar; see, for instance, Kennedy 2002; Voorhees 2012), Giddings and Kennedy's consideration of the fluid exchange of control and submission between human and machinic bodies begins to nudge at a materialist account of the embodied pleasures of digital play. Again in their words, "gameplay is an intense event, a set of intimate circuits between human bodies and minds, computer hardware and the algorithms and affordances of the virtual worlds of videogames" (19). Their micro-ethnographic attention to "the ripples of pleasure" that "run through gameplay events, triggered by and interfering with the imbricated agencies" of gaming apparatuses offers a conceptual fold into which we can work a more materialist understanding of the technoerotics of digital play.

Likewise, James Ash (2013), writing about the ways that expert first-person shooter (FPS) players become affectively "attuned" to the somatic and perceptual demands of competitive *Call of Duty*, reframes expertise in terms of *vulnerability*—an openness and enhanced susceptibility to external stimuli—rather than *agency*. Acknowledging that this account of the body as vulnerable and permeable runs counter to narratives that associate "war games and toys" (and, certainly, competitive games) to the hypermasculine valorization of toughness, resilience, and strength, Ash writes that "opening the body to sensory feedback from the game is necessary in order to be able to respond fast enough to events that occur in the game" (45). As productive as this insight is, it frames the body's perceptual and somatic "opening up" (can gamers blossom?) as "necessary" in order to attain a level of proficiency in the overtly masculinized domain of competitive FPS play—a tendency that Ward sees in many accounts of straight men's heteroerotic homosexual encounters, wherein the pleasure of such encounters must go unacknowledged in order to preserve heteronormativity. In this case, however, the threat to heteronormativity comes not from direct contact with other male bodies, but via digitized encounters wherein players' bodies are vulnerable to external stimulation both from the semiotic and technical apparatus of play, and from other players' actions within and through this apparatus.

To fully acknowledge both the layered eroticisms of these encounters, we might productively (re)turn to feminist theories of the cyborg, and to cyberfeminism's engagements with techno-eroticism, reading these alongside more heteronormative treatments of game controllers as sexual objects.

While somewhat dated, cyberfeminist theory might provide a useful perspective of gauging ways that our machinic extensions can extend our desire. Donna Haraway (1990) argues that humans have been slowly transformed into cyborgs, hybrid of machine and organism and suggests that rather than resisting this transformation we focus on its potential pleasures. Haraway writes:

A cyborg body is not innocent; it was not born in a garden; it does not seek unitary identity and so generate antagonistic dualisms without end (or until the world ends); it takes irony for granted. One is too few, and two is only one possibility. Intense pleasure in skill, machine skill, ceases to be a sin, but an aspect of embodiment. The machine is not an *it* to be animated, worshipped, and dominated. The machine is us, our processes, and aspect of our embodiment. We can be responsible for machines; *they* do not dominate or threaten us. We are responsible for boundaries; we are they. (p. 180)

So, to wrap this back into our theoretical model of straight male desire in gaming, the sexual binaries that we might typically encode into bodies (i.e., male/female or homo/heterosexual) cease to sustain relevance with the cyborg. They give us opportunities to revise our existing boundaries as a form of desire.

The Harder Cyberfeminism Gets

One of the central conceits of cyberfeminist theory is the use of "irony"—how postmodern bodies take on ironic meaning through their intersections and collapses. If "irony" is the cornerstone of cyberfeminism, then there is nothing more suitable than thinking about how cyberfeminist theory can be operationalized in terms of the masculinities of gaming.[5] Thus, we are deploying the notion of cyberfeminism, not as a route to empower women, but as a consideration of how machines (and games, in particular) are capable of making intersectional bodies. Like all intersectional bodies, these cyborged creations are not necessarily willing parties; they do not acknowledge their own intersections or own bodily ironies. But given the overwhelming masculinity of the video game industry and the subsequent pushbacks via feminist theory, it is worth considering the transformative aspects of combining human with machine, via game controller.

Game controllers become proxies for body parts, both extending our own bodies and penetrating ourselves (and others) with the sleek fetishized plastics, metals, and wires in ways that it is theoretically less acceptable to do in the real world. Comparisons between game controllers and sexual organs are by no means new or original. Certainly, game companies quickly caught on to the phallic imagery of joysticks, popularized from the 1970s and 1980s. The comparison was so obvious that Sega—a company which relished in marketing to young men—chose to include it in their advertising with slogans like, "Something to do with your hands that won't make you go blind" and "The more you play with it, the harder it gets." In both of these vintage advertisements, the artwork used sketch drawings of young men with a joystick in place of the penis. Similarly, a Zine circulated internally in the early days of Atari, *The Gospel According to St. Pong* (1973), makes passing jokes and comments about the inherent masculinity of the joystick. But if the joystick is an extension of the phallus, then what of the dualshock controller, a more recent—and for some time now, dominant—iteration on console controls? In many ways, we can start to see this style of game controller as the vagina to the phallic joystick. The subtler, rounded features seem to resemble the intricacies and subtleties of women's bodies in ways that the singular shaft of the joystick-penis is incapable of. Indeed, the art of button mashing in the modern game controller seems to imply the process of a player en route to achieving some sort of clitoral ecstasy. The mastery of the modern game controller is the mastery of *othered* bodies—bodies that are not necessarily prioritized by the video game industry, writ large.

In sum total, these game controllers allow for an outwards externalization of genitalia—penises, vaginas—it makes no difference because to the game controller; our cyborg bodies are indifferent. In this way, game controllers become an acceptable mode of public masturbation, wherein players can try on cyborg prostheses in order to implement their own (potentially substandard) body parts. As such, the previously quoted marketing slogan is misleading—game controllers would never make us go blind, they are extending our sexualized bodies, not limiting them.

So where do we put all of this? If gaming bodies require the excess of sexual organs—those without reproductive capability, but full of pleasure-making capacity, then we might see how interactions with material apparatuses of gaming, via the controller, become a site of erotic and potentially queering pleasure. Game controllers remind us that in game worlds we can extend our sex organs in the queerest possible sense, whilst button mashing and masturbating to no avail. We can perform sexualities, without actually having to permanently embody them. In this, Cyberfeminist theory might shed light on emancipatory potential of machinist articulations in gaming. Queer content (or queer readings of allegedly straight content) is not the only possible way to think about homosexuality within gaming contexts. Ruberg (2015) has written about the queer potential of failure in games. Co-author Chess (2016) has described the entire narrative structure of games as being full of potential for queerness (within opposition to traditional narrative structure). Further, we would like to argue that the kind of homosexual contact within gaming can occur at a material level. Returning to the Chatroulette example that began this chapter, we would like to suggest that the mechanisms of gaming themselves might be supple with opportunities for homoerotic play. Seen from this perspective, gaming between straight white men involves both a homoerotics and technoerotics, "materializing" players' bodies to be both agential and vulnerable, and imbricating them into flows of affect between other bodies, both human and non-human—even while what plays out on screens are hypermasculine fantasies of domination and violence. To that end, the heterogeneous circuitry of play means that straight white men (the core market for the business) are able to game together and touch, move, penetrate each other, and provoke responses in each other's bodies, without directly touching each other.

Some Finishing Touches

Our materialist account of homoeroticism among straight white male gamers has deliberately avoided attention to the symbolic and representational aspects of digital games, which—to paraphrase Karen Barad (2003)—we feel have been "granted too much power" in accounts of gender and gaming. Rather, our attention is to the erotic circuitries of human and non-human entities through which agency and affect circulate, acting both on and through players' bodies. Following contemporary theorizations that regard *all* experiences with media as material (Hayles 2010; Packer and Wiley 2012), players may not be *physically* touching each other, but they are nonetheless *really* doing so. In-game actions originate in the (potentially queering) co-mingling of thumbs, fingers, and controllers, and play out on and in each other's bodies, registering as pleasure, desire, frustration, and pain. These interpenetrating affects (Shinkle 2005) certainly are pleasurable, but are nonetheless problematic to the project of maintaining a heteronormative masculine identity, premised as contemporary discourses of masculinity are on the presentation of an impenetrable body (Connell 2005)—and one that is, moreover, firmly in control of technology (Hacker 1989; Wajcman 2010).

The Magic Circle Jerk

The notion of the "magic circle jerk," while cheeky, is also meant to underscore the serious role that *ritual* plays here. Both Johan Huizinga's (1970) theorization of the "play element in culture" and the circle jerks of fratboyhood denote special times and places constituted for rituals of belonging. The magic circle, though it has passed out of favour among game studies scholars when (perhaps erroneously) understood as an ontological claim about games' non-reality, remains a potent means for acknowledging the roles that games play in reaffirming normative power relations even as (and precisely because) these relations may be temporarily subverted through the game. And the circle jerk, as a ritual in which heteronormative injunctions against male sexual contact are temporarily ignored, allows for currents of erotic pleasure to travel between straight men's bodies, nonetheless couched in (and legitimized by) structures of competition, abjection, and revulsion.

Coupling these together, "magic circle jerk" is meant to express the possibility that gaming between straight white male bodies combines the cultural functions of both these rituals. It discursively confirms a heteronormative masculine mastery of digital media, particularly as expressed through representations of violence and domination, while materially acting as a way for participants to jerk each other's bodies—again, in ways that are rarely (directly) corporeal in the sense of direct physical contact between players, but are nonetheless material, as pulses of affect registered by and inscribed upon players' bodies.

It is at this point that we turn back to the representational aspects of the practices we address here—the moment of gamified Chatroulette at the LAN party, and similar acts of homosexual incorporeal contact. We argue that the representative dimensions of these practices operate to ensure that these acts are not *seen as* homosexual contact. Like the forms Jane Ward considers, such as hazing in frat houses and embassies, straight men looking for hookups with other men on Craigslist, these gaming practices are embedded in misogynist and homophobic scripts—rituals of the magic circle jerk—that signal their participants' heterosexual status.

Extending Ward's analysis, we see gaming between straight white men as ritualized events in which there are both homoerotic and technoerotic pleasures at play—erotics which blow open hypermasculine discourses of the invulnerable, agential male body and see it instead as porous, prosthetized, and penetrated, and which therefore must be buttressed with misogyny and homophobia. This may help explain why, in intensely homosocial domains like e-sports tournaments, LAN parties, arcades, and man caves, the pleasures of incorporeal homosexual contact are moulded, legitimized, and given intelligibility via a discursive matrix that persistently insists on gamers' heterosexuality and hypermasculinity. This is how straight white males take the gay out of gaming: through exclusionary politics that so vociferously alienate non-straight, non-male bodies that we must wonder whether there is more at stake than just games.

Very early on in the writing of this chapter, we recounted the story of the Chatroulette incident to various colleagues of ours, rhetorically asking, "what do we do with this?" One colleague—without a moment's hesitation, putting himself in the seat of the mark who has just started jerking off in front of a bunch of gamers—responded, "you look them in the eyes and finish." There's a surprising amount of insight here, if we extrapolate: one way to confront the rigidly exclusionary politics of contemporary straight white male gamer culture is to fully acknowledge the dangerously queering undercurrents of pleasure that such politics mask. This seems like a suitable ending for this analysis: like our colleague's answer, it is messy, it leaves us vulnerable, but it certainly has been a long time coming.

Notes

1. We are also curious as to whether and how gamified porn consumption by straight males, such as Jerk Off Challenges and "Cock Hero," might be incorporated into this theorization, since these practices seem to heavily involve homoerotic elements (Stadler 2015). But this is beyond the scope of this chapter.
2. Katherine Hayles (2010), among others, insists on the materiality of digital media; data is always embodied in and by something. Following this, the forms of contact we describe here may not be *physical*, but they are always *material*.
3. Following Jeremy Packer and Stephen Wiley, we use the term "materialist" in regard to communication and media studies, to signal an attempt to move beyond "textualist" paradigms and instead theorize communication in terms of "infrastructure, space, technology, and the body" (Packer and Wiley 2012, 3).
4. It is interesting to note that many of the paradigmatic representations of hypermasculinity in digital games involve rugged outlaws, militaristic super-soldiers, and sports athletes—paragons of the very domains where we most often find instances of ritualized homosexual contact between straight white men.
5. Although Susanna Paasonen (2011) suggests moving beyond that irony, perhaps there is still some usefulness within it.

Bibliography

Alloway, Nola, and Pam Gilbert. 1998. Video Game Culture: Playing with Masculinity, Violence and Pleasure. In *Wired-up: Young People and the Electronic Media*, ed. Sue Howard, 95–114. London: University College London Press.

Ash, James. 2013. Technologies of Captivation: Videogames and the Attunement of Affect. *Body & Society* 19 (1): 27–51.

Atari, Inc. 1973. *The Gospel According to St. Pong* 1 (2), July 25. http://ftp.pigwa.net/stuff/collections/Atari%20newsletters/(The%20Gospel%20According%20to)%20St.%20Pong/st_pong_v1n2.pdf.

Barad, Karen. 2003. Posthumanist Performativity: Toward an Understanding of How Matter Comes to Matter. *Signs: Journal of Women in Culture and Society* 28 (3): 801–831.

Belkin, Aaron. 2012. *Bring Me Men: Military Masculinity and the Benign Facade of American Empire, 1898–2001*. Oxford: Oxford University Press.

Chess, S. 2016. The Queer Case of Video Games: Orgasms, Heteronormativity, and Video Game Narrative. *Critical Studies in Media Communication* 33 (1): 84–94.

Chess, Shira, and Adrienne Shaw. 2015. A Conspiracy of Fishes, or, How We Learned to Stop Worrying About #GamerGate and Embrace Hegemonic Masculinity. *Journal of Broadcasting & Electronic Media* 59 (1): 208–220.

Connell, Raewyn W. 2005. *Masculinities*. Berkeley, CA: University of California Press.

Consalvo, Mia. 2003. Hot Dates and Fairy-Tale Romances: Studying Sexuality in Games. In *The Video Game Theory Reader*, ed. Mark J.P. Wolf and Bernard Perron, 171–194. New York: Routledge.

———. 2012. Confronting Toxic Gamer Culture: A Challenge for Feminist Game Studies Scholars. *Ada: A Journal of Gender, New Media, and Technology* 1. https://doi.org/10.7264/N33X84KH.

Cross, Katherine A. 2014. Ethics for Cyborgs: On Real Harassment in an "Unreal" Place. *Loading...* 8 (13): 4–12.

Fron, Janine, Tracy Fullerton, Jacquelyn Morie, and Celia Pearce. 2007. *The Hegemony of Play*. Paper read at Situated Play: Proceedings of the Digital Games Research Association Conference, Tokyo, Japan, September 24–28.

Giddings, Seth, and Helen Kennedy. 2008. Little Jesuses and Fuckoff Robots: On Aesthetics, Cybernetics, and Not Being Very Good at *Lego Star Wars*. In *The Pleasures of Computer Gaming: Essays on Cultural History, Theory and Aesthetics*, ed. Melanie Swalwell and Jason Wilson, 13–32. Jefferson, NC: McFarland.

Gray, Kishonna L. 2012. Intersecting Oppressions and Online Communities. *Information, Communication & Society* 15: 411–428. https://doi.org/10.1080/1369118X.2011.642401.

Hacker, Sally. 1989. *Pleasure, Power and Technology*. Boston, MA: Unwin Hyman.

Haraway, Donna. 1990. *Simians, Cyborgs, and Humans*. New York: Routledge.

Harper, Todd. 2014. *The Culture of Digital Fighting Games: Performance and Practice*. New York: Routledge.

Hayles, Katherine. 2010. *How We Became Posthuman*. Chicago: University of Chicago Press.

Huizinga, Johan. 1970 [1938]. *Homo Ludens: A Study of the Play Element in Culture*. London: Temple Smith.

Humphreys, Laud. 1970. *Tearoom Trade: Impersonal Sex in Public Places*. New Brunswick, NJ: Transaction.

Kennedy, Helen. 2002. Lara Croft: Feminist Icon or Cyberbimbo? On the Limits of Textual Analysis. *Games Studies* 2 (2). http://gamestudies.org/0202/kennedy/.

Kirkland, Ewan. 2009. Masculinity in Video games: The Gendered Gameplay of *Silent Hill*. *Camera Obscura* 24 (271): 161–183.

Kocurek, Carly. 2015. *Coin-operated Americans: Rebooting Boyhood at the Video Game Arcade*. Minneapolis: University of Minnesota Press.

Leonard, David J. 2005. To the White Extreme: Conquering Athletic Space, White Manhood, and Racing Virtual Reality. In *Digital Gameplay: Essays on the Nexus of Game and Gamer*, ed. Nathan Garrelts, 110–129. Jefferson, NC: McFarland.

Mechling, Jay. 2008. Paddling and the Repression of the Feminine in Male Hazing. *Thymos: Journal of Boyhood Studies* 2 (1): 60–75.

Messner, Michael A. 2001. Friendship, Intimacy and Sexuality. In *The Masculinities Reader*, ed. Stephen M. Whitehead and Frank J. Barrett, 253–265. Cambridge, UK: Polity Press.

———. 2002. *Taking the Field: Women, Men, and Sports*. Minneapolis: University of Minnesota Press.

Nettleton, Pamela H. 2016. No Girls Allowed: Television Boys' Clubs as Resistance to Feminism. *Television & New Media*: 1–16. https://doi.org/10.1177/15274764 16630300.

Paasonen, Susanna. 2011. Revisiting Cyberfeminism. *Communications: The European Journal for Communication Research* 36: 335–352. https://doi.org/10.1515/ COMM.2011.017.

Packer, Jeremy, and Stephen B. Crofts Wiley. 2012. Introduction: The Materiality of Communication. In *Communication Matters: Materialist Approaches to Media, Mobility, and Networks*, ed. Jeremy Packer and Stephen B. Crofts Wiley, 3–16. New York: Routledge.

Pronger, Brian. 1999. *The Arena of Masculinity: Sports, Homosexuality, and the Meaning of Sex*. New York: St. Martin's.

Rich, Adrienne. 1980. Compulsory Heterosexuality and Lesbian Existence. *Signs* 5 (4): 631–660.

Ruberg, Bonnie. 2015. No Fun: The Queer Potential of Video Games that Annoy, Anger, Disappoint, Sadden, and Hurt. *QED: A Journal of GLBTQ Worldmaking* 2 (2): 108–124.

Sabo, Don, Terry Kupers, and Willie London. 2001. *Prison Masculinities*. Philadelphia: Temple University Press.

Salter, Anastasia, and Bridgett Blodgett. 2012. Hypermasculinity and Dickwolves: The Contentious Role of Women in the New Gaming Public. *Journal of Electronic Media* 56 (3): 401–416.

Sedgwick, Eve. 1995. *Between Men: English Literature and Male Homosocial Desire*. New York: Columbia University Press.

Shinkle, Eugenie. 2005. Corporealis Ergo Sum: Affective Response in Digital Games. In *Digital Gameplay: Essays on the Nexus of Game and Gamer*, ed. Nathan Garrelts, 21–35. Jefferson, NC: McFarland.

Smith, David Harris, and Deborah Fels. 2012. The Disintegrated Erotics of Second Life. *The International Journal of the Image* 2 (3): 125–138.

Stadler, John P. 2015. Designing Compulsion. -empyre-: soft_skinned_space, October. http://empyre.library.cornell.edu/phpBB2/viewtopic.php?t=992&highl ight=john+stadler+designing+compulsion.

Taylor, T.L. 2012. *Raising the Stakes: E-sports and the Professionalization of Computer Gaming*. Cambridge, MA: The MIT Press.

Taylor, Nicholas, Jennifer Jenson, and Suzanne de Castell. 2009. Cheerleaders, Booth Babes, Halo Hoes: Pro-gaming, Gender, and Jobs for the Boys. *Digital Creativity* 20 (9): 239–252.

Voorhees, Gerald. 2012. Criticism and Control: Gameplay in the Space of Possibility. In *CtrlAltPlay: Essays on Control in Video Gaming*, ed. Matthew Wysocki, 9–20. Jefferson, NC: McFarland.

———. 2014. Identification or Desire? Taking the Playeravatar Relationship to the Next Level. *First Person Scholar*. http://www.firstpersonscholar.com/identifica-tionordesire/.

Wajcman, Judy. 2010. Feminist Theories of Technology. *Cambridge Journal of Economics* 34 (1): 143–152. https://doi.org/10.1093/cje/ben057.

Ward, Jane. 2015. *Not Gay: Sex Between Straight White Men*. New York: New York University Press.

Witkowski, Emma. 2013. Eventful Masculinities: Negotiations of Hegemonic Sporting Masculinities at LANs. In *Sports Videogames*, ed. Mia Consalvo, Konstantin Mitgutsch, and Abe Stein, 217–235. New York: Routledge.

Zeeland, Steven. 1996. *The Masculine Marine: Homoeroticism in the U.S. Marine Corps*. New York: Routledge.

Index

© The Author(s) 2018

N. Taylor, G. Voorhees (eds.), *Masculinities in Play*, Palgrave Games in Context,
https://doi.org/10.1007/978-3-319-90581-5

CPI Antony Rowe
Eastbourne, UK
November 26, 2019